ORIGINS AND DEVELOPMENT OF THE ARAB-ISRAELI CONFLICT

**Other Titles in the
Greenwood Press Guides to
Historic Events of the Twentieth Century**
Randall M. Miller, Series Editor

ORIGINS AND DEVELOPMENT OF THE ARAB-ISRAELI CONFLICT

Ann M. Lesch
and
Dan Tschirgi

Greenwood Press Guides to
Historic Events of the Twentieth Century
Randall M. Miller, Series Editor

Greenwood Press
Westport, Connecticut • London

Library of Congress Cataloging-in-Publication Data

Lesch, Ann Mosely.
    Origins and development of the Arab-Israeli conflict / Ann M.
Lesch and Dan Tschirgi.
        p.   cm.—(Greenwood Press guides to historic events of the
twentieth century, ISSN 1092–177X)
    Includes bibliographical references (p.   ) and index.
    ISBN 0–313–29970–6 (alk. paper)
        1. Arab-Israeli conflict.   2. Arab-Israeli conflict—1993–
I. Tschirgi, Dan.   II. Title.   III. Series.
DS119.7.L4665   1998
956.05′3—dc21   97–49481

British Library Cataloguing in Publication Data is available.

Library of Congress Catalog Card Number: 97–49481
ISBN: 0–313–29970–6
ISSN: 1092–177X

First published in 1998

Greenwood Press, 88 Post Road West, Westport, CT 06881
An imprint of Greenwood Publishing Group, Inc.

Printed in the United States of America

∞™

The paper used in this book complies with the
Permanent Paper Standard issued by the National
Information Standards Organization (Z39.48–1984).

10 9 8 7 6 5 4 3 2 1

Front cover photo: Yasir Arafat and Benjamin Netanyahu. AGENCE FRANCE PRESSE/
CORBIS-BETTMANN.

Back cover photo: New apartment blocs in Ma'ale Adumin. By Ann Lesch.

Copyright Acknowledgments

Contents

A photo essay follows page 70

Series Foreword

As the twenty-first century approaches, it is time to take stock of the political, social, economic, intellectual, and cultural forces and factors that have made the twentieth century the most dramatic period of change in history. To that end, the Greenwood Press Guides to Historic Events of the Twentieth Century presents interpretive histories of the most significant events of the century. Each book in the series combines narrative history and analysis with primary documents and biographical sketches, with an eye to providing both a reference guide to the principal persons, ideas, and experiences defining each historic event, and a reliable, readable overview of that event. Each book further provides analyses and discussions, grounded in both primary and secondary sources, of the causes and consequences, in thought and action, that give meaning to the historic event under review. By assuming a historical perspective, drawing on the latest and best writing on each subject, and offering fresh insights, each book promises to explain how and why a particular event defined the twentieth century. No consensus about the meaning of the twentieth century emerges from the series, but, collectively, the books identify the most salient concerns of the century. In so doing, the series reminds us of the many ways those historic events continue to affect our lives.

Each book follows a similar format designed to encourage readers to consult it both as a reference and a history in its own right. Each volume opens with a chronology of the historic event, followed by a narrative overview, which also serves to introduce and examine briefly the main themes and issues related to that event. The next set of chapters is composed of topical essays, each analyzing closely an issue or problem of interpretation introduced in the opening chapter. A concluding chapter suggesting the long-term implications and meanings of the historic event brings the strands of the preceding chapters together while placing the event in the larger historical context. Each book also includes a section of short biographies of the principal persons related to the event, followed by a section introducing and reprinting key historical documents illustrative of and pertinent to the event. A glossary of selected terms adds to the utility of each book. An annotated bibliography—of significant books, films, and CD-ROMs—and an index conclude each volume.

The editors made no attempt to impose any theoretical model or historical perspective on the individual authors. Rather, in developing the series, an advisory board of noted historians and informed high school history teachers and public and school librarians identified the topics needful of exploration and the scholars eminently qualified to examine those events with intelligence and sensitivity. The common commitment throughout the series is to provide accurate, informative, and readable books, free of jargon and up to date in evidence and analysis.

Each book stands as a complete historical analysis and reference guide to a particular historic event. Each book also has many uses, from understanding contemporary perspectives on critical historical issues, to providing biographical treatments of key figures related to each event, to offering excerpts and complete texts of essential documents about the event, to suggesting and describing books and media materials for further study and presentation of the event, and more. The combination of historical narrative and individual topical chapters addressing significant issues and problems encourages students and teachers to approach each historic event from multiple perspectives and with a critical eye. The arrangement and content of each book thus invite students and teachers, through classroom discussions and position papers, to debate the character and significance of great historic events and to discover for themselves how and why history matters.

The series emphasizes the main currents that have shaped the modern world. Much of that focus necessarily looks at the West, especially Europe and the United States. The political, commercial, and cultural expansion of the West wrought largely, though not wholly, the most fundamental changes of the century. Taken together, however, books in the series reveal the interactions between Western and non-Western peoples and society, and also the tensions between modern and traditional cultures. They also point to the ways in which non-Western peoples have adapted Western ideas and technology and, in turn, influenced Western life and thought. Several books examine

such increasingly powerful global forces as the rise of Islamic fundamentalism, the emergence of modern Japan, the Communist revolution in China, and
the collapse of communism in eastern Europe and the former Soviet Union.
American interests and experiences receive special attention in the series, not
only in deference to the primary readership of the books but also in recognition
that the United States emerged as the dominant political, economic, social,
and cultural force during the twentieth century. By looking at the century
through the lens of American events and experiences, it is possible to see why
the age has come to be known as "The American Century."

Assessing the history of the twentieth century is a formidable prospect.
It has been a period of remarkable transformation. The world broadened
and narrowed at the same time. Frontiers shifted from the interiors of Africa
and Latin America to the moon and beyond; communication spread from
mass circulation newspapers and magazines to radio, television, and now
the Internet; skyscrapers reached upward and suburbs stretched outward;
energy switched from steam, to electric, to atomic power. Many changes
did not lead to a complete abandonment of established patterns and practices
so much as a synthesis of old and new, as, for example, the increased use
of (even reliance on) the telephone in the age of the computer. The automo-
bile and the truck, the airplane, and telecommunications closed distances,
and people in unprecedented numbers migrated from rural to urban, industrial, and ever more ethnically diverse areas. Tractors and chemical fertiliz-
ers made it possible for fewer people to grow more, but the environmental
and demographic costs of an exploding global population threatened to
outstrip natural resources and human innovation. Disparities in wealth
increased, with developed nations prospering and underdeveloped nations
starving. Amid the crumbling of former European colonial empires, Western
technology, goods, and culture increasingly enveloped the globe, seeping
into, and undermining, non-Western cultures—a process that contributed to
a surge of religious fundamentalism and ethno-nationalism in the Middle
East, Asia, and Africa. As people became more alike, they also became more
aware of their differences. Ethnic and religious rivalries grew in intensity
everywhere as the century closed.

The political changes during the twentieth century have been no less
profound than the social, economic, and cultural ones. Many of the books in
the series focus on political events, broadly defined, but no books are confined
to politics alone. Political ideas and events have social effects, just as they
spring from a complex interplay of non-political forces in culture, society, and
economy. Thus, for example, the modern civil rights and women's rights
movements were at once social and political events in cause and consequence.

Likewise, the Cold War created the geopolitical framework for dealing with competing ideologies and nations abroad and served as the touchstone for political and cultural identities at home. The books treating political events do so within their social, cultural, and economic contexts.

Several books in the series examine particular wars in depth. Wars are defining moments for people and eras. During the twentieth century war became more widespread and terrible than ever before, encouraging new efforts to end war through strategies and organizations of international cooperation and disarmament while also fueling new ideologies and instruments of mass persuasion that fostered distrust and festered old national rivalries. Two world wars during the century redrew the political map, slaughtered or uprooted two generations of people, and introduced and hastened the development of new technologies and weapons of mass destruction. The First World War spelled the end of the old European order and spurred communist revolution in Russia and fascism in Italy, Germany, and elsewhere. The Second World War killed fascism and inspired the final push for freedom from European colonial rule in Asia and Africa. It also led to the Cold War that suffocated much of the world for almost half a century. Large wars begat small ones, and brutal totalitarian regimes cropped up across the globe. After (and in some ways because of) the fall of communism in eastern Europe and the former Soviet Union, wars of competing cultures, national interests, and political systems persisted in the struggle to make a new world order. Continuing, too, has been the belief that military technology can achieve political ends, whether in the superior American firepower that failed to "win" in Vietnam or in the American "smart bombs" and other military wizardry that "won" in the Persian Gulf.

Another theme evident in the series is that throughout the century nationalism has continued to drive events. Whether in the Balkans in 1914 triggering World War I or in the Balkans in the 1990s threatening the post–Cold War peace—or in many other places—nationalist ambitions and forces would not die. The persistence of nationalism is yet another reminder of the many ways that the past becomes prologue.

We thus offer the series as a modern guide to and interpretation of the historic events of the twentieth century and as an invitation to consider how and why those events have defined not only the past and present but also charted the political, social, intellectual, cultural, and economic routes into the next century.

Randall M. Miller
Saint Joseph's University, Philadelphia

Preface

This study of the Arab-Israeli conflict seeks to provide a succinct overview of the main issues and events since the late nineteenth century, when Zionist and Arab nationalist aspirations began to collide. It reflects on three principal themes. First, it traces the shifts between ideologically rooted policies and pragmatic approaches on the part of both Arabs and Israelis. Second, it examines the internal tensions within both sides over the nature of the conflict and the ways to resolve it. And third, it stresses the role that external actors have played in either bolstering ideological intransigence or encouraging pragmatic accommodation. In that sense, it is an extended essay on the interplay among the policies of Arabs, Israelis, and third parties as they promote confrontation or accommodation.

The book is structured to examine these issues by initially presenting a wide-ranging historical overview, followed by topical chapters. The first topical chapter considers the growth of Zionism and Palestinian nationalism during the period of British rule in the first half of the twentieth century, as the clash between the two peoples intensified to the point of all-out confrontation. The succeeding topical chapters look separately at Israel, the Palestinians, and U.S. policy toward the Arab-Israeli conflict, in order to focus more precisely on the changing views and policies of key parties concerning the dispute. Finally, the conclusion evaluates the situation as of mid-1997, ending with an assessment of the issues that must still be resolved in order to obtain a comprehensive peace.

We have interspersed poems and quotations from political actors and observers throughout the text, in order to bring a sense of immediacy to the issues being analyzed. These include Egyptian president Anwar Sadat's reflections on his visit to Jerusalem in 1977, Leah Rabin's recollections of her deepening sense of Jewish nationalism as a teenager in the 1930s, and Hanan Ashrawi's anguished poem about a Palestinian girl injured by an Israeli soldier in 1988. We have also highlighted people who are not likely to be known in the United States, such as an Israeli soldier who wrote home after he viewed the Western Wall in the Old City of Jerusalem in June 1967, and a Palestinian poet who expressed the anguish of exile. These writings voice in different ways the intense feelings that characterize both peoples.

The reader will find excerpts from a large number of documents that mark critical moments in the Arab-Israeli conflict. They range from the Basel Declaration at the founding conference of the World Zionist Organization and the Balfour Declaration, by which Great Britain pledged support for the concept of a Jewish national home, to the guidelines for the Israeli government formed in June 1996. They include passages from the PLO's National Covenant in 1964/1968, which called for armed struggle against Israel, alongside the PLO's declaration of principles in 1988 and Arafat's statements that autumn, which called for peace with Israel and an end to terrorism. Diplomatic mileposts are marked by UN Security Council Resolution 242 (1967), the Egyptian-Israeli accords in 1977–1978, the Israel-PLO Declaration of Principles in 1993, and the peace treaty between Israel and Jordan in 1994. These documents enable the student to address directly the words of policymakers and the substance of the negotiated accords. They are complemented by a detailed chronology that includes many more events than we could mention in the text.

Biographical sketches profile key political figures, providing a flavor of their lives and personalities as well as a discussion of their importance on the Middle East stage. The annotated bibliography features sources that provide a starting point for conducting further research on the Arab-Israeli conflict. Memoirs, biographies, novels, and videos also offer a feeling for the ways in which individuals have been buffeted by the conflict and have struggled to surmount the suffering that it has caused to everyone.

By using multiple sources and varying approaches, we hope to avoid leading students to particular conclusions. Rather, we seek to expose them to divergent views on a complex topic that is the subject of heated debate.

This book is dedicated to Conchita, John, and Mark, and to Ann's brave sister Patricia, who died while we were still completing the manuscript.

Map I
The Middle East Today

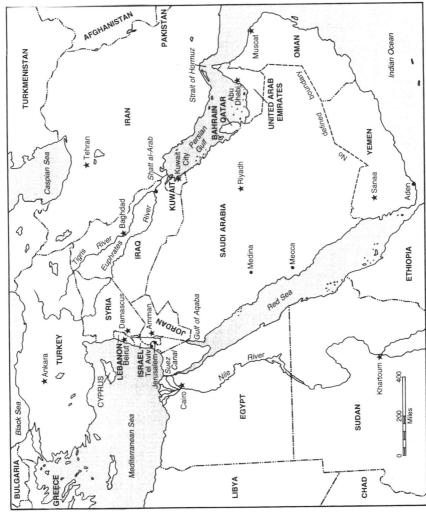

Source: Daniel C. Diller, *The Middle East*, 8th ed. (Washington, DC: Congressional Quarterly, 1994). Used by permission of Congressional Quarterly, Inc.

Chronology of Events

1516/1517	Ottoman rule begins in Syria, Mount Lebanon, Palestine, and Egypt.
1869	Suez Canal opens.
1882	The first Lovers of Zion group travels from Russia to Jaffa; Ottoman government restricts Jewish immigration to Palestine.
1882	Britain occupies Egypt.
1888	Constantinople Treaty provides for international transit of Suez Canal.
1894	Trial of Alfred Dreyfus in France.
1896	Herzl proposes statehood as the solution to anti-Semitism in *The Jewish State*.
1897	World Zionist Organization formed at First Zionist Congress in Basel, Switzerland.
1901	Establishment of Jewish National Fund.
1904	Theodor Herzl dies.
1909	Founding of Tel Aviv.
November 1914	Ottoman Empire enters World War I on the side of Germany.

July 1915– March 1916	Hussein-McMahon correspondence: Britain promises independence to the Arabs.
May 1916	Sykes-Picot agreement between Britain and France.
June 1916	Arab revolt begins.
November 2, 1917	Balfour Declaration offers Jews a national home in Palestine.
December 9, 1917	British General Edmund Allenby captures Jerusalem.
October 1918	British and Arab troops capture Damascus.
November 1918	World War I ends.
March 1920	Arab congress proclaims Faisal king of Syria.
April 1920	San Remo conference assigns mandates to Britain and France; Arabs protest in Jerusalem.
July 1920	French army expels Faisal from Syria.
August 1920	France separates Lebanon from Syria.
March 1921	Britain appoints Faisal king of Iraq and Abdullah ruler of Transjordan.
May 1921	Arab attacks on Jewish immigrant hostel in Jaffa; Haganah formed.
February 1922	Britain declares Egypt independent but retains military bases and economic privileges.
July 1922	League of Nations ratifies Palestine mandate, with Balfour Declaration and a separate Transjordan.
May 1923	Britain declares Transjordan a self-governing state.
1924	Ibn Saud captures the Hijaz (Mecca) from Hussein.
August 1929	Riots at Western (Wailing) Wall in Jerusalem; Jews killed in Jerusalem, Safed, and Hebron.
October 1932	Iraq becomes independent, joins League of Nations; Britain keeps military bases and oil interests.
January 30, 1933	Adolf Hitler assumes power in Germany.
September– November 1935	Nuremberg Laws against Jews are passed in Germany.
October 1935	Italy invades Ethiopia.
April–October 1936	Arab general strike in Palestine.

July 1937	Peel Commission report recommends partition of Palestine.
October 1937	Palestinian Arab revolt resumes.
February 1939	Anglo-Arab Conference on Palestine in London.
May 1939	British White Paper restricts Jewish land purchases and immigration to Palestine, rescinds recommendation to partition Palestine.
September 1, 1939	World War II begins.
September 1940	Italian forces invade Egypt from Libya.
June 1941	Britain reoccupies Iraq and seizes Syria and Lebanon from (Vichy) France.
May 1942	Biltmore Declaration calls for Jewish state in all of Palestine.
November 1942	Allied victory at Al-Alamein (Egypt).
November 1943	Lebanon declares independence.
February 1945	President Franklin D. Roosevelt meets with King Ibn Saud of Saudi Arabia on the Red Sea.
March 22, 1945	Arab League founded in Cairo.
May 25, 1945	Germany surrenders.
March 22, 1946	Transjordan gains independence.
May 1, 1946	Anglo-American Committee of Inquiry recommends admitting one hundred thousand Jews to Palestine.
July 22, 1946	British headquarters in King David Hotel (Jerusalem) bombed by the Irgun, right-wing Jewish nationalists.
May 13, 1947	UN General Assembly establishes Special Committee on Palestine (UNSCOP).
November 29, 1947	UN General Assembly Resolution 181 supports the partition of Palestine.
April 9, 1948	Irgun attacks Deir Yassin (Palestinian village).
April 13, 1948	Arab attack on Jewish bus convoy to Mt. Scopus.
April 22, 1948	Haganah captures Haifa.

May 14, 1948	Israel becomes an independent state.
May 15, 1948	Arab armies attack Israel.
September 17, 1948	UN mediator Count Folke Bernadotte assassinated by a Jewish militant.
January 25, 1949	Israeli elections; Ben-Gurion becomes prime minister.
February 24, 1949	Israel and Egypt sign armistice agreement at Rhodes.
March 11, 1949	Israel and Transjordan sign cease-fire.
July 20, 1949	Syria and Israel sign armistice.
January 1, 1950	Israel annexes West Jerusalem.
April 24, 1950	King Abdullah annexes East Jerusalem and the West Bank, renames his state the Hashemite Kingdom of Jordan.
July 20, 1951	King Abdullah assassinated in East Jerusalem.
July 23, 1952	Free Officers' coup d'état in Egypt.
August 1953	Hussein becomes King of Jordan.
July 1954	Lavon affair exposes Israeli sabotage mission in Egypt.
July 27, 1954	Anglo-Egyptian accord to complete the withdrawal of British forces from Egypt (ratified in October).
February 28, 1955	Israel attacks Gaza.
April 1955	Nasser attends Bandung nonaligned conference.
November 1955	Baghdad Pact is completed: Britain, Iraq, Turkey, Iran, and Pakistan.
September 27, 1955	Gamal Abdel Nasser announces Egyptian purchase of Soviet-bloc arms.
May 1956	Egypt recognizes the Peoples Republic of China.
June 13, 1956	British troops leave the Suez Canal.
July 19, 1956	Secretary of State John Foster Dulles withdraws U.S. financing for High Dam at Aswan.
July 26, 1956	Nasser nationalizes the Suez Canal Company.
October 29, 1956	Israel invades Sinai.
October 31, 1956	Britain and France bomb Egyptian airfields on Canal.

November 6/7, 1956	Britain, France, and Israel agree to cease-fire under U.S. and UN pressure.
November 21, 1956	Britain and France withdraw from Canal.
January 5, 1957	United States announces Eisenhower Doctrine to counter communism in the Middle East.
March 1, 1957	Israel withdraws from Gaza Strip; UN Emergency Force placed between Gaza Strip and Israel and at Sharm al-Sheikh.
February 1, 1958	Egypt and Syria form United Arab Republic (UAR).
July 14, 1958	Monarchy overthrown in Iraq.
July 15, 1958	United States sends Marines to Lebanon.
July 17, 1958	British troops land in Jordan.
March 24, 1959	Iraq leaves Baghdad Pact, renamed Central Treaty Organization (CENTO).
1959	Yasir Arafat and colleagues in Kuwait form Fatah, a Palestinian nationalist group.
June 19, 1961	Kuwait becomes independent.
September 29, 1961	Syria withdraws from UAR.
September 1962	Civil war begins in Yemen.
September 1962	United States' first sale of arms to Israel.
January 1964	Arab League summit conference establishes Palestine Liberation Organization (PLO) and plans to divert the headwaters of the Jordan River.
May 1964	Founding conference of the PLO in East Jerusalem.
January 1, 1965	Fatah's first raid targets Israeli National Water Carrier.
February 25, 1966	Baathists seize power in Syria.
November 4, 1966	Egypt and Syria sign mutual defense pact.
November 13, 1966	Israeli army raids Jordan at as-Samu (West Bank).
April 1967	Armed clashes between Israel and Syria.
May 20/22, 1967	Nasser demands withdrawal of UNEF, then closes Gulf of Aqaba to Israeli shipping.
May 30, 1967	Egypt and Jordan sign mutual defense pact.

June 5, 1967	Israel attacks Egypt, then Syria and Jordan.
June 7, 1967	Israel captures East Jerusalem.
June 8, 1967	Israeli planes attack *USS Liberty*.
June 10, 1967	Israel captures Golan Heights from Syria.
June 10, 1967	Cease-fire; Israel controls East Jerusalem, West Bank, Gaza Strip, Sinai, and Golan Heights.
June 28, 1967	Israel extends jurisdiction of West Jerusalem municipality over East Jerusalem.
September 1967	Arab summit conference at Khartoum.
September 24, 1967	Israel approves first Jewish settlement on the West Bank, at Gush Etzion.
November 22, 1967	UN Security Council unanimously passes Resolution 242, which proposes a "land-for-peace" formula.
March 21, 1968	Israeli-PLO battle of Karameh, east of Jordan River.
July 10–17, 1968	Palestine National Council (PNC) revises PLO covenant.
February 1969	Arafat becomes chairman of PLO at fifth PNC.
1969–1970	"War of attrition" along the Suez Canal.
August 3, 1969	Israeli Prime Minister Golda Meir announces Israel will keep Golan, Gaza, and part of Sinai.
December 1969	United States announces Rogers Plan.
June 25, 1970	United States announces Rogers Initiative.
August 7, 1970	United States negotiates cease-fire along Suez Canal.
September 6, 1970	Popular Front for the Liberation of Palestine (PFLP) hijacks civilian airplanes to Jordan.
September 16, 1970	King Hussein declares martial law; Jordan army attacks PLO bases and refugee camps.
September 27, 1970	PLO-Jordan cease-fire mediated by Nasser.
September 28, 1970	Nasser dies of heart attack; Anwar Sadat becomes president of Egypt.
November 13, 1970	Syrian Defense Minister Hafiz al-Asad seizes power.
July 18, 1972	Sadat expels Russian military advisers.

September 5, 1972	Israeli athletes murdered at Munich Olympics by Black September (Fatah).
October 6, 1973	October War begins with Egyptian and Syrian attacks against Israeli forces in Sinai and the Golan Heights.
October 15, 1973	United States begins arms airlift to Israel.
October 17, 1973	Arab members of OPEC impose oil embargo on United States.
October 22, 1973	UN Security Council Resolution 338 calls for direct negotiations based on Resolution 242.
October 23, 1973	Israeli troops cut off Egyptian army in Sinai.
October 25, 1973	U.S. forces on nuclear alert.
October 27, 1973	Egypt and Israel, then Syria, agree to cease-fire.
December 21, 1973	Peace conference opens in Geneva.
January 18, 1974	Israel and Egypt sign first disengagement accord.
February 28, 1974	United States and Egypt resume diplomatic relations.
May 31, 1974	Israel and Syria sign disengagement accord.
June 16, 1974	United States and Syria resume diplomatic relations.
October 28, 1974	Arab League summit conference at Rabat recognizes the PLO as the sole legitimate representative of the Palestinian people.
November 13, 1974	Arafat addresses UN General Assembly.
April 1975	Civil war begins in Lebanon.
June 5, 1975	Suez Canal reopens.
September 4, 1975	Israel and Egypt sign second disengagement accord.
November 10, 1975	UN General Assembly adopts resolution defining Zionism as "a form of racism."
May 31, 1976	Syrian troops enter Lebanon.
July 4, 1976	Israeli commandos raid airport at Entebbe (Uganda) to free passengers of airliner hijacked on June 27.
March 16, 1977	President Jimmy Carter endorses a Palestinian "homeland."
May 17, 1977	Menachem Begin (Likud) wins Israeli elections.

November 20, 1977	Sadat addresses Israeli Knesset.
December 25, 1977	Begin and Sadat meet in Ismailiyya, Egypt.
March 14, 1978	Israel invades Lebanon in "Operation Litani" in retaliation for Fatah bus hijacking.
June 13, 1978	Israel withdraws from Lebanon, except for six-mile "security zone."
September 17, 1978	Camp David peace accords signed by Begin, Sadat, and Carter.
February 1, 1979	Ayatollah Rouhollah Khomeini arrives in Iran.
March 22, 1979	Egypt-Israel peace treaty signed in Washington, D.C.
March 31, 1979	Egypt expelled from Arab League, which moves its headquarters from Cairo to Tunis.
April 30, 1979	First Israeli freighter passes through Suez Canal.
May 25, 1979	Israel begins withdrawal from Sinai Peninsula.
July 16, 1979	Saddam Hussein becomes president of Iraq.
November 4, 1979	American diplomats seized at U.S. embassy in Tehran.
July 30, 1980	Knesset declares all Jerusalem permanently Israeli.
September 22, 1980	Iraq attacks Iran.
June 7, 1981	Israel bombs Iraqi nuclear reactor at Osirak.
July 17, 1981	Three hundred civilians die in Israeli bombing of Beirut.
July 24, 1981	Israel-PLO cease-fire mediated in Lebanon.
October 6, 1981	Sadat assassinated; Hosni Mubarak becomes president of Egypt.
November 30, 1981	United States-Israel strategic cooperation memorandum.
December 14, 1981	Israeli Knesset annexes Golan Heights.
December 18, 1981	United States temporarily suspends strategic cooperation with Israel.
April 25, 1982	Israel returns Sinai (except Taba) to Egypt.
June 3, 1982	Israeli ambassador in London wounded.
June 6, 1982	Israel invades Lebanon.
August 13, 1982	Beshir Gemayel elected president of Lebanon.

August 21, 1982	PLO withdrawal from Beirut, completed by September 1.
September 1, 1982	Reagan Initiative.
September 9, 1982	Fez Peace Proposal.
September 14, 1982	Gemayel assassinated, allegedly by a Syrian agent, then Israeli troops seize West Beirut.
September 18, 1982	Sabra and Shatila massacres of Palestinian refugees.
September 20, 1982	Amin Gemayel becomes president of Lebanon.
April 18, 1983	Bomb partly destroys U.S. embassy in Beirut.
August 29, 1983	Menachem Begin resigns, replaced by Yitzhak Shamir.
September 16, 1983	U.S. Navy begins hitting targets in Lebanese hills.
October 23, 1983	Two hundred forty-one U.S. Marines killed in truck bomb in Beirut.
February 21, 1984	U.S. peacekeeping forces depart Lebanon.
July 23, 1984	Israeli elections: Labor-Likud government with Shimon Peres as Prime Minister formed September 13.
January 20, 1985	Israel begins initial withdrawal from Lebanon.
February 22, 1985	Jordanian-PLO peace plan.
June 10, 1985	Israel withdraws from most of Lebanon.
June 14, 1985	TWA airliner hijacked by Lebanese group to Beirut (released June 30).
October 1, 1985	Israel bombs PLO headquarters in Tunis.
October 7, 1985	Cruise ship *Achille Lauro* hijacked by Abu Abbas's group.
October 20, 1986	Shamir (Likud) becomes Israeli prime minister under rotation arrangement with Labor.
November 1987	Arab League summit in Amman focuses on Iran-Iraq war.
December 9, 1987	Palestinian intifada begins in Occupied Territories.
April 16, 1988	Israel assassinates PLO military head Abu Jihad in Tunis.
July 31, 1988	King Hussein renounces claims to West Bank.
August 20, 1988	Iraq-Iran cease-fire.
September 29, 1988	Taba is returned to Egypt by international arbiters.

November 15, 1988   Palestine National Council proclaims Palestinian state and accepts UN Security Council Resolution 242 (1967).

December 14, 1988   After Arafat's press conference, United States opens dialogue with PLO.

May 22, 1989   Egypt is readmitted to Arab League.

October 24, 1989   Lebanese parliament endorses Taif peace plan.

May 30, 1990   Israel captures Abu Abbas's boats on way to attack Israeli beach.

June 8, 1990   Likud-right coalition government in Israel.

June 20, 1990   United States suspends dialogue with PLO.

August 2, 1990   Iraq invades Kuwait.

November 29, 1990   UN authorizes use of "all necessary means" to expel Iraq from Kuwait and sets January 15, 1991, as the deadline.

January 16, 1991   United States-led coalition begins air attack on Iraq.

January 18, 1991   Iraq's first use of Scud missiles against Israel.

February 27, 1991   Kuwait is liberated.

October 18, 1991   Soviet Union reestablishes diplomatic relations with Israel (broken in 1967).

October 30, 1991   Arab-Israel peace conference opens in Madrid.

December 3, 1991   Last U.S. hostage in Lebanon is freed.

December 16, 1991   UN General Assembly overturns Zionism-is-racism resolution.

February 16, 1992   Israel kills Hizballah leader in South Lebanon.

June 23, 1992   Israeli elections: Yitzhak Rabin (Labor) becomes prime minister, Peres becomes foreign minister.

December 17, 1992   Israel deports 415 Hamas members to south Lebanon.

January 16, 1993   Knesset repeals law banning contact with PLO.

March 25, 1993   Benjamin Netanyahu replaces Shamir as head of Likud.

July 25, 1993   Israel attacks Lebanon, retaliating for Hizballah rockets, displaces 250,000 civilians; United States mediates ceasefire.

August 30, 1993   Peres announces Israel-PLO Declaration of Principles (DOP) negotiated in Oslo.

September 10, 1993   United States resumes dialogue with PLO.

September 13, 1993   Israel and PLO sign DOP on Palestinian Interim Self-Government in Washington, D.C.

December 13, 1993   Target date passes for beginning Israeli withdrawal from the Gaza Strip and Jericho.

January 16, 1994   Asad says he will negotiate a treaty with Israel.

February 25, 1994   Jewish settler kills Palestinian worshipers in Hebron.

April 6, 1994   Hamas bombs bus in Afula (Israel).

May 4, 1994   Arafat and Rabin sign Gaza-Jericho Accord in Cairo.

July 1, 1994   Arafat arrives in Gaza, assumes presidency of Palestinian Authority (PA).

July 25, 1994   King Hussein and Rabin end state of war between Jordan and Israel.

August 26, 1994   Hamas stabs two Israelis to death in Tel Aviv.

September 11, 1994   Israeli-Syrian negotiations reopen in Washington, D.C.

September 26, 1994   Israel approves housing for settlements on West Bank.

October 2, 1994   Israel and Tunisia agree to exchange economic liaison offices.

October 11, 1994   Hamas kidnaps Israeli soldier (killed on October 14).

October 11–13, 1994   U.S. Secretary of State Warren Christopher shuttle in Middle East.

October 19, 1994   Hamas blows up Israeli bus in Tel Aviv.

October 26, 1994   Israeli-Jordanian peace treaty signed near Aqaba.

October 30, 1994   Casablanca economic summit conference.

November 18, 1994   Clash between Palestinian police and Islamic militants in Gaza (accord to end violence November 21).

December 5–7, 1994   Christopher shuttle to Middle East.

December 22, 1994   Israel-Syria talks in Washington, D.C.

January 19, 1995   Rabin and Arafat meet; Rabin agrees to halt new settlements and confiscate land only for roads.

January 22, 1995   Car bombs at Bet Lid (Israel); Israel-PLO negotiations suspended.

January 25, 1995	Israel approves building 2,200 housing units on the West Bank.
February 2, 1995	Arafat, Rabin, Hussein, Mubarak summit in Cairo.
June 1, 1995	Rabin says he will submit Israel-Syria treaty to a referendum.
July–August 1995	Israeli settlers try to seize land on West Bank.
July 24, 1995	Hamas bombs bus in Ramat Gan (Israel).
August 31, 1995	Hamas bus bombing in Jerusalem.
September 28, 1995	Israel-PLO Oslo-II accord signed in Washington, D.C.
October 26, 1995	Israel assassinates Fathi Shiqaqi, leader of Islamic Jihad, in Malta.
November 4, 1995	Israeli kills Rabin in Tel Aviv; Peres becomes acting prime minister.
December 1995	Palestinian Authority assumes control in towns on West Bank, issues passports.
December 1995–March 1996	Syria-Israeli talks at Wye Plantation (United States).
January 5, 1996	Israel kills Hamas's "The Engineer" with booby-trapped cellular phone in Gaza.
January 20, 1996	Palestinian legislative and presidential elections on West Bank and Gaza Strip.
January 22, 1996	Israel and Tunisia set up interests sections.
January 27, 1996	Israel and Oman establish economic liaison offices.
February 23, 1996	Hamas bomb on bus in Jerusalem.
March 3, 1996	Hamas bomb on bus in Jerusalem.
March 4, 1996	Hamas suicide bomb in Tel Aviv.
March 13, 1996	Sharm al-Sheikh conference on terror: Arafat, King Hussein, Peres, Clinton, Mubarak.
April 11, 1996	Israel begins air raids on Lebanon after Hizballah shelling; four hundred thousand Lebanese displaced.
April 18, 1996	Israel shells UN post at Qana in Lebanon.
April 20, 1996	Christopher begins shuttle in Middle East, finalizes cease-fire in Lebanon on April 27.

April 22–24, 1996   PNC meets in Gaza, revokes clauses of PLO Charter that call for Israel's destruction.

May 3, 1996   Peres delays troop withdrawal from Hebron until after Israeli election.

May 29, 1996   Netanyahu elected prime minister of Israel.

June 16, 1996   Netanyahu states that Israel will retain sovereignty over the Golan.

June 21, 1996   Arab summit in Cairo calls on Israel to honor its commitments.

July 12, 1996   Qatar cancels plan to open trade mission in Israel.

September 4, 1996   Netanyahu and Arafat meet for first time.

September 24, 1996   Israel opens door of tunnel in Jerusalem; clashes spread through West Bank and Gaza: fifty-six Palestinians and fourteen Israeli soldiers die.

October 1–2, 1996   Netanyahu, Arafat, King Hussein, and Clinton meet in Washington, D.C.

November 18, 1996   Talks on Israeli redeployment in Hebron reach an impasse; Israeli military court sentences four Israeli soldiers to one hour's jail for shooting to death a Palestinian youth on the West Bank on November 13, 1993.

November 20, 1996   Consultative Group, meeting in Paris, pledges support for the PA's investment program.

November 22, 1996   Israeli Infrastructure Minister Ariel Sharon draws up plans to construct 900 housing units on the Golan Heights as first phase in building 2,500 units over three years.

November 25, 1996   Arafat letter to Netanyahu urges a halt in the expansion of settlements.

November 26, 1996   PA announces boycott of multilateral talks, except refugee group, due to lack of progress in Hebron negotiations and Israeli nonimplementation of provisions in the 1995 accords.

December 2, 1996   Israeli government approves construction of new housing units in settlements on the West Bank.

December 3, 1996   Oman suspends ties with Israel and recalls its representative, due to lack of progress on Hebron.

December 6, 1996   Palestinian military court sentences to life in prison a guard who killed a prisoner on December 3.

December 8, 1996   Israel boycotts meeting of quadripartite refugee committee (Egypt, Jordan, PA, and Israel) in Bethlehem.

December 11, 1996   PFLP kills two Israeli settlers from Beit El in response to renewed settlement construction.

December 13, 1996   Israeli cabinet restores top-level priority to settlements; Hamas antisettlement rally in Gaza.

December 15, 1996   Palestinian military court sentences to death two Hamas members for killing two Palestinian policemen a year ago.

December 16, 1996   Netanyahu rejects Clinton's criticism of renewed expansion of settlements; Tunisia suspends relations with Israel, due to its nonfulfillment of the accords with the PLO.

December 18, 1996   Palestinian State Security Court in Ramallah convicts three PFLP members for killing two settlers on December 11.

December 24, 1996   Netanyahu and Arafat meet at Erez junction (Gaza-Israel border).

January 1, 1997   Off-duty Israeli soldier wounds six Palestinians in Hebron; soldier discharged but not tried.

January 6, 1997   Second Netanyahu-Arafat meeting at Erez junction.

January 12, 1997   King Hussein flies to Gaza and Israel, breaks diplomatic impasse.

January 14, 1997   Army begins forced removal of four hundred Jahalin bedouin from lands near Ma'ale Adumim settlement on Jerusalem-Jericho road.

January 15, 1997   Hebron protocol initialed at Erez, then ratified by PA Executive Authority, PLO Executive Committee, Palestinian legislature, Israeli cabinet, and Knesset.

January 17, 1997   Israel completes redeployment from 80 percent of Hebron.

February 4, 1997   Two Israeli helicopters collide in northern Israel on their way to Lebanon, with all seventy-three soldiers on board killed.

February 9, 1997   Netanyahu and Arafat meet at Erez and agree to start talks on implementing the September 1995 accords.

February 10, 1997	Israeli armed forces present "final status" map to the cabinet in which 51.8 percent of the West Bank would remain under Israel.
February 11, 1997	Israel releases the twenty-seven female Palestinian prisoners; four thousand men remain in jail.
February 15, 1997	Netanyahu says that he will not rule out a "cosmetic withdrawal" from the Golan Heights.
February 23, 1997	Netanyahu and Clinton meet in Washington, D.C., focus on restarting Syrian-Israeli talks.
March 7, 1997	Israeli cabinet approves a troop deployment on the West Bank that accords the PA 2 percent more land.
March 13, 1997	Jordanian border guard kills seven Israeli schoolgirls in joint Israeli-Jordanian controlled park.
March 18, 1997	Bulldozers break ground at Har Homa (Jebel Abu Ghneim), Jewish settlement in East Jerusalem bordering Bethlehem.
March 21, 1997	Suicide bomb in Tel Aviv café kills three Israeli women and the Hamas militant.
March 22, 1997	Israeli closure of Israel to residents of the West Bank and Gaza Strip leads to a week of clashes between Palestinians and Israeli soldiers in Bethlehem, Hebron, Nablus, and Ramallah.
March 31, 1997	Arab League decision to suspend participation in the multilateral working groups and reactivate the economic boycott of Israel, due to the construction of Har Homa.
May 7–16, 1997	U.S. envoy Dennis Ross fails to restart the peace process.
June 8, 1997	Israeli and Palestinian negotiators meet in Cairo.
June 16, 1997	Nineteen Palestinians are wounded in Hebron during clashes with Israeli soldiers.
June 28, 1997	Israeli woman arrested for putting up posters in Hebron that insult the Prophet Muhammad.
July 13, 1997	Protests resume in Hebron.
July 30, 1997	Two suicide bombers kill fifteen Israelis in market in West Jerusalem; Israel closes West Bank and Gaza, suspends financial transfers to the Palestinian Authority, and arrests two hundred Palestinians.

August 9, 1997   Dennis Ross arrives in Israel to restore Israeli-Palestinian
                    security coordination.

September 4, 1997   Three suicide bombers kill four Israelis in West
                    Jerusalem, prompting renewed closure of the West Bank
                    and Gaza; Lebanese kill twelve Israeli soldiers attacking a
                    village between Sidon and Tyre.

September 9, 1997   U.S. Secretary of State Madeleine Albright begins her
                    first trip to the Middle East.

THE ARAB-ISRAELI CONFLICT EXPLAINED

I

Historical Overview

The Middle East has long been an area of brilliant civilizations and severe conflicts. Its strategic location—a true crossroads linking Europe, Asia, and Africa—facilitated the spread of ideas and commerce but also provoked local and foreign powers to seize its valuable territory. The lands on the eastern Mediterranean between Mesopotamia and the Nile Valley were contested fiercely by Canaanites, Phoenicians, Hebrews, Philistines, and Nabateans. Greek armies swept across those lands on their way from Egypt to Persia, followed by the powerful Roman and Byzantine empires.

In the seventh century, adherents of the new Islamic religious movement challenged the declining Byzantine empire and founded Muslim Arab empires whose centers of power soon shifted from Arabia to the eastern Mediterranean and Mesopotamia. A gradual process of Arabization and Islamization blended the varying Middle Eastern peoples. Arab rulers survived the ravages of the Crusaders and the Mongols but succumbed to the Ottoman armies in the early sixteenth century. Although the Ottoman Empire brought stability for nearly four centuries, the strategic balance had shifted decisively against the Ottomans by the time Napoleon conquered Egypt in 1798. His invasion heralded Europe's competitive scramble for territory throughout the Middle East and North Africa. By the end of World War I, only Turkey, Persia, and Arabia remained outside the direct political control of Europe. And when the Europeans departed after World War II, they left behind a legacy of local conflicts and a deepset bitterness against foreign domination.

The years after World War II have seen the world become used to what is often called "*the* Middle East conflict": the Arab-Israeli conflict. For the past fifty years, this struggle has predominated in news about events in the Middle East. In terms of the prolonged suffering and bloodshed inflicted on all sides, the Arab-Israeli conflict is the most pressing political problem challenging the region—and all who interact with it.

Two decades ago, as will be seen in the following pages, hope that the conflict could be resolved began to spread, with the arrival of peace between Egypt and Israel. Within the last half-decade, such hopes have been boosted by other agreements between Israel and major Arab political actors. However, full peace does not yet exist between Israel and the Arab world. It is notable that some people conclude that such a peace, one characterized by mutual acceptance and cordial relations, will never arrive. It is even more notable that among those who are most convinced of this view are Israelis and Arabs—those "rejectionists" in each camp who see no possibility of enduring compromise.

Because of this pessimism some observers argue that the conflict between Israel and the Arabs is so deep-rooted, intense, and multifaceted that a comprehensive resolution is impossible. They cite the Arabs' hostility to Zionism in the first half of the twentieth century and the series of wars that began upon Israel's birth in 1948. Such observers argue that Arabs will never really accept Israel's legitimacy and its permanent presence in the region and that Israelis will never accept the right of the Palestinians to national self-determination and statehood. This view holds that the conflict is zero-sum: Victory by one side means defeat by the other. No compromise is possible between the parties, and therefore positions remain inflexible. Because core values are at stake in the conflict over the very existence of Israel and Arab rights to Palestine, strife will be unending.

A contrasting approach maintains that the conflict cannot be seen as zero-sum. Rather, both sides gain from negotiations and the resolution of basic issues. In this positive-sum situation, success for one side is not at the expense of the other. Diplomatic flexibility and political pragmatism can yield positive results in the management and resolution of issues dividing the parties.

In tracing the history of the Arab-Israeli conflict, this chapter makes three key points. First, Arabs as well as Israelis have alternated between pursuing ideologically rooted policies and attempting pragmatically motivated approaches. Second, both sides have frequently faced internal divisions over the nature of the conflict and the ways to resolve it. Third, external third-party actors have played important and varying roles in either bolstering ideological intransigence or encouraging pragmatic accommodation. Overall, the chapter argues that the Arab-Israeli conflict can be understood by looking at the interplay among the policies of Arabs, Israelis, and third parties in order to determine the factors that have promoted or hindered confrontation or accommodation.

THE EUROPEAN CONTEST TO CONTROL THE ARAB WORLD

The Arab-Israeli conflict originated in the contest among European powers to control the Arab territories of the Ottoman Empire. Just at the time that Arabs began to develop their own sense of nationalism, they found their dreams contested by European ambitions and by the counterclaims of the new Jewish nationalist movement that arose in Europe.

The Ottoman Empire spread from Anatolia (now Turkey) along the eastern Mediterranean coast to Morocco and down the Arabian peninsula to the Muslim holy cities of Mecca and Medina. Ottoman rule even reached into Europe as far as Vienna by 1529. But the empire weakened economically and politically by the nineteenth century. European powers seized territory in Europe and North Africa. Great Britain was anxious to control the sea routes to India, its prize colony. By World War I, Great Britain controlled all the key sites along those routes: Gibraltar, Malta, Cyprus, Egypt, Sudan, Aden, and South Africa. Britain also established special relations with local Arab rulers along the Persian Gulf. France countered by seizing Algeria, Tunisia, and Morocco, and Italy grabbed Libya. The Ottoman Empire shrank to Anatolia and the Arab provinces on the eastern Mediterranean (Syria, Lebanon, Palestine), the Red Sea coast (Hejaz, Yemen), and Mesopotamia (Iraq). (See Map 2.)

In addition to fearing European colonialism, residents of Arab provinces began to fear the Zionist movement. A sense of Jewish nationalism was emerging in Europe in the 1880s, in reaction to deep-seated anti-Semitism and to the difficulty that Jews faced assimilating into European society. As will be discussed in Chapter 2, Zionists felt that Jews could not be fully accepted in Europe and that they needed to rule their own independent state. Although Zionism attracted limited support in the formative period, Jewish immigration to Palestine from 1882 to 1914 increased the number of Jewish residents from 6 percent to 10 percent of the population there. The World Zionist Organization (WZO), founded in 1897 (Document 1), assisted immigrants and bought land with the aim of creating a Jewish state in Palestine. When the Palestinian residents protested against these political aims, the Ottoman rulers tried to restrict Jewish immigration and purchase of land. This Jewish nationalism clashed with the nationalism of the Palestinian Arabs, who comprised 90 percent of the residents.

Map 2
Ottoman Palestine and Syria, 1910

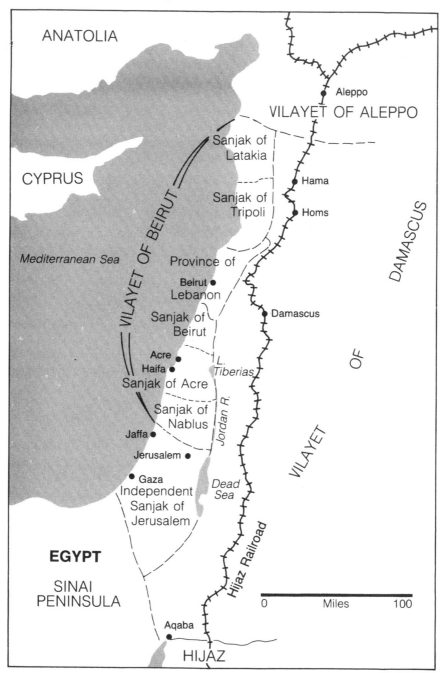

ANATOLIA

CYPRUS

Mediterranean Sea

Aleppo

VILAYET OF ALEPPO

Sanjak of
Latakia

Sanjak of
Tripoli

Hama

Homs

DAMASCUS

VILAYET OF BEIRUT

Province of
Beirut
Lebanon

Sanjak of
Beirut

Damascus

OF

Acre
Haifa
Sanjak of Acre

L.
Tiberias

Sanjak of
Nablus

Jordan R.

Jaffa

Jerusalem

VILAYET

Gaza
Independent
Sanjak of
Jerusalem

Dead
Sea

EGYPT

SINAI
PENINSULA

Hijaz Railroad

0   Miles   100

Aqaba

HIJAZ

Source: Charles D. Smith, *Palestine and the Arab-Israeli Conflict*, 2nd ed. (New York: St. Martin's Press, 1992), p. 33. Copyright © 1992. Reprinted with permission of St. Martin's Press, Inc.

World War I transformed the political map in the Middle East. When the Ottoman Empire entered the war on the side of Germany and the Austro-Hungarian Empire in November 1914, the three countries that sought to carve up its territory—Russia, France, and England—competed for the potential spoils from the war. Because Britain ruled Egypt, its troops were poised to occupy the remaining Arab provinces. To achieve its ambitions, Britain concluded three contradictory agreements: the first with the Arabs, the second with France, and the third with the Zionist movement. These contradictory promises have haunted the Middle East ever since.

First, the Hussein-McMahon Correspondence from July 1915 to May 1916 (Document 2): To secure its position in the region, Britain recognized the value of gaining the support of the ruler of the Hejaz, who was also the religious leader of Mecca and Medina, the most holy cities in Islam. That support would undermine the Ottoman claim that Muslims had a religious obligation to fight Christian Europe. Through a lengthy correspondence, Britain persuaded Sharif Hussein of Mecca to launch an Arab revolt that would help destroy the Ottoman Empire and achieve Arab independence. Sharif Hussein and Arab nationalists in Syria and Palestine thought that this would ward off European rule. However, the British carefully excluded certain territories from the area of Arab independence. They insisted that Britain rule oil-rich Iraq, keep its protectorates over the Arab principalities along the Persian Gulf, and retain its colony in Aden. They hinted that France would gain a special role in Lebanon, where it was already the guardian of the Maronite (Catholic) community and had extensive commercial interests. Palestine was not mentioned as a territory to be excluded from the Arab zone, and therefore the Arabs assumed that they would rule it. This, and additional public declarations by British officials to the Arab peoples, caused Sharif Hussein's forces to help Britain conquer Palestine, Transjordan, and Syria during 1917–1918. At the same time, British troops from India seized Iraq. Hussein's son, Faisal, was installed in Syria as the ruler of a provisionally independent Arab state.

Second, the Sykes-Picot Agreement of May 16, 1916: This was a secret agreement between Britain and France that included a plan to carve up the Arab provinces. France would control Lebanon, Syria, and northern Iraq, and Britain would dominate Transjordan and central and southern Iraq. The accord placed Palestine under international control rather than within the Arab areas that would receive independence. The Arab area shrank to only a portion of the Arabian peninsula. When the new Bolshevik government in Russia published—and denounced—the Sykes-Picot agreement in December 1917, Arabs were furious over the secret imperial designs. But the Arabs had no effective lobby in western Europe, and they had no presence at the peace table at Versailles, which was redrawing the global political map. The British and French had their way inasmuch as the Sykes-Picot Agreement served as the basis for the postwar settlement that the new League of Nations ratified.

Third, the Balfour Declaration of November 2, 1917 (Document 3): The British government informed the Zionist movement that it favored the establishment of a "national home for the Jewish people" in Palestine. Britain hoped that the Declaration would encourage American and Russian Jews to press their governments to fight harder in Europe. Forming a Jewish national home under British protection would circumvent both the promise to the French to internationalize Palestine and the inclusion of Palestine in the Arab zone. By offering to help the Zionists establish this home, Britain could place its own troops in Palestine and thereby control that strategic prize near the Suez Canal as well as preside over the holy places in Jerusalem.

These deals were sanctioned in a series of international conferences that Britain and France dominated. As a result, the new international organization called the League of Nations gave France authority over Syria and Lebanon, and confirmed Britain's control over Iraq, Palestine, and Transjordan. As "mandatory" powers, Britain and France did not have exclusive control but were entrusted by the League to rule on behalf of the residents. The Balfour Declaration was written into Britain's mandate over Palestine. The imperial powers thereby used the League of Nations to establish a new international order that they designed to fulfill their ambitions.

The three sets of promises contained deep contradictions. Overall, European colonial rule prevailed, at the expense of Arab independence. Jewish nationalism was given priority over the rights of the Palestinians. Arabs felt betrayed and bitter at the carving up and colonization of their territories. Even the Zionists felt betrayed when they realized, many years later, that the British pledge to help them create a national home did not necessarily mean that Britain would support the formation of a fully independent state.

The British tried to mollify Sharif Hussein after the French expelled his son Faisal from Syria in July 1920; they placed Faisal on the throne in Iraq in 1921 and let another son, Abdallah, rule Transjordan. But Hussein refused to sanction the colonial land-grab and the Balfour Declaration. The British then withdrew financial support from Hussein, who was soon forced from power by his rival, Ibn Saud.

During the 1920s and 1930s the contradictions in Palestine became starkly evident, as Chapter 2 stresses. Jewish and Palestinian nationalists, each seeking statehood in the same territory, struggled against each other.

Arabs could not stem Jewish immigration, which became increasingly urgent once Adolph Hitler and the Nazis seized power in Germany in 1933. The Palestinians' plight contrasted with the independence gained by other Arabs. North Yemen had become independent as soon as the Ottoman Empire fell in 1918. Ibn Saud quickly unified the central Arabian peninsula as Saudi Arabia. Iraq and Egypt gained independence in 1932 and 1936, respectively. Transjordan and Lebanon attained self-governing status in 1926 and received full independence in 1945–1946, along with Syria. Arab governments became actively concerned about the Palestine problem and anxious to complete the decolonization process. They articulated Arab grievances in meetings with the British government in 1937–1939, and after World War II they formed the League of Arab States to coordinate their foreign policies.

The Arabs' bitterness over the Palestinians' fate began to be matched by Zionist hostility to British rule at the end of the 1930s. Britain had proposed a partition plan in 1937 that would have created a Jewish state on a quarter of the land (Document 4) but rescinded that offer in 1939 due to escalating Arab opposition. Impelled by the growing possibility of war in Europe, London tried to shore up its position in the Arab world by limiting the development of the Jewish national home in Palestine through restricting immigration and the purchase of land. The Jewish community felt betrayed. Although the official Zionist leadership decided not to engage in armed struggle against British rule while Britain was fighting Hitler's Germany, some Zionist splinter groups waged a campaign of terrorism against the mandatory administration, even during World War II. After the war ended, official Zionist-British relations in Palestine deteriorated into a tense, and sometimes violent, confrontation.

World War II led to a groundswell of support in the United States and Europe for a Jewish state, as a result of shock at the Nazis' near annihilation of European Jewry. Zionists hardened their political position, insisting that the Jewish state must encompass all of Palestine because that state would serve as the haven for world Jewry. The war also created a massive problem of displaced persons in Europe, over one hundred thousand of whom were Jews. Zionist leaders pointed to the legal barriers hindering the immigration of Jews to the United States and other countries, and strongly supported the recommendation of the Anglo-American Committee of Inquiry in 1946 that those one hundred thousand Holocaust survivors settle in Palestine.

That Committee of Inquiry also proposed that Palestine become a joint Jewish-Arab state. By then, however, the Arab and Jewish communities were each determined to create their own state. Moreover, U.S. President

Harry Truman would not commit himself to the proposed joint state or to assisting the British in resolving the Arab-Jewish conflict.

Partition, rather than sharing power, reemerged as a way to resolve the dilemma. This idea, which had been proposed in 1937, resurfaced in 1947 after Britain turned the problem over to the United Nations—the successor to the League of Nations. UN General Assembly Resolution 181 of November 29, 1947, endorsed a plan to establish separate Jewish and Arab states. At that time, Palestine's Jewish community totaled 30 percent of the population and owned 7 percent of the land. However, the partition plan allotted 55 percent of the land to the Jewish state. Jerusalem and its environs, some 5 percent of Palestine's area, would form an international enclave under UN control. The Arab state would comprise 40 percent of Palestine's land. Palestinians and the Arab states rejected that partition plan, insisting that Palestine gain full independence as an Arab state, in keeping with the clear desire of the majority of its inhabitants. Although many Zionists strongly believed that no compromise should be made on their claim to all of Palestine, the Zionist leadership accepted the partition plan as "the indispensable minimum."[1]

As Chapter 2 indicates, when assessing the evolution of the conflict from the late nineteenth century to 1948, it is evident that the lines of tension deepened and hardened dramatically. By the mid-1940s, Arabs and Zionists were in the grip of desperate passions. For the former, these were fueled by the growing threat to their land and established way of life; passions among the latter were immeasurably intensified by the Holocaust and the postwar homelessness of European Jews. Strong feelings developed on both sides that their maximal demands could not be reduced, that no compromise was possible.

Yet, history shows that we cannot be sure that no possibility of compromise existed by 1948. The Zionist leadership, after clinging fiercely to its demand for all of Palestine, modified its stand when presented with the option of partition in 1947. At the same time, Arab governments, after having repeatedly emphasized that only a united Arab Palestinian state was acceptable, indicated in late 1947, at first in private and then openly, that a federal option would be acceptable. Could a compromise between partition and federation have been achieved? Could the Arab governments have convinced the Palestinians to accept a compromise? We shall never know, for time ran out and Arab-Zionist relations were to be shaped for the next fifty years by the war that broke out in 1948.

An analysis of the conflict before 1948 would be incomplete without examining the role of external states that shaped the context in which the

Arab-Zionist struggle developed. Chief among these was Great Britain's role. From the outset, Britain's contradictory promises to Arabs and Zionists created a conflictive environment. Moreover, signs that Britain could be pressured by events into altering its policy on Palestine—such as occurred in 1939 when London limited the development of the Jewish homeland—were not infrequent. For both Arab and Zionist leaders, this made extremist rhetoric a logical tactic designed to elicit favorable British reactions. Inevitably, these tactics inflamed the passions of rank-and-file Arabs and Zionists; just as inevitably, the inflamed sentiments tended to restrict the flexibility that could be shown by their leaders. Britain's shifts in its stand on Palestine's future helped foment a vicious circle of rising militancy on the part of both Arabs and Zionists.

Washington's entry into the Palestine equation after World War II had the same effect. By verbally, but not practically, supporting the demand that one hundred thousand Jewish displaced persons (DPs) be permitted to enter Palestine and by delaying supporting any specific political arrangement, the Truman administration invited extremist stands intended to sway a final U.S. decision.

In the final analysis, then, the major impact of external states on the Arab-Zionist conflict was to exacerbate, rather than moderate, tension. The ensuing explosion gave new impetus to enduring animosities between the newly proclaimed state of Israel and the Arab states.

CREATION OF AN INTER-STATE CONFLICT

Israel proclaimed its independence on May 15, 1948, just as the last British troops departed. By then the Jewish army had seized most of the territory allotted to the Jewish state and had even captured major Palestinian towns such as Jaffa and Acre that the UN partition plan placed outside its borders. Thousands of Palestinians fled, fearful of Haganah and Irgun attacks. In early May 1948, the Arab states finally agreed to defend the Palestinians. On the same day that Israel was born, Egypt sent troops into the Gaza Strip and the Negev, Transjordan dispatched its Arab Legion to the West Bank, the Syrian army approached the Sea of Galilee, and Lebanon sent token forces into northern Galilee. However, their forces were uncoordinated and ill-prepared for combat.

The fighting lasted from May through December 1948, after which armistice agreements between the warring parties left Israel in control of three-quarters of Palestine. An unwritten secret agreement between Israel and Transjordan enabled Transjordan's King Abdullah to retain the West

Bank. Israel feared that Britain might intervene militarily on behalf of Egypt, and so it left the Gaza Strip under the Egyptian army. Syria was the only Arab country whose army controlled land along the Jordan River and the Sea of Galilee that had been allotted to the Jewish state in the partition plan. (See Map 3 regarding the changing borders of Israel.)

The UN partition plan had called for Jerusalem to be an international city. Nonetheless, both Israel and Transjordan rejected internationalization, and their armies fought bitterly to control the holy city. The fighting resulted in East Jerusalem remaining under Jordanian control and West Jerusalem remaining under Israel.

The loss of Palestine embittered Arabs against the European colonial powers that had carved up their land and aided Zionism. But the defeat also led to self-criticism. Arab peoples denounced their rulers for corruption, and Arab soldiers denounced their military officers for incompetence. This led to *coups d'état* in Syria in 1949, the assassination of King Abdullah of Jordan in 1951, and a 1952 military *coup d'état* in Egypt that was led by Colonel Gamal Abdel Nasser.

Israel used its victory to consolidate its hold territorially and politically. Some 750,000 Palestinians had fled or been expelled by the Israeli army, and the Israeli government settled Jewish immigrants in their homes and took over their vacant farms and shops. Financial assistance came from the United States as well as West Germany, which paid restitution for the Holocaust. That aid helped the new country overcome the Arab trade boycott, which was designed to choke Israel economically by preventing it from trading with the neighboring countries. Meanwhile, as Jews migrated to Israel from Europe and the Middle East, Israel's Jewish population grew rapidly. The 650,000 Jewish residents in 1948 doubled to 1.3 million in 1952.

The United Nations (UN) admitted Israel as a member in 1949, conditional upon its repatriating or compensating Palestinian refugees and internationalizing Jerusalem. Less than a year later Israel defied those terms by proclaiming West Jerusalem its capital. Jordan's King Abdullah responded by annexing East Jerusalem and the West Bank, and renaming his enlarged country the Hashemite Kingdom of Jordan. Israel resisted U.S. pressure to readmit 40 percent (three hundred thousand) of the Palestinian refugees in the context of a peace agreement. Israeli Prime Minister David Ben-Gurion argued that letting them return would be political suicide, because they would oppose the Jewish state. Israel also refused to alter the armistice lines in order to provide more living space for the refugees in Gaza and the West Bank, claiming that all its postwar territory was needed to settle Jewish immigrants. Furthermore, Israel would not turn over the funds held by

Map 3
The Changing Borders of Israel: 1947, 1949, 1967, and 1982

Jewish state as proposed by the United Nations, 1947

Israel after the Arab War, 1949

Areas taken and held after the Six-Day War, 1967

Area returned to Egypt by 1982, Auja and Taba excepted

Beirut

LEBANON
Sidon

Tyre

GOLAN HTS.

SYRIA

Haifa

ISRAEL — Nablus

Mediterranean Sea

Tel Aviv
Jaffa

JORDAN

Amman

Jerusalem

Nile Delta

Gaza

Hebron   Dead
          Sea

GAZA STRIP

Port Said

El Arish

Suez
Canal   Qantara

Auja

NEGEV

Ismailiya

Great Bitter
Lake

Cairo

Suez

SINAI PENINSULA

Eilat

Taba   Aqaba

E   G   Y   P   T

UNITED ARAB REPUBLIC

Jordan R.

Gulf of Aqaba

SAUDI
ARABIA

Gulf of Suez

Mt. Sinai

El Tor

Tiran Is.

Str. of Tiran

Sharm el Sheikh

0   Miles   50

Source: Charles D. Smith, *Palestine and the Arab-Israeli Conflict*, 2nd ed. (New York: St. Martin's Press, 1992), p. 207. Copyright © 1992. Reprinted with permission of St. Martin's Press, Inc.

Palestinians in bank accounts inside Israel, even though that disbursement would have eased refugees' financial distress. The poorest refugees were sheltered in UN-operated camps in Lebanon, Syria, the West Bank, and the Gaza Strip.

During the 1950s and early 1960s, there were continual outbreaks of limited violence between Israel and its Arab neighbors. On their own, the immediate causes were relatively minor. But in the context of embittered relations and deep mutual suspicion, each incident became significant. Indeed, many Israelis viewed the government policy of instant retaliation as a crucial way to overcome their sense of powerlessness during the Holocaust. In that context, a young Israeli soldier, who had been born in Palestine during World War II, viewed his own participation in a paratroop unit as a reaction to the Holocaust, rather than as a measured response to the immediate conflict he faced with the Palestinians and the Arab governments:

I am a product of what we can call the reprisal generation. . . . I think that one of the reasons that the State of Israel went over to reprisal raids can be expressed in the saying: "It doesn't matter what the Gentiles say: what counts is what the Jews do." I think it derives from . . . the deep shame we've experienced throughout history. For me, the "final solution" is the essence of that shame. . . . The sense of insult and pain may have been one of the unconscious reasons why I joined the [paratroop] unit. . . . I didn't think in terms of "showing the Arabs." . . . My thinking and my motives had their starting point in the destruction of the Jews in Europe. To "show" the Gentiles afar, and not those close at hand.[2]

The lack of monitoring of the armistice lines separating the warring states caused continual problems. Palestinian refugees crossed those lines to pick their crops and search for belongings. Later they attacked Israeli civilians who lived in their former homes. The Israeli army shot them on sight, mined their former fields, and conducted retaliatory raids into the Gaza Strip and the West Bank. Large-scale Israeli raids in 1953, for example, killed about fifty civilians each in the Bureij refugee camp (Gaza) and Qibya village (West Bank). On February 28, 1955, the raids culminated in an Israeli attack on Egypt's main military post in Gaza. Humiliated by this raid, Egyptian president Nasser began to let Palestinian guerrillas operate more freely across the armistice lines, and he anxiously sought arms from abroad. That search led to Egypt's first arms deal with the Soviet Union, which Nasser announced in September 1955. Cross-border tensions contributed significantly to heating up the arms race between Egypt and Israel.

Israel and Syria contested for control of demilitarized zones (DMZs) along the armistice lines that divided them. The Syrian army evacuated three DMZs along the Jordan River on condition that Palestinian farmers remain on their lands. Nonetheless, Israel claimed sovereignty over the DMZs, ousted the Palestinian villagers, and brought in Jewish settlers to farm their lands. Expelled farmers could see their homes from their refuge on the Golan Heights and joined the Syrian army in shooting at armed Israelis who illegally cultivated their fields. Israel also denied Syrian and Palestinian fishermen access to the Sea of Galilee, stating that it would restore this historic right only if Syria signed a peace treaty. Israel retaliated whenever Syrian gunners shot at Israeli patrol boats on the lake. In Jerusalem, Israeli attempts to smuggle arms into the UN-controlled DMZ on Mount Scopus similarly caused tension with Jordan and the UN.

Another set of problems arose concerning Israeli access to the Suez Canal and the Gulf of Aqaba. Israel argued that its ships should be allowed to pass through the Egyptian-controlled Suez Canal, on the grounds that the Constantinople Convention of 1888 required that the Canal be kept open to all countries, whether in peace or war. Egypt refused to let Israeli vessels—and even ships bound for Israel—transit the Canal. When the UN Security Council supported Israel's position in 1951, Egypt desisted from detaining third-country ships that carried cargo to Israel. However, when an Israeli merchant vessel tried to enter the Canal in September 1954, Egypt stopped the ship and detained its crew for several months.

Israel was also worried that Egypt would block Israeli ships from sailing from its port at Eilat through the Gulf of Aqaba to the Red Sea, because Egypt claimed that the Gulf was not an international waterway. Although Egypt searched only 3 of 267 vessels that entered the Gulf from 1951 to 1955, Israel feared its vulnerability to a blockade and stressed that it would go to war if its access were denied.

Israeli efforts to destabilize Arab regimes helped keep the atmosphere tense. The most famous of these was the Lavon Affair of 1954, which was named for the then Israeli defense minister. Israeli operatives sabotaged British and American property in Egypt, hoping that the attacks would be blamed on Egypt and would undermine negotiations for an accord to withdraw British troops from Egypt. The plot was exposed just before the Anglo-Egyptian Treaty was signed in July 1954. The attempt mentioned earlier to send an Israeli vessel through the Suez Canal was part of this effort to foil Nasser's negotiations: The ship arrived at the Canal in September 1954, just before the Anglo-Egyptian Treaty was ratified in October.

These irritating tensions culminated in a major Syrian-Israeli military confrontation in December 1955 and Israel's bombardment of Gaza in April 1956, which killed fifty-six Palestinian civilians. Meanwhile, the Cold War intruded into the Middle East, and lingering colonial tensions exacerbated Arab-Israeli relations.

The Cold War initially intruded when the United States tried to get Arab countries to join an anti-Soviet military alliance that included the non-Arab Muslim countries of Turkey, Iran, and Pakistan. The pro-British government of Iraq joined the alliance in April 1955, which was then named the Baghdad Pact. Most Arab countries had no interest in the Cold War, because they were preoccupied with confronting Israel and completing the process of decolonization. In fact, Nasser turned to the Soviet Union in September 1955 only after the Israeli raid on Gaza in February 1955 and after the United States and West European governments refused to sell him arms. Nonetheless, the Egyptian-Soviet arms deal frightened the United States, because it enabled Moscow to gain influence in the heart of the Arab world. The United States also became angry when Egypt extended diplomatic recognition to the Communist Chinese government in May 1956.

European colonialism lingered on in the contests for control over Algeria and the Suez Canal. A nationalist revolution broke out in Algeria in 1954, whose people sought to overthrow France's 120-year rule. France correctly accused Nasser of arming the Algerian revolutionaries—and retaliated by selling arms to Israel.

On July 26, 1956, Nasser nationalized the administration of the Suez Canal, which had opened in 1869 under international management. Nationalization helped provide revenue for Egypt to construct the Aswan High Dam, which the United States, Britain, and the World Bank had refused to fund. The United States recognized Nasser's right to nationalize the Suez Canal Company so long as Egypt compensated the stockholders. Washington sought to resolve the crisis by diplomacy—not force. In contrast, France and Britain, who were the major shareholders in the Canal Company, were determined to regain control of the canal. Britain denounced Nasser as a new Hitler, who would dominate the Middle East if appeased. Britain and France assembled naval and air forces in the eastern Mediterranean to invade Egypt.

Israel shared the British and French desire to overthrow Nasser. The Canal crisis provided an opportunity for Israel to seize the Gaza Strip, gain control of the Sinai coast along the Gulf of Aqaba, try to force Egypt to sign a peace treaty, and perhaps to cause Nasser's fall from power. Leaders of Britain, France, and Israel secretly met in Paris on October 16, 1956, and invented an elaborate cover story to disguise their plans. This resulted in Israel attacking Egypt on October 29, with the stated purpose of stopping guerrilla raids from Gaza and opening the Gulf and the Suez Canal to Israeli shipping. Britain and France then issued an ultimatum to both Israel and Egypt to withdraw from the Canal, which would have left Israeli forces in control of Sinai. They also demanded that Nasser accept a temporary Anglo-French occupation of the Canal to protect international shipping. When Nasser, as expected, rejected the ultimatum, France and Britain attacked Egypt.

They hoped that the United States would condone the attack because the American public generally sympathized with Israel, and Washington was preoccupied with the Soviet crackdown on Hungary as well as with its own presidential elections. However, President Dwight D. Eisenhower sternly opposed the invasion of Egypt, viewing it as a throwback to colonial-era gunboat diplomacy. He also found it objectionable because the West had just condemned Moscow's invasion of Hungary. Both the United States and the Soviet Union supported UN resolutions that condemned the three countries' attack on Egypt, called for an immediate cease-fire, and demanded their withdrawal. The United States encouraged the establishment of a UN Emergency Force (UNEF) to police the Israel-Egypt border.

Britain, France, and Israel had to give in to this pressure. British and French troops departed on November 21, 1956, and Israel withdrew from Sinai and the Gaza Strip on March 1, 1957, after France and Canada threatened to withhold military aid and the United States assured Israel that its free passage through the Gulf of Aqaba would be guaranteed. UNEF was stationed in the Gaza Strip and at the southern end of the Gulf of Aqaba. UNEF prevented Palestinian raids into Israel and ensured that Israeli shipping could pass through the Gulf. But Israel did not gain the use of the Suez Canal, and its political conflict with Egypt festered.

A variety of political interests coincided and clashed in a dramatic fashion during the Suez Crisis. The former colonial powers, who wanted to retain their privileged status, worked with Israel to bring down Nasser. That collaboration seemed to validate Arab perceptions of Israel as a western puppet. The United States and the U.S.S.R. set aside their Cold War rivalry to oppose the invasion and uphold Egypt's right to nationalize the Canal. Nasser emerged as the hero of the Arab world, and Britain's closest Arab allies were severely weakened. Pro-Nasser Arab nationalists challenged the monarch in Jordan and overthrew the Iraqi king in a military *coup d'état* in 1958. That was a serious blow to the Baghdad Pact. Meanwhile, France solidified its ties with Israel and helped Israel construct a secret nuclear power plant at Dimona.

Soviet influence increased markedly in Egypt, Syria, and Iraq. Moscow became the major arms supplier and a significant trading partner for those states. Eisenhower's support for Egypt during the Suez Crisis encouraged Arab nationalists, but U.S. preoccupation with the Cold War dampened that support because Arab regimes were more concerned about Israel than about potential Communist threats. Nonetheless, Britain and the United States landed troops in Jordan and Lebanon, respectively, in 1958 in response to alleged Communist scares. Lebanon's internal tensions were actually caused by the country's president, who sought a second term in office, even though the constitution permitted only one term. The U.S. Marines' arrival defused the constitutional crisis and enabled the Lebanese to elect a new president. British troops in Jordan helped keep King Hussein in power against restive supporters of Nasser and pan-Arabism as well as discontented Palestinians.

Inter-Arab differences between 1957 and 1964 caused the Arab-Israeli conflict to become a low priority in the Arab world. Arab politicians were preoccupied with their search for political identity. Under the banner of pan-Arabism, politicians in Egypt and Syria attempted to achieve political unity. They formed the United Arab Republic (UAR), which lasted only from February 1958 until September 1961 because Syrians resented their junior role in the union. Many Syrians also criticized Egypt's one-party political system and its state-controlled economy. When Damascus left the union, Nasser did not try to force Syria to remain in the UAR against its will.

Arab rulers sometimes resolved their conflicts through diplomacy. This approach succeeded, for example, when Iraq threatened to invade and absorb Kuwait soon after the country gained independence in June 1961. Other Arab regimes sent troops under the umbrella of the Arab League to deter the Iraqis, and diplomacy defused the threat. But in another case, regional states polarized severely: When military officers overthrew the monarch in North Yemen in 1962, Egypt backed the new military regime and Saudi Arabia supported the ousted ruler. Egypt committed nearly half of its ground and air forces to the Yemeni war. The war in Yemen exacerbated tensions between the conservative Arab monarchies and radical Arab military regimes.

During those years, Arab rulers avoided confrontation with Israel. UNEF's presence helped Nasser keep the Egyptian-Israeli border quiet. Israel welcomed the breathing space, which gave it time to integrate the diverse Jewish immigrants and strengthen its economy. Nonetheless, flareups along the armistice lines separating Israel, Syria, and Jordan occasionally created new crises.

Arabs and Israelis made no progress toward resolving their conflict, for they disagreed on how to negotiate: Arabs wanted indirect negotiations under UN auspices; Israel insisted on direct talks. They also disagreed on negotiating priorities. Arabs viewed the Palestinian refugee problem as key: The refugees' status must be resolved before Arabs would recognize Israel and agree on borders. On the other hand, recognition was Israel's top priority: Only after achieving diplomatic recognition would Israel discuss the refugees. Even then, Israel would not consider allowing refugees to return to their pre-1948 homes. Israelis hoped that, over time, refugees would assimilate into the surrounding countries. Instead, the refugee problem festered, and the armistice lines remained unstable.

THE SIX-DAY WAR IN JUNE 1967

The Arab-Israeli conflict suddenly heated up after Israel began to construct its National Water Carrier, through which water flowed from the Jordan River to the Negev desert. Israel viewed the water carrier as vital for its economic growth and for Jewish settlement in the arid south. Arabs saw the water carrier as proof that Israel was a permanent entity that could not be wished away. Moreover, the leaders of the Baath party that had ruled Syria since 1963 used the issue to pressure other Arab governments to approve radical action against Israel. Nasser tried to contain the situation by convening summit conferences of the Arab League, in January and September 1964, at which he urged the Arab leaders to formulate a long-term strategy rather than rush into a war for which they were not prepared.

The strategy that the Arab League devised included denying water to Israel by diverting that part of the headwaters of the Jordan River that is located on the Syrian Golan Heights. However, instead of delaying confrontation, this strategy accelerated conflict by threatening Israel's vital interests. Without water, Israel could not survive. Israel promptly bombed Syria's diversion works. Damascus then heated up its rhetoric and allowed Palestinian commando groups to attack sites within Israel, including the water carrier. Jordan was also disturbed by the water carrier, which would deprive its farmers of Jordan River water and undermine its own economic development plans. Jordan's King Hussein supported the Arab League plan to divert the headwaters, although he correctly feared that the project—together with Palestinian guerrilla strikes—would provoke Israeli attacks on Jordan. When Israeli troops raided a Palestinian village on the Jordan-controlled West Bank in November 1966, the king faced riots by Palestinians who demanded arms to defend themselves against Israeli attacks.

This escalation of Syrian-Israeli tensions coincided with the revival of Palestinian national militancy. Until then, Palestinians had relied on Arab rulers and political movements to lead the effort to regain their homeland. But the rulers did not seem to do anything on their behalf. Palestinians began to complain that the rulers lacked the will and the capacity to fight Israel. Some formed political cells in which they argued that Palestinians must act independently. The most important group was Fatah, founded by young professionals in Kuwait who questioned the Arab regime's commitment to fight. Led by Yasir Arafat, Fatah made a tacit alliance with Syria that enabled the group to send armed squads across the border into Israel. Those were mere pinpricks, but they signaled renewed Palestinian activism and self-awareness. Not wanting to be dragged into a war with Israel for which he was not ready, Nasser tried to contain such independent activism by promoting the birth of the Palestine Liberation Organization (PLO) in 1964 and carefully circumscribing its political and military operations (Document 5).

Arab-Israeli tensions steadily mounted during 1966 and 1967. The final push toward war came in April 1967 when Israel and Syria engaged in aerial dogfights and Syria shelled Israeli farmers inside the DMZ. When Israel threatened to strike Damascus, Syria signed a defense accord with Egypt. After Moscow falsely informed Nasser that Israeli troops were mobilizing along the Syrian border, Egypt issued threats against Israel and sent tanks into Sinai.

Because other Arabs taunted Egypt for hiding behind UNEF, Nasser requested the partial withdrawal of UNEF on May 16. The UN Secretary General responded that there could not be a partial withdrawal—all the forces must depart. That left the entire Egypt-Israel border exposed. On May 22 Nasser announced the blockade of the Gulf of Aqaba to Israeli ships. This was an act of major significance because it was well known that Israel viewed such a blockade as a legal justification for going to war.

Whereas the United States urged caution, Israel mobilized its armed forces in preparation for war, arguing that it was justified in light of the blockade of the Gulf of Aqaba and tensions on the Syrian border. On June 5 Israel launched air strikes against Egypt, followed by a land offensive into the Gaza Strip and the Sinai peninsula that overwhelmed the Egyptian troops. Egypt signed a cease-fire on June 9, after Israeli forces reached the Suez Canal. The fighting on the Israeli-Syrian front resulted in Israel's occupation of the Golan Heights. Jordan's entry into the war led to Israel's seizure of the entire West Bank, including East Jerusalem.

The war caused a seismic shock in the Middle East, equal to the impact of the fighting in 1948–1949. The Arabs' swift defeat destroyed Nasser's credibility as the preeminent Arab leader and undermined the Syrian regime's claim to be the Arab world's radical savior. Egypt faced economic collapse when it lost revenue from oil wells in Sinai and from the Suez Canal. King Hussein's credibility was also destroyed because he lost the holy sites in Jerusalem and failed to protect Palestinians on the West Bank. Moreover, thousands of Palestinians fled to Jordan from the West Bank in the wake of the fighting.

Israel strengthened its position dramatically by tripling in size and gaining strategic depth. Dominating the Golan Heights meant commanding the headwaters of the Jordan River, ending Syrian shelling of Israeli farms below the Heights, and dominating the road to Damascus. Occupying the east bank of the Suez Canal blocked that waterway and provided leverage over Egypt. Controlling the entire city of Jerusalem enabled Israelis to regain access to Jewish holy places, which had been denied them since 1948, and to assert their political claim to all of Jerusalem. By controlling the Gaza Strip and the West Bank, Israel ruled all of Palestine. But Israel had to contend with a large, hostile Palestinian population, which it placed under military rule.

Israelis reacted with amazement, jubilation, and relief to their victory. After feeling besieged by the Arab armies, they now seemed to have won space and security. They flooded East Jerusalem to visit the holy places and hoped that Arabs would quickly agree to peace. But talk of trading the newly occupied territories for peace soon shifted to talk of keeping certain territories—all of East Jerusalem, security zones, and Jewish settlements along the Jordan River as well as former Jewish sites on the West Bank, such as Gush Etzion and Hebron. Security, religious, and nationalist claims merged in the thinking of many Israelis. The government could not formulate a coherent policy—some members viewed the lands as bargaining chips to be relinquished in return for peace, and others wanted Israel to keep the territories permanently in order to deepen the buffer zone around Israel or to incorporate land that had been part of the ancient Jewish kingdoms. The depth of the emotional reaction and the strength of the view that God had ordained Israel's victory are illustrated in this excerpt from a letter written by a soldier soon after the fighting ended:

I believe that the hand of God was in my participation in the battle for the liberation . . . of Jerusalem. . . . Do you know the significance of Jerusalem for a religious man . . . "And return speedily to Jerusalem, Thy city, in mercy, and dwell within it as Thou hast spoken"? . . . I felt as if I had been granted the great privilege of acting as an agent of God, of Jewish history. . . .

When we broke into the Old City and I went up to the Temple Mount and later to the Western Wall . . . I saw the [soldiers'] tears, their wordless prayers, and I knew they felt as I did: a deep feeling for the Temple Mount where the Temple once stood, and a love for the Wall on whose stones so many generations have wept.[3]

After the 1967 war, key Arab countries began to hint that they would endorse pragmatic approaches toward the conflict. Even though the Arab League, at its summit conference in Khartoum in September 1967, opposed negotiations and peace, it approved the use of diplomacy to achieve tangible results. Egypt and Jordan sought a diplomatic resolution and accepted the framework for a comprehensive accord that the UN Security Council established in its Resolution 242 of November 22, 1967 (Document 6).

That framework has remained the basis for all subsequent negotiations. Under its "land-for-peace" formula, the resolution called for Israel to withdraw from territories occupied in the June 1967 war. The resolution did not demand withdrawal from all the territories; rather, it recognized that negotiated boundaries must be "secure." In return, Arab states should end their state of belligerency with Israel and recognize Israel's right to live in peace. The resolution also called for freedom of navigation through international waterways, which meant the Gulf of Aqaba and the Suez Canal, and a "just settlement" to the refugee problem. In that context, Palestinians were merely refugees, not a nation. The resolution did not specify the content of a "just settlement" of the refugee problem.

FROZEN DIPLOMACY

Although UN Security Council Resolution 242 provided a framework for negotiations, little diplomatic movement occurred until the next war in October 1973. The imbalance in power—as well as the political differences—between Israel and its Arab neighbors were so extreme that meaningful negotiations proved to be impossible. Bolstered by U.S. military and economic aid, Israel felt strong enough to avoid making concessions in return for peace. Arab states refused to consider concluding peace without regaining all their land. Moreover, Israel demanded face-to-face talks, which Arab regimes continued to refuse.

The regional tension was exacerbated by the Cold War. During the fighting in 1967 Egypt and Syria broke diplomatic relations with the United States. The Soviets broke relations with Israel. Because each superpower had its client states, Cold War polarization complicated efforts to foster diplomacy.

Two key developments took place between 1967 and 1973. The first involved the mounting tension between Palestinians and their Arab hosts. The second development was the onset of sustained fighting between Egypt and Israel along the Suez Canal. The latter escalated to the point of risking war if external powers did not intervene.

Tensions between Palestinians and Arab regimes were manifested in Jordan, where Palestinian guerrillas established bases in pursuit of their goal of replacing Israel with a Palestinian state. The PLO had been transformed in 1968–1969, when Fatah and other guerrilla groups wrested power away from old-line politicians. Yasir Arafat became chairman of the PLO executive committee, as detailed in Chapter 4. With the Arab armies discredited, the Palestinian guerrillas gained popularity for mounting armed resistance, particularly in the Gaza Strip, where arms had been hidden during the war and guerrillas could hide in the huge refugee camps and slums. When the guerrillas withstood an Israeli attack in March 1968 on their base in Karameh, on the East Bank of Jordan, thousands of young Palestinians flocked to join them.

Palestinian raids from Jordan into Israel and the West Bank caused Israel to retaliate with land and air strikes on Jordan itself. Moreover, radical Palestinian groups such as the Popular Front for the Liberation of Palestine (PFLP) called for the overthrow of King Hussein as the first step toward liberating Palestine. Arafat preferred to cooperate with the king, but he could not control the PFLP. Arafat also could not contain Palestinian anger after Egypt and Jordan accepted a U.S. peace plan in the summer of 1970.

King Hussein had to balance his sympathy for the Palestinians with the need to maintain his own power and prevent another war with Israel. This underscored the growing division among Arabs over whether they should take an ideological or a pragmatic approach to their conflict with Israel.

The showdown came when the PFLP hijacked three airplanes to Jordan on September 9, 1970. The hijacking showed that the king could not control events in his own country. The officers in the Jordanian army insisted on attacking the PFLP—and the Palestinian community as a whole. The army's attack on the PLO, which began on September 18, killed thousands of Palestinian refugees and PLO fighters, who were outgunned by the Jordanian tanks and air power. Neither Iraq nor Syria assisted the PLO, largely for fear that Israel would intervene. Nasser hastily mediated a cease-fire between Jordan and the PLO on September 27, in an atmosphere so tense that it may have triggered his fatal heart attack on September 28.

During the coming year, Palestinian guerrillas were forced to move to south Lebanon, where they camped in the hills just north of Israel. The PLO-Jordanian showdown forced the PLO to face the limitations of guerrilla struggle in a situation in which the host regimes had interests that differed from the Palestinians' priorities. It provided an indication that fighting would not undermine Israel or compel Arab states to support the PLO. A diplomatic strategy would have to be developed.

The second major development after the 1967 war was an escalation of fighting along the Suez Canal during 1969 and 1970. Nasser launched this "war of attrition" in order to spur diplomatic action on the part of the United States and the Soviet Union. In December 1969 the United States announced a peace proposal, known as the Rogers Plan, that had been developed after consultation with the Soviet Union as well as with Britain and France. Secretary of State William Rogers called for indirect negotiations among Israel, Egypt, and Jordan that would lead to an Israeli withdrawal from nearly all occupied territories in exchange for Arab recognition of Israel's sovereign right to exist in peace. The plan was dropped when only Jordan received it favorably.

In the meantime, the "war of attrition" escalated, and Soviet pilots began flying MiG jets near the Canal in early 1970. The fear of a Soviet-Israeli clash led Rogers to undertake a new effort. In late June, the Rogers Initiative called for a cease-fire as a prelude to indirect Arab-Israeli negotiations aimed at exchanging an unspecified amount of territory for peace. Although the cease-fire was accepted by all parties and went into effect in August— shortly after Israeli warplanes shot down four Soviet-piloted MiGs over the Canal—the proposed indirect negotiations did not materialize.

Nasser nonetheless viewed the outcome of the "war of attrition" as a victory, because he had enlisted the Soviets militarily and the United States diplomatically in the effort to negotiate a solution. However, the Rogers Initiative split Israelis, who were still led by the National Unity government formed on the eve of the 1967 war. The right-wing Gahal bloc (later known as the Likud) quit the government, because it opposed territorial withdrawal on any front. Even the ruling Labor party emphasized the importance of retaining Jerusalem, all the Gaza Strip, most of the Golan, and the eastern third of the West Bank along the Jordan River, citing both security and religious reasons. As noted earlier, Rogers' Initiative increased Palestinian-Jordanian tension, because Palestinians realized that Jordan and Egypt would not support their maximal goals of complete repatriation to a free Palestinian state.

Nasser's diplomatic efforts were pursued by his successor, Anwar Sadat. In February 1971, Sadat renewed Egypt's acceptance of the Rogers Initiative. When Israel refused to withdraw to the prewar borders, Sadat offered partial peace in return for a partial Israeli pullback in Sinai, which would have allowed the Suez Canal to reopen. Israel rejected that partial withdrawal, too.

Israel's lack of interest in Sadat's proposals made him realize that the Jewish state would not respond so long as the Arabs lacked both military credibility and U.S. diplomatic support. Therefore, he expelled Egypt's Soviet military advisers in 1972 and strengthened his armed forces. Sadat also attempted to achieve a diplomatic solution when he sent a special envoy to Washington in early 1973 to repeat the offer of partial peace in return for partial withdrawal. By then, Henry Kissinger dominated U.S. diplomacy. As discussed in Chapter 5, Kissinger believed that the Arabs could not confront Israel militarily and that a prolonged stalemate in the Middle East served U.S. interests. He therefore brushed off Sadat's proposal. In his memoirs Kissinger later expressed regret that he missed this opportunity

PRAGMATIC ACCOMMODATION

In an effort to catch Israel offguard, Egypt and Syria launched simultaneous attacks across the Suez Canal and the Golan Heights, respectively, on October 6, 1973. Israel was observing Yom Kippur, the Day of Atonement, a day of fasting and prayer that is the holiest day of the year for Jews. The war therefore became known as the October War, the Yom Kippur War, or Ramadan 10, because it began on the anniversary of a battle fought by the Prophet Muhammad during the Islamic month of fasting. Syria initially seized most of the Golan Heights, but Israeli troops then pushed the Syrian forces east toward Damascus. Egypt gained control over the east bank of the Canal, but Israeli forces later crossed to the west bank, where they cut off and surrounded Egyptian troops in Suez City.

Israel managed to turn the tide of battle against the Arabs, partly because the United States engaged in a massive effort to provide it with military supplies. By utilizing those weapons and the strategic depth provided by the Sinai and Golan buffers, Israel emerged victorious on the battlefield. But the war was traumatic for Israel, not only because it took the country by surprise but also because some 2,500 Israeli soldiers died—far more than the 700 soldiers who died in 1967.

Two new elements entered into this war. First, oil was used as a diplomatic weapon by the Arab states. Second, the United States and Soviet Union, frightened by their near confrontation during this crisis, cooperated to bring the war to an end.

The Organization of Petroleum Exporting Countries (OPEC), formed in 1960, had gained influence internationally by the 1970s. Moreover, its Arab members sought to coordinate their policies within OPEC. During the October War, Saudi Arabia and other oil-rich Arab countries instituted a 25 percent cutback in oil production and increased the posted price of oil by 50 percent. They also refused to sell oil to the United States and other countries such as the Netherlands and Portugal that armed Israel or allowed U.S. supply planes to refuel in their airports on the way to Israel. Those measures were instituted within hours of the U.S. dispatch of arms to Israel. Production cutbacks, price increases, and embargoes led to long lines at gas stations in the West and increased the pressure on the United States and Europe to resolve the crisis diplomatically.

When Israeli forces overran Syrian and Egyptian positions in the third week of fighting, the Soviets invited Kissinger to Moscow to press for a cease-fire that would avert the Arabs' collapse. At that time, the U.S. government was in disarray because of the Watergate crisis. Moreover, the United States feared that the Soviets might send troops or even nuclear weapons to Egypt.

In that crisis atmosphere, the United States and Soviet Union reached a common understanding that resulted in UN Security Council Resolution 338 of October 24, 1973, which called for a cease-fire in place and immediate negotiations on the basis of UN Security Council Resolution 242 (1967). Egypt, Israel, and Syria accepted the resolution. Egypt had already accepted Resolution 242, but this was the first time that Syria endorsed it. Israel resented the cease-fire, because its forces had trapped a sizable part of the Egyptian army. But Kissinger felt that Sadat was more likely to make peace if the war ended in stalemate rather than in complete defeat.

When there were no results from either the meetings of Egyptian and Israeli commanders in Egypt during November and December or an international peace conference that convened briefly in Geneva, Kissinger undertook urgent diplomatic missions to disengage the combatants. Kissinger preferred solo shuttles because he could exclude the Soviets and place the United States in the pivotal position.

Kissinger secured three bilateral disengagement agreements:

- Sinai I of January 18, 1974, resulted in Israel's withdrawal from the west side of the Suez Canal and the establishment of a new armistice line twenty miles east of the Canal. Egypt reopened the Canal in June 1975. UNEF troops patrolled the buffer zone. This resembled Sadat's proposal of February 1971. As payoffs to the United States, Egypt restored diplomatic relations with Washington, and Saudi Arabia lifted the oil embargo in March 1974.

- The Golan Accord of May 31, 1974, resulted in Israel's withdrawal from the land captured from Syria in the October War and from the city of Qunaitra, which Israel had occupied in 1967. Israel retained control over Mount Hermon and several hills where it set up electronic observation posts. UN troops patrolled the buffer zone west of Qunaitra, whose buildings Israel demolished as its army departed. The United States and Syria restored diplomatic relations.

- Sinai II of September 1, 1975, yielded further Israeli pullbacks east of the mountain passes in Sinai and from the oil fields in the Gulf of Suez. The accord widened the buffer zone between the two sides, and Egypt renounced the use of force against Israel. In a secret annex between the United States and Israel, the United States pledged to neither recognize nor negotiate with the PLO as long as the PLO did not recognize Israel's right to exist and did not accept UN Security Council Resolutions 242 and 338.

The three bilateral agreements secured Kissinger's aim of separating the parties, promoting negotiations, and reinforcing U.S. centrality to any agreements. However, they also exacerbated political tensions involving the PLO, Jordan, and Lebanon.

For example, as discussed in Chapter 4, the U.S. pledge not to recognize the PLO prevented the United States from exploring directly the hints the PLO sent during the 1970s and 1980s that it might negotiate an accord to achieve a Palestinian state on the land occupied by Israel in 1967. By tying its own hands, the United States could not explore possibilities for mediating the Israeli-Palestinian conflict even after President Jimmy Carter supported the idea of a "Palestinian homeland" in March 1977.

Moreover, the United States weakened King Hussein's diplomatic standing when Kissinger failed to press Israel to negotiate a disengagement accord in the Jordan Valley. The king's inability to regain territory on the West Bank—coupled with his crackdown on the PLO in September 1970—persuaded the Arab League to set aside the king's claims to represent the Palestinians. Instead, at a summit conference in September 1974, the Arab League recognized the PLO as the sole representative of the Palestinian people.

The accords also intensified tensions inside Lebanon. Many of the Maronites, who comprised a quarter of the population, resented the thousands of Muslim Palestinian refugees in Lebanon. They also feared that the PLO's political and military presence would undermine their own political dominance, because the PLO aligned with Muslim and left-wing groups that sought to restructure the Lebanese political system. Moreover, Palestinian raids into Israel triggered Israeli retaliatory strikes on the south and even on Beirut. Maronite leaders feared that the accords on Sinai and the Golan would freeze the Palestinian issue permanently, which was intolerable to them. These fears coincided with Syria's anger at Sadat for pledging that he would never fight Israel again. Syria feared that this undermined its political leverage and eliminated Israel's incentive to undertake additional pullbacks on the Golan Heights.

In that highly charged atmosphere, civil war broke out in Lebanon in April 1975, engulfing the PLO as well as the Lebanese political forces. Syrian troops entered Lebanon in June 1976, ostensibly to restore order. Syrian President Hafiz al-Asad sought to restrain intra-Lebanese fighting, control the PLO, and warn Israel to stay out of Lebanon.

Meanwhile, political crises erupted inside Israel, as the public asked why the armed forces had been unprepared for the October War. Although Israelis benefited from the disengagement accords, which created demilitarized buffer zones and reduced the prospect of fighting with Egypt and Syria, they felt isolated internationally. Many countries broke diplomatic relations with Israel after the war, and the UN General Assembly adopted a resolution in November 1975 that defined Zionism as "a form of racism." Israelis' sense of personal vulnerability was heightened by Palestinian terrorism, notably the killing of Israeli athletes at the Munich Olympics in 1972 and the hijacking of an airliner to Entebbe, Uganda, in 1976. The successful rescue mission at Entebbe undertaken by Israeli commandos underscored Israelis' view that they must act alone to protect their people.

Within Israel, polarization grew between political groups that believed Israel must recognize Palestinian nationalism and those that insisted on retaining the Palestinian-inhabited West Bank and Gaza Strip. Religious Zionism became the core of the latter ideology: historical, biblical, and security reasons blended to support the goal of retaining those territories and settling large numbers of Israeli Jews there. In May 1977 this trend led to the election of the first Likud government, headed by the former Irgun commander and long-established right-wing political leader, Menachem Begin. There was sad irony in the fact that just as the PLO was moderating its stance, official Israeli policy became more insistent that Israel should absorb all the occupied lands. As ideology became less important in Arab politics, it became more important in Israeli policies. Those contradictory shifts complicated international efforts to foster negotiations.

U.S. President Jimmy Carter thought that reconvening the short-lived Geneva peace conference would be the best way to renew the search for peace. Chapter 5 discusses how this effort collapsed because of various factors, including U.S. domestic opposition, rivalries among Arab rulers, and Israel's preference for a framework that would exclude the Soviets and Palestinians. On November 9, 1977, Sadat issued a startling declaration: He would go anywhere to achieve peace—even to Israel. Ten days later he landed at the airport near Tel Aviv and, on November 20, he addressed the

Israeli parliament in Jerusalem. He spoke movingly of the need to break through the psychological barriers between the two peoples in order to achieve a comprehensive peace that would provide security for Israel as well as Palestinian independence:

I realized that we were . . . caught up in a terrible vicious circle. . . . And the root cause was . . . the psychological barrier . . . that huge wall of suspicion, fear, hate, and misunderstanding that has for so long existed between Israel and the Arabs. It made each side simply unwilling to believe the other. . . . [Traveling to Jerusalem would] make it absolutely clear to Premier Begin that we were determined to [negotiate] seriously. . . .

In less than forty minutes [my plane] landed at Lod airport. I was in Israel. Disbelief prevailed. . . . The minute I stepped out of the plane, I found myself face to face with Mrs. Golda Meir. . . . I saw Dayan next . . . and General Ariel Sharon. . . . Next I spotted Mordechai Gur, the Israeli Chief of Staff, who had warned that my visit was a trick designed to camouflage an imminent attack. . . .

I had reckoned that my Jerusalem trip would break the vicious circle. . . . On this my calculations proved accurate enough. For, just as my people's reception was remarkable . . . so too the Israeli people . . . danced for joy. . . . They respect a man who . . . can say: "Let the October War put an end to all wars! And now let us sit down together like civilized men around the negotiating table to discuss what you want—security—instead of resorting to force."[4]

Sadat believed that his gesture would quell Israeli fears and transform the negotiating climate. He also felt encouraged by Carter's personal request that he break the diplomatic stalemate. Perhaps most importantly, secret meetings in Morocco between Israeli and Egyptian envoys had given Sadat reason to think that Israel would withdraw from Sinai in return for peace. Sadat was also anxious to cement Cairo's ties with the West and to overcome the economic stagnation that caused major riots in Egyptian cities in January 1977. He did not anticipate, however, the anger that his move would cause in the rest of the Arab world. Indeed, he expected that—despite momentary criticism—Arab governments would fall in line behind Egypt.

Only when Sadat began direct negotiations with Begin did he realize how difficult those talks would be. Begin was ready to relinquish Sinai but insisted on driving a hard bargain on the West Bank and Gaza Strip. Palestinians might gain administrative self-rule, but Israel would control the land and water, continue to construct settlements, and claim ultimate sovereignty. This contrasted with the American view that Israel should not claim sovereignty over the territories and that the construction of Jewish settlements should be suspended. Egypt's perspective diverged further, because Egypt supported the Palestinian goal of independence and viewed Jewish settlements as illegal.

Sadat was further embarrassed when Israel attacked Lebanon in March 1978, in response to Fatah commandos, who hijacked a bus near Tel Aviv and killed Israeli civilians. Israel's attack on Lebanon confirmed Lebanese and Syrian apprehensions that Egypt's willingness to make peace would free Israel to act without fear of any Arab response. Although the United States pressured Israel to withdraw in June 1978, Israeli forces retained a security zone in south Lebanon.

To prevent Israeli-Egyptian negotiations from collapsing, Carter brought Sadat and Begin to his retreat at Camp David for a last-ditch effort in September 1978 (Document 7). The agreements hammered out there had two aspects: The first agreement, a framework for Egyptian-Israeli peace, called for Israel's full withdrawal from Sinai in return for diplomatic, economic, and cultural relations with Egypt and the placement of multilateral forces in Sinai. These provisions were enshrined in a peace treaty signed in Washington in March 1979, after months of intensive U.S. diplomacy (Document 8). The first Israeli freighter passed through the Suez Canal in April 1979, and Egypt confirmed that the Gulf of Aqaba was an international waterway. The United States pledged huge economic and military aid packages to both countries. In a special annex to the treaty, Egypt promised to sell oil to Israel, replacing the oil that Israel lost when the pro-West Iranian regime collapsed in January 1979.

In the second part of the Camp David accord, the parties agreed to enter into negotiations over the establishment of a self-governing authority for the West Bank and Gaza Strip, based on UN Resolution 242 and the "legitimate rights of the Palestinian people" (Document 7). They anticipated that Jordan and Palestinians from the West Bank and Gaza would join the talks, although they had not consulted those parties beforehand. The accord did not stop settlement construction or resolve Jerusalem's status.

The other Arab governments were shocked at the terms, which they believed satisfied Egypt's interests at the expense of the Palestinians. An Arab League summit convened in Baghdad in November 1978 to organize opposition. When the Egypt-Israel peace treaty was signed in 1979, all the Arab states—except Oman and Sudan—broke diplomatic relations with Egypt and suspended Egypt from the Arab League. They also expelled Egypt from inter-Arab banks and investment companies, banned the sale of oil to Egypt, and closed their airspace to Egyptian planes.

Sadat failed to achieve gains in the West Bank negotiations that would have restored his credibility. The Israeli government accelerated the construction of Jewish settlements on the West Bank and Gaza Strip, and declared unified Jerusalem the eternal capital of Israel in July 1980. During his final year in office, Carter was preoccupied with the Soviet invasion of Afghanistan and revolutionary Iran's seizure of U.S. hostages. When Ronald Reagan replaced Carter in the White House, Reagan distanced himself from his predecessor's policies. He signaled to Israel that his priority was U.S. support for a strategic partnership to curtail Soviet influence in the Middle East. By the time that Egyptian Islamist militants assassinated Sadat on October 6, 1981, Sadat was unpopular within his own country and isolated regionally.

RENEWED TENSION UNTIL THE GULF CRISIS

The diplomatic arena remained largely frozen from 1979 to 1991. During those years, Israel and the Arab countries focused their attention on the civil war in Lebanon and the drawn-out war between Iraq and Iran that Iraq's President Saddam Hussein launched in September 1980. However, clashes between Israeli forces and Palestinian guerrillas based in Lebanon kept tensions high along the Israel-Lebanon border.

Israel invaded Lebanon in June 1982, immediately after the Israeli ambassador in London was wounded by a bomb set by a renegade Palestinian group that was not a member of the PLO. Israeli armed forces occupied the entire southern third of Lebanon, encircling Beirut and shelling the city for weeks. They aimed to destroy the PLO and to ensure that Bashir Gemayel, head of the Maronite Lebanese Forces, would become president of Lebanon. The United States finally mediated an accord that led to the evacuation of the PLO from Beirut, but not from northern Lebanon, and implicitly endorsed Gemayel's election. That accord failed to stop Israel from occupying all of Beirut and then allowing units of the Lebanese Forces to massacre several hundred Palestinian civilians in the Sabra and Shatila refugee camps. That massacre occurred immediately after Gemayel was assassinated on September 14, 1982, apparently by a Lebanese supporter of the Syrian government. Egypt was embarrassed by the carnage in Lebanon, which began only six weeks after Israel completed its withdrawal from Sinai. Cairo withdrew its ambassador from Tel Aviv after the massacre of civilians in the refugee camps, but continued to sell oil to Israel, as specified in an annex to the peace treaty.

The United States then unsuccessfully tried to achieve peace between Lebanon and Israel as well as to resolve the civil war. Although the two governments signed a U.S.–brokered peace accord in May 1983, it was never ratified, due to overwhelming opposition inside Lebanon as well as opposition by Syria, whose troops controlled much of Lebanese territory. Moreover, siding with the Lebanese army, U.S. peacekeepers became the target of opposition forces. That culminated in the killing of 241 Marines by a suicide truck bomb near the Beirut airport on October 23, 1983. Reagan evacuated the Marines in February 1984, but not before U.S. citizens began to be seized as hostages in the newly internationalized crisis. Israeli forces, who also suffered from suicide bombers, withdrew to a ten-mile-wide "security zone" in south Lebanon by June 1985.

By this time the Iran-Iraq war had deteriorated into exhausting trench warfare, with thousands of casualties on both sides. Arab fears that Iran would overrun Iraq caused all the Arab governments except Syria to coalesce behind Saddam Hussein's regime. Because they needed Egypt's strategic weight, they quietly ended the diplomatic and economic boycott of Cairo. After the war ended in August 1988 with a partial victory for Iraq, Saddam Hussein projected himself as the pivotal leader in the Arab world.

During the 1980s the United States did not pursue a coherent strategy to promote negotiations. As discussed in Chapter 5, there was no follow-up to the Reagan Initiative for a comprehensive peace that the United States launched in September 1982, even though an Arab summit later that month floated an alternative peace proposal, the Fez Plan, in an effort to generate a dialogue with Washington (Document 9). Similarly, the United States did not respond to King Hussein's and Arafat's common negotiating position, articulated in 1985, which proposed creating some form of Jordanian-Palestinian confederation alongside Israel. The U.S.-Israeli strategic relationship tightened despite Israeli policies on the West Bank and Gaza Strip that accelerated the construction of Jewish settlements and the dismantling of Palestinian institutions.

Terrorism by extreme Palestinian groups—notably the hijacking of the *Achille Lauro* cruiseship in October 1985 and attacks in European airports in December 1985—continued to taint the PLO. Finally, the underlying problems exploded into the *intifada* (uprising) on the West Bank and Gaza in December 1987, described in Chapter 4. The daily spectacle of Palestinian civilians using rocks to battle heavily armed Israeli troops eventually helped produce diplomatic movement. The key diplomatic outcomes of the uprising were the PLO's acceptance of UN Security Council Resolution 242 in November 1988 and the opening of a U.S. dialogue with the PLO the next month (Documents 10 and 11). Suddenly, the peace process seemed to be moving again. In that context, Arab mediators worked out a political formula to end the Lebanese civil war, based on enhancing the influence of the Muslim communities and disarming the militias. However, no further progress was made toward solving the Arab-Israeli conflict. Hopes further dimmed after the United States suspended its dialogue with the PLO in June 1990, following an attempted commando operation against Israel by the same Iraqi-supported Palestinian group that had hijacked the *Achille Lauro*.

Change came with explosive impact in August 1990, when Iraq's invasion of Kuwait sowed deep discord in the Arab world. The United States responded by organizing a massive international coalition that prepared to restore Kuwait's sovereignty by force. Arabs were divided in their reactions, although virtually all criticized the perceived double standard of a world that condemned Iraq's occupation of Kuwait while accepting Israel's occupation of Arab lands. The Soviet Union, weakened by the collapse of its control over eastern Europe and facing internal political and economic crises, preferred a negotiated settlement to the Gulf crisis but was not in a position to checkmate or even stall the determined U.S. president George Bush. Indeed, no longer able to arm and bolster diplomatically its allies, Moscow even accepted financial assistance from Saudi Arabia and other oil-rich countries in the midst of the Gulf crisis.

When the U.S.–led international coalition began air strikes against Iraq on January 16, 1991, and Iraq launched missile attacks on Israel, the Arab-Israeli issue once again became central. In this case, however, Israel agreed to not respond militarily to Iraq, because that might disrupt Arab participation in the coalition that the United States had assembled against Baghdad. Under President George Bush, the United States capitalized on its leading role in the international operation to call for comprehensive negotiations between Israel and its Arab neighbors. That led to the Madrid Peace Conference, which opened on October 30, 1991. For the first time, Syrian, Lebanese, Jordanian, and Palestinian delegates sat down with Israeli representatives to address their fundamental problems. The altered climate was signaled by the Soviets' restoration of diplomatic relations with Israel and by the UN General Assembly's repeal of the Zionism-is-racism resolution in December 1991.

STEPS TOWARD PEACE

Following the Madrid conference, bilateral negotiations opened between Israel and each of Lebanon, Syria, and a Jordanian-Palestinian team. As part of the peace process, multilateral negotiations involving a wide range of states from around the world as well as from the Middle East region were also launched. These, however, were decidedly secondary and unlikely to yield substantial results until progress was achieved on the far more signficant bilateral track.

The bilateral talks were initially deadlocked, for two reasons. One reason was that Israel's Likud government adhered to a posture that precluded relinquishing any land, even in the context of peace. The other was that the Palestinians' status in the talks remained vague for a long time. Because Israel refused to deal officially with the PLO and because the Arab states supported the PLO's claim to be the official voice of the Palestinians, negotiations could not be very productive in the PLO's absence.

Even when the Labor party formed a new Israeli government in July 1992, negotiations barely moved forward. However, appearances were deceiving. Recognizing that the official Palestinian negotiators, who came from the West Bank and Gaza, could not finalize an accord without PLO approval, Israel opened secret talks directly with the PLO under the auspices of the Norwegian foreign ministry. In September 1993 these culminated in an announcement that surprised the world. The Israelis and the PLO agreed in their Declaration of Principles to recognize each other's legitimacy and, moreover, to establish Palestinian self-rule within the West Bank and Gaza Strip (Document 12).

A second agreement in May 1994 enabled the PLO to form a Palestinian Authority in Jericho and the Gaza Strip. Arafat and the PLO leadership returned from exile to preside over limited Palestinian self-rule. As discussed in Chapter 4, Palestinians elected Arafat president and elected a legislative council in January 1996. They also gained partial authority over villages on the West Bank but remained subject to stringent Israeli security controls.

The limited extent of Palestinian self-rule angered many Palestinians, who had hoped for more extensive powers and for a definitive pledge that they would achieve statehood at the end of the five-year interim period. In particular, the Islamist movements Hamas and Islamic Jihad tried to torpedo negotiations during the summer of 1995 by setting off bombs that killed Israeli civilians. Although that failed to derail the accords, those groups returned to terrorism in February and March 1996, in revenge for Israel's assassination of two of their key leaders. Moreover, renewed terror in the spring and summer of 1997 capitalized on Palestinian disappointment with the lack of economic improvements since the Oslo accords and anger at Israel's renewal of expanding Jewish settlements in East Jerusalem and on the West Bank.

The breakthrough in Israel-PLO relations had immediate consequences for relations between Israel and the Arab world. Jordan quickly used its bilateral negotiations with Israel to conclude a formal peace treaty on October 26, 1994 (Document 13). That accord delineated their territorial border; established complementary security arrangements; specified their allocations of water in the Jordan River basin; and opened up trade, communications, and tourism. King Hussein then became an important intermediary between Israeli and Palestinian negotiators. He attempted to ease tensions and persuade Israeli officials to implement the provisions of its accords with the PLO.

Other Arab regimes also cautiously contacted Israel. Israel exchanged economic liaison offices with Tunisia and Oman in early 1996 and negotiated with Qatar to purchase natural gas. Israeli businessmen met their Arab counterparts at international economic summits in Casablanca, Amman, and Cairo. The implementation of economic agreements remained hostage, however, to fluctuations in the regional political climate.

In contrast to the accords involving Israel, the PLO, and Jordan, Israel and Syria failed to reach complete agreement on the terms of a peace treaty. The basic issue dividing Syria and Israel was clear: the future of the Golan Heights. The issue was complicated because of the Golan's strategic importance to both sides as well as the changes that Israel had made on the ground since 1967. Those changes included the construction of thirty-three Jewish settlements (see Map 4) and the Knesset's extension of Israeli law and administration to the Golan in December 1981. Syria demanded the full restoration of Syrian political sovereignty on the Golan, while accepting the possibility that Israel's security would be guaranteed through demilitarization and other monitoring arrangements. Israel's Labor government agreed in principle to restore Syrian administrative control on the Golan. However, by the time negotiations ended in early 1996, negotiators had not agreed on the precise border to be established, the fate of Jewish settlements, the exact forms of monitoring, or the full extent of demilitarization. Due to public sensitivity over the Golan, Israeli Prime Minister Yitzhak Rabin also stated that the public would vote on any Israel-Syria accord in a referendum.

Meanwhile, Syrian President Hafiz al-Asad signaled that he sought a settlement by calling for a "peace of the brave" between the two countries. He also made a goodwill gesture by allowing Jewish citizens to leave Syria. Within a short time, nearly all of Syria's four thousand Jews moved to Israel or the United States. However, Asad remained noncommittal as to whether peace would include economic and cultural relations as well as the exchange of ambassadors. Moreover, the Israel-PLO agreement in 1993 was a setback for Asad, who felt that Syria had now been isolated. Jordan's peace treaty in 1994 had the same effect. Nonetheless, agreement on key points was

Map 4
The Golan Heights after 1967

— *Golan Heights* —

LEBANON

Mt. Hermon

Majdal
Shams

al-Ghajar Neve Ativ
Baniyas

Mas'adah

1949 Armistice Line / International Boundary

Ayn
Kiniah

Buq'ata

Odem

Elrom

Merom
Golan

Bruhim
Golan

Sha'al

Dor Ortal Ein Zivan
HaGolan

UN Disengagement
Observer Forces (UNDOF)
(established 1974)

al-Qunaytirah

Golan Heights

Kidmat
Zvi

Alonei Habashan

S Y R I A

*(Occupied by Israel
1967; annexed 1981)*

Katzrin

Keshet

ISRAEL

*Jordan
River*

Aniam

Hadnes

Yonatan

Ma'ale Gamla

Kanaf

Ramat
Magshimin

Ramot Natur Hispin

Sea of

Nov

Givat Geshur
Yoav Eliad

Avnei
Eitan

Galilee

Bnei Yehuda
Neot Golan

Afik

Kfar
Haruv Metzar

Mevo
Hama

JORDAN

LEGEND

▲ Israeli settlement

● Syrian village

Occupied by Israel (June 1967)

UNDOF

Demilitarized Zone (1949)

0   5 kilometers

0   5 miles

Source: Foundation for Middle East Peace, *Report on Israeli Settlement in the Occupied Territories,* 7 September 1996, p. 3. Used by permission of the Foundation for Middle East Peace. By Andy Hemstreet.

reached by early 1996, particularly during intensive negotiations at the Wye Plantation in Maryland. Those talks halted after Palestinian Islamist militants killed Israeli civilians in Tel Aviv and Jerusalem—bombings that many Israelis blamed on Syria. Then, the election of a Likud government in May 1996 precluded fruitful negotiations, because the Likud reverted to a "peace for peace" formula that maintained that Syria should make peace without regaining any land (Document 14).

Without an accord between Israel and Syria, little progress could be achieved in negotiations between Israel and Lebanon. Prior agreement on the Golan Heights was necessary because Syria viewed southern Lebanon as an extension of its security zone. Moreover, Syria wanted to retain its pressure on Israel by supporting armed Lebanese groups such as the Islamist movement Hizballah.

Therefore, even though Israel agreed to carry out UN Security Council Resolution 425 (1978), which required its withdrawal to the international border, the situation in Lebanon remained inflamed. Hizballah continued its decade-long effort to expel Israel from the security zone by force. In the wake of Hizballah's attacks on Israeli soldiers in the security zone and its shelling of Israeli civilians across the border, Israel launched air and land strikes on south Lebanon in July 1993 and April 1996. These displaced nearly four hundred thousand civilians and demolished entire villages.

Finally, the Madrid peace process that began in October 1991 included the formation of five multilateral working groups related to refugees, environment, water resources, economic development, and arms control and regional security. Those working groups were intended to resolve regional problems, simultaneously with the bilateral peace negotiations. Syria refused to participate in the working groups on the grounds that it was premature to discuss regional issues before signing peace accords. The working groups met sporadically in various Arab and world capitals during the following years. The environmental working group moved furthest in its deliberations by developing a code of conduct to protect natural resources. The water resources working group planned research projects on ways to enhance the production and distribution of water within the region. However, the other working groups were hostage to the progress—or setbacks—in bilateral negotiations. In March 1997 the Arab League called on its members to suspend participation in the working groups, following the Israeli government's decision to construct a new Jewish settlement in East Jerusalem.

ASSESSMENT

The Arab-Israeli conflict has been placed on a new footing. In the past, Arab states refused to recognize Israel's legitimacy and each side remained inflexible, even on minor issues. Today, Egypt, Jordan, the PLO, and Israel explicitly recognize each others' legitimacy and right to peace. Syria and Lebanon, by attending the Madrid conference and entering into direct negotiations with Israel, implicitly extend recognition to Israel. So long as their differences do not propel them into armed clashes, the relationship between Israel and these Arab actors stands a good chance of becoming ever more solidly based on pragmatic considerations of national interest rather than being afflicted by ideological differences.

Looking at the half-century of strife between Israel and the Arab world, it is clear that a chief element in the dynamic has been a change in the Arab perspective toward the conflict. From an original outlook that rejected the admissibility of a Jewish state on the grounds of an absolute vision of justice for the Palestinians, Arab states have moved toward a pragmatic position that takes into account the reality of Israel. Arab governments seek concrete improvements in their security and economic well-being, which must be based on compromises with Israel. Although some Arab governments—and many Arab peoples—continue to reject contact with Israel, that ideological rejectionism would probably not prevail if negotiations resumed and the Palestinians achieved tangible gains.

Israel's position has become more complex. The state's founders expressed a pragmatic willingness to partition Palestine and remained open to deals with Arab states that would consolidate Israel's victory in the 1948 war. However, they refused to compromise their fundamental ideological claim to statehood or to concede that they had caused any injustice to the Palestinians. After 1967, Israel's pragmatism waned. The return to pragmatism in the Egypt-Israel and Jordan-Israel treaties has only been partly repeated on the Syrian and Palestinian fronts. The accord between the PLO and Israel was a milestone, giving hope that a mutually beneficial compromise might be achieved, but was balanced by heightened ideological demands inside Israel to retain the West Bank. Today, Israel suffers from acute ideological polarization that has resulted in a virtual freeze in forward movement on the Palestinian-Israeli front. The re-ideologizing of Israeli foreign policy has also helped freeze negotiations between Israel and Syria, even though their differences lack the emotional depth of the Israeli-Palestinian dilemma and are, in principle, more amenable to diplomatic bargaining.

NOTES

1. Cited in J. C. Hurewitz, *The Struggle for Palestine* (New York: Schocken Books, 1976), 301.

2. *The Seventh Day: Soldiers' Talk about the Six-Day War*, recorded and edited by a group of young kibbutz members (London: Penguin Books, 1971), 205–6.

3. *The Seventh Day*, 274–76.

4. Anwar El-Sadat, *In Search of Identity* (New York: HarperCollins, 1978), 360–70.

2

Contradictory Nationalist Movements

Arabs and Jews began to experience a growing sense of national identity more than a hundred years ago, which led them to seek cultural self-realization and political independence. Because Jewish nationalism focused on Palestine, which was already inhabited by Arabs, the two peoples clashed intensely and severely. This chapter covers the period until 1948, by which time most Arab states gained independence and Jewish nationalists achieved their goal of establishing a Jewish nation-state, but the Palestinians were defeated and dispersed. First, it is important to understand what is meant by nationalism and a nation-state.

Scholars frequently use the term "nation-state" to indicate that one "nation" should rule one "state." The idea of a state is straightforward: It basically means the governing system in an independent, sovereign territory. However, there is often disagreement and confusion about the concept of a "nation." In the United States, all persons born in the United States are American citizens by right of birth, and immigrants may become citizens through a process of naturalization. National identity derives from shared ideas embodied in the Constitution rather than loyalty to an ethnic, racial, or religious group. Allegiance is accorded to the Constitution of the territory known as the United States of America. This form of civic or territorial nationalism ideally embraces all who qualify to be citizens, irrespective of religion, race, or ethnicity.

However, the concept of a nation that prevails in most of the world conceives of a nation as an ethnic group that has a distinct language, religion, physical characteristics, and/or history. According to that approach, the members of a clearly demarcated ethnic group are likely to want to—and

to have the right to—establish their own state. This form of ethnic nationalism was evident in the past century in Europe. German nationalists, for
example, talked of including all German speakers within the borders of a
reunited German state. What began as a cultural-linguistic concept deepened into a racial and religious ethnic nationalism that excluded Jews, Slavs,
and other non-German ethnicities and reached its extreme form in the
discriminatory laws of the 1930s and the Holocaust during World War II.
More recently, ethnic nationalism has rent the formerly multiethnic Yugoslavia into smaller states. Ethnonationalist politicians emphasize the religious differences and historical tensions among Serbs, Croats, and Muslim
Bosnians in order to argue that each group needs its own nation-state and
to rationalize the expulsion of persons of different faiths from their national
enclaves.

Ethnic nationalists tend to argue that ethnicity is deep-seated and virtually unchanging. Nonetheless, identity can be manipulated in order to
mobilize people behind political goals. Conscious action can be taken to
develop a national language that unifies people and to produce literature
and political symbols that inculcate a sense of nationhood. In that process,
differences with other ethnic groups are stressed in order to reinforce the
sense of selfhood and distinctiveness. All too often that sense of difference
can be transformed into hostility as each group constructs a rival history
and politicizes religion, language, or race.

In the Middle East, nationalist movements and political-legal systems have
incorporated both territorial/civic nationalism and ethnic nationalism. Within
a given country, the two approaches are often contested fiercely. In Egypt, for
example, civic nationalism is strengthened by a constitutional system that
defines all native residents as Egyptian by nationality and citizenship, irrespective of religion. Although 90 percent of the population is Muslim, the
Egyptian nation includes Christian communities that have deep roots in the
Nile Valley. The national identity of Lebanon is based on constitutional
concepts that accord each religious community a specifically defined status
within the political system. Palestinian nationalism is even more clearly a form
of territorial nationalism, based on historical ties to that land, even though
many Palestinians now live outside the land they consider their own. Loyalty
to a particular territorial state is therefore an important concept in the region.

However, powerful elements of ethnic nationalism overlap or challenge
such territorial nationalism. For example, a broad pan-Arab nationalism has
called for Arab unity based on a common language and a common culture.
Arabic-speaking countries stretch from Morocco, on the Atlantic Ocean, to
Iraq on the Tigris-Euphrates river system. When politicians call for a

politically united state, Arab nationalism challenges the legitimacy of the individual states. In practice, however, Arabs only took serious steps toward political unity from 1958 to 1961 when Egypt and Syria formed a short-lived union called the United Arab Republic.

Arab nationalism also raises questions concerning the status of non-Arab groups inside the borders of its lands. The Kurdish minority in Iraq, for example, cannot embrace the Arab identity espoused by the government in Baghdad. Kurds have developed their own ethnic nationalism that calls for self-rule within Iraq and aspires to an independent Kurdish state that would unite the Kurdish territories of Iraq, Syria, Turkey, and Iran.

Religious-based ethnicity also challenges the concept of a territorial nation-state. In Lebanon, the developing civic nationalism collapsed under the pressure of religio-ethnic identity. The country was then embroiled in a bitter civil war that pitted members of the many Muslim, Christian, and Druze factions against each other. After a dozen years of fighting, Lebanese political forces reaffirmed the territorially defined basis of citizenship and attempted to reform the political structures in order to hold together the diverse communities. In this sense, they rejected the partitioning into ethnic enclaves that was the outcome of the ethno-religious strife in the former Yugoslavia.

In recent decades another type of ethnic nationalism has been espoused by fundamentalist Islamic movements that seek to establish Islamic states whose constitutions would be based on religious law. Non-Muslims would not have the same legal and political rights as Muslims. In that way, one religious community would be privileged over the others. Such movements have gained power in Iran and the Sudan and contest the secular constitutional systems in, for example, Egypt and Algeria.

Zionism is the strongest ethnic nationalism in the Middle East. This concept of a Jewish nation, articulated initially in late nineteenth-century Europe, led to the development of a political movement to return to the ancient Jewish homeland in Palestine. By 1948 the movement was strong enough to create the independent nation-state of Israel. Ethnic nationalist Zionism clashed with the civic nationalism of the Palestinians and the ethnic nationalism of the Arab world to create an enduring conflict that is still not fully resolved.

ZIONISM

The Concept of a Jewish Nation

The Zionist movement arose in late nineteenth-century Europe as a part of, and a reaction to, the nationalist ferment that was sweeping the continent.

It received a strong impetus from the increasingly intolerable conditions facing the large Jewish community in czarist Russia. Jews endured government restrictions over their residency and jobs, exclusion from the Slavophile nationalism that was identified with the Russian Orthodox church, and violent *pogroms* (armed attacks) in 1881 and 1903, in which forty-five Jews were killed and nearly six hundred wounded in the city of Kishinev. Jewish intellectuals became disillusioned with the prospect of assimilating into Russian society. Some of them concluded that anti-Semitism would be rampant so long as Jews lacked a government and land of their own: They could not have any security as a religious community, and they could not merge with the Christian majority. Those intellectuals formed Lovers of Zion, a movement of young idealists who left Russia and founded a dozen small agricultural settlements in Palestine in the 1880s.

Theodor Herzl, an assimilated Hungarian-born Jewish journalist, developed this approach much further. His belief in the possibility of assimilating into European society was dashed when he witnessed virulent anti-Semitism during the treason trial in Paris in 1894 of the Jewish Captain Alfred Dreyfus. Herzl concluded that the only way to counter anti-Semitism was to create a Jewish nation-state. In 1897 he joined forces with the Lovers of Zion and other groups to form the World Zionist Organization (WZO) at a conference in Basel, Switzerland. The 197 delegates at that meeting articulated the goal of attaining a Jewish nation-state and established institutions to bring about that goal (Document 1).

Herzl's book *The Jewish State* (1896) analyzed the elements of anti-Semitism and outlined his ideas for statehood:

I can see in [anti-Semitism] the elements of . . . common commercial rivalry, of inherited prejudice, of religious intolerance. . . . It is a national question. . . .

We are a people—*one* people.

We have sincerely tried everywhere to merge with the national communities in which we live. . . . In vain are we loyal patriots. . . . We are still decried as aliens. . . .

The whole plan is essentially quite simple. . . . Let Sovereignty be granted us over a portion of the globe adequate to meet our rightful national requirements; we will attend to the rest. . . .

Palestine is our unforgettable historic homeland. The very name would be a marvelously effective rallying cry. . . . We should there form a part of a wall of defense for Europe in Asia, an outpost of civilization against barbarism.[1]

This modern concept of a Jewish nation was both new and controversial. Assimilationist Jews in western Europe believed that citizens' religious beliefs should be a private matter and feared that Zionism could jeopardize their civil rights and political equality by setting Jews apart as a political group. In contrast, the tightly knit orthodox Jewish communities in eastern Europe sought to maintain their beliefs and distinct rituals and viewed the Jewish exile from the Holy Land as God's punishment for their sins. God would restore them to the land in a miraculous ingathering when He decided that their term of punishment should end. Those orthodox Jews viewed Jewish nationalists as false messiahs because the nationalists urged Jews to move to Palestine to establish a secular state in the Holy Land.

Nonetheless, a few orthodox rabbis supported the idea of a religion-based nationalism. In particular, Rabbi Abraham Isaac Kook argued that Zionism was part of the divine plan and embodied the necessary human preparation for the coming of the Messiah and the Final Redemption. Through his influential position as chief rabbi of Jerusalem (1919–1935), Kook emphasized that living in the Holy Land would restore the "organic holiness of Jewry" and unleash Jews' creativity, which was stifled in exile. Kook affirmed God's promise to Abraham, which underlined the Jews' claim to a territorial state: "I will give to you and to your seed after you . . . all the land of Canaan, for an everlasting possession."2

Over time, the religious and secular dimensions of Jewish nationalism reinforced each other. Religious Zionists used the Bible to claim that there was a divine promise of the land to the tribes of Israel. Secular Zionists argued that they should restore the ancient Jewish nation-state and maintained that statehood was the sole way to ensure that Jews were strong enough to combat anti-Semitism. Even secular Zionists recognized the special resonance of the longing for the return to Zion voiced in the greeting recited by Jews every year at the Passover seder: "Next year in Jerusalem."

The sense of overwhelming need for a nation-state reached its apex after the Holocaust. Zionists argued that they could have saved European Jewry from extermination had Jews achieved statehood before World War II. Without a state of their own, Jews had no haven to which to flee and no way to defend themselves. *They all would have left Germany.*

Former Israeli Prime Minister Yitzhak Shamir's address to the Madrid Peace Conference in 1991 provides a recent example of how these religious and secular arguments merge. Shamir stressed that the persecution of Jews and the horrors of the Holocaust occurred because the Jews were homeless and therefore defenseless. He asserted that "no one wanted" the Land of Israel except Jews, who have an "immemorial" claim to the land:

We are the only people who have lived in the Land of Israel without interruption for nearly 4,000 years. We are the only people, except for a short Crusader kingdom, who have had an independent sovereignty in this land. We are the only people for whom Jerusalem has been a capital. We are the only people whose sacred places are only in the Land of Israel.[3]

Shamir clearly linked national-political claims with religious tenets in his call for Jewish primacy over that land.

Practical Zionism

Shamir's statements represented the culmination of the long process of creating a Jewish national identity. That process began at the turn of the century with the initiation of a political movement that helped Jews move to Palestine and then purchased land and created governing structures there. The process also involved basing the new national culture on the revival of Hebrew as a daily language, instilling the idea that the return to the land and physical labor were morally uplifting, and emphasizing the concept of self-reliance. The establishment of an all-Jewish Hebrew-language educational system became an essential component of Jewish nationalism. The use of Hebrew promoted a common language among the diverse immigrants that would help to create a cohesive national ethos.

Even before the British government's Balfour Declaration of November 1917 (Document 3) gave international force to the claim of a Jewish national home in Palestine, the Zionists took practical steps on the ground. WZO set up the Jewish National Fund in 1901 to pay for land purchases; opened an office in Jaffa in 1907 to assist immigrants; founded the first all-Jewish town, Tel Aviv, in 1909; and set up the first *kibbutz* (collective agricultural settlement) in the same year. The early colonists made clear their political aims. A young settler from Russia stated succinctly in 1882: "The final goal is eventually to gain control of Palestine and to restore to the Jewish people the political independence of which it has been deprived for 2,000 years."[4]

In February 1919 WZO's president, Chaim Weizmann, argued to the Versailles peace conference at the end of World War I that Jews would soon become the majority in Palestine as the result of large-scale Jewish immigration. Once they became the majority, they would form an independent government: Palestine would be "as Jewish as England is English."[5]

In the meantime, the British government ruled Palestine under a mandate from the League of Nations. The British declared that a Jewish Agency—controlled by WZO—would advise its administration on matters affecting the Jewish national home and the general development of the country. During the thirty years of British rule, the Zionist movement laid the groundwork for a separate Jewish state. Its activists built political structures that could assume state functions, including an elected community council, executive body, administrative departments, and religious courts. This organized collective was known as the *Yishuv*.

They also created a defense force (*Haganah*) that guarded Jewish residential areas in the towns and rural areas. The Haganah was tacitly recognized by the British, which worked closely with its units during the Arab uprising of 1937–1939. This cooperation deepened during World War II, when Jewish volunteers joined the British forces and the Haganah assisted British forces fighting in Lebanon. After the war, the Haganah expanded rapidly and engaged in extensive arms-buying in the United States and Europe in preparation to fight for Jewish independence.

Large-scale immigration from Europe was a key means to build the national home. Between 1922 and 1931, the Jewish population of Palestine increased from 11 percent to 17 percent—two-thirds due to net immigration. Immigration peaked in 1935–1936, shortly after Adolph Hitler came to power in Germany. In 1939 the British imposed a quota on Jewish immigration to Palestine that reduced access to that haven just as Hitler's anti-Semitic persecutions intensified. Nonetheless, the Jewish community grew to 30 percent of Palestine's total population by 1946. That dramatic demographic shift gave the Jewish Agency the population base to demand statehood.

Zionist-affiliated companies bought land to found rural settlements and stake territorial claims. They owned 162,000 acres in 1920 and 475,000 acres in 1947. Even so, this represented only 7 percent of the land surface of Palestine. The Jewish National Fund held that land as the inalienable property of the Jewish people on which only Jewish labor could be employed. The concepts of manual labor and the "return to the soil" were key to Jewish nationalism. The *Histadrut* (The General Federation of Jewish Labor), which was headed by David Ben-Gurion, pressured Jewish enterprises to adhere to this policy of *Avodat Ivrit* (Jewish labor).

Political considerations often determined the placement of settlements. Outposts constructed in 1937–1938 in the north, for example, sought to prevent the British government from placing that area in the Arab state in any territorial partition. Similarly, outposts set up in 1946 in the south ensured that the Negev would be part of the Jewish state.

Attitudes toward the Arab Community

The practical policies of the Zionist movement resulted in the creation of a compact and well-rooted community by the late 1940s. The Yishuv had its own political, educational, economic, and military institutions. It minimized its contact with the Arabs, who still comprised Palestine's majority in 1948.

The Zionist movement's focus on achieving Jewish statehood clashed with the indigenous Arabs on both the political and practical levels. On the political level, the Zionists' aims meant that Palestinian Arabs could not achieve their own national goal of independence. Leaders such as Weizmann and Ben-Gurion did not acknowledge the authenticity of Palestinian nationalism. They recognized Arab nationalism as a legitimate liberation movement, but they argued that the Arab residents of Palestine lacked a separate identity and must reconcile themselves to becoming a minority in a Jewish state. Weizmann argued in 1930 that

The Balfour Declaration and the Mandate have definitely lifted [Palestine] out of the context of the Middle East and linked it up with the world-wide Jewish problem. . . . The rights which the Jewish people has been adjudged in Palestine do not depend on the consent, and cannot be subjected to the will, of the majority of its present inhabitants.[6]

Indeed, leaders of the Yishuv quickly recognized the depth of the gap between the aims of the two peoples. They feared that a clash was unavoidable. Ben-Gurion stated bluntly in 1919:

There is no solution to this question. No solution! . . . I do not know what Arab will agree that Palestine should belong to the Jews. . . . We, as a nation, want this country to be *ours*; the Arabs, as a nation, want this country to be *theirs*.[7]

Twenty years later, Ben-Gurion underscored the gap when he commented that the Arab Revolt "is an active resistance by the Palestinians to what they regard as a usurpation of their homeland by the Jews. . . . And politically we are the aggressors and they defend themselves."[8] Therefore, Ben-Gurion concluded, the Zionist movement must strengthen its armed forces and prepare for all-out confrontation.

The difficulty in recognizing Palestinian aspirations was also due to the Zionist leaders' belief that European civilization was superior to the cultures of Asia and Africa. Herzl argued that the Jewish state would serve as "part of a wall of defense for Europe in Asia, an outpost of civilization against barbarism," as he wrote in *The Jewish State*, quoted earlier in this chapter. Similarly, Weizmann declared that the Zionist movement could bring progress to the allegedly backward Arabs.[9] He could not imagine that Palestinians could govern themselves within the context of their own national culture.

Weizmann even suggested in 1930 that Palestinian peasants be moved to Transjordan and Iraq to make room for Jewish immigrants. That concept of population transfer led to the Jewish Agency's insistence in 1937 that the

Arabs leave the territory of any Jewish state. (See the discussion of the 1937 partition plan, later in this chapter, and Document 4.)

Even that limited accommodation to Arab interests was rejected by the Revisionist movement, which consistently demanded the entire territory of Palestine as the Jewish state and refused to cooperate with Britain. In the 1940s, under the leadership of Menachem Begin, the Revisionists' armed wing, Irgun Zvai Leumi, used terror tactics against British troops and Arab civilians in order to achieve independence. This split between Ben-Gurion's Mapai/Labor movement and Begin's Revisionism (now embodied in the Likud party) has continued to polarize the Jewish state.

On the practical level, policies that were essential for creating a Jewish state widened and deepened the gap with the Arab community. Making land inalienable meant that no Arab could lease or purchase the land. The land was lost to the individual Arab and to the Arab national community as a whole. Similarly, Histadrut's "conquest of labor" deprived Arabs of employment and meant that Arabs could not benefit directly from the expanding Jewish economy. Establishing separate Hebrew schools meant that Jewish and Arab children did not study together and that the two communities lacked a common language that might promote dialogue and mutual understanding.

Zionism embodied the concept of ethnic nationalism. Zionists viewed the Jewish people as a nation that should establish a state on the land that constituted their historic and religious heritage. They adopted cultural, economic, political, and military measures to achieve that dream of a nation-state. The formation of a cohesive ethnic nation-state necessarily collided with the nationalism of the Palestinian Arabs, who shared the same territory.

ARAB AND PALESTINIAN NATIONALISMS

Palestinian political self-awareness can be traced back to the late nineteenth century, when the area was part of the Ottoman Empire. Palestinian and other Arab elites played prominent roles in local government and religious institutions as well as in the imperial government in Istanbul. They viewed the empire as a multinational entity, in which neither Arabs nor Turks were dominant. That perception began to change before World War I, when the rulers in Istanbul started to emphasize their Turkish ethnic origins and the preeminence of Turks inside the empire. Arabs felt discriminated against in the allocation of government jobs and resented the preference accorded to the Turkish—as against the Arabic—language in the educational and ruling systems.

Some Arabs pressed for the decentralization of the empire, so that they could have local autonomy. They did not dare call for Arab independence, partly because the government quickly jailed anyone who made that demand and partly because they feared that dismantling the empire would enable European powers to seize Arab territories. They also feared Zionism. As early as 1891, a group of Muslim and Christian notables in Jerusalem urged the Ottoman rulers to prohibit immigration and land purchases by European Jews, because they feared that this would displace Arabs and lead to a Jewish state.

The British army conquered Palestine and Syria during World War I, supported by Arab armed forces. The Hussein-McMahon Correspondence (1915–1916)—and other British declarations in the late 1910s—promised the Arabs their independence in most of the Ottoman lands as well as the Arabian peninsula. Arab politicians argued that this included Palestine. (See Document 2.)

However, the proclamation of the Balfour Declaration in November 1917 undermined those aspirations. The Declaration referred to Arabs merely as the resident "non-Jewish communities," even though they constituted 90 percent of the population. The Declaration emphasized Jewish national claims and was silent on Arab political and national rights. (See Document 3.)

In the face of Britain's direct rule and the rapidly expanding Jewish community, Palestinian Arabs insisted that Palestine remain an Arab country. They argued that they had the same right to self-determination and independence as the British accorded Egypt, Transjordan, and Iraq. Palestinians also maintained that their territory should not be used to solve the plight of the Jews in Europe. Jewish national aspirations should not override the Arabs' own political rights.

At first, Palestinian politicians articulated a version of territorial nationalism in which all indigenous residents would have equal rights. Over time, their views shifted toward ethnic nationalism, because the Zionist movement rejected a civic nationalism that would enable the Arab majority to play the principal role in governance. Thus, in reaction to Zionist ethnic nationalism, Palestinian nationalism began to include an ethnic dimension. Nonetheless, the fundamental definition of the Palestinian nation remained civic-territorial and included, in principle, those Jewish residents who did not seek a separate state.

Practical Measures

Members of the Arab middle and upper class reactivated and expanded political and cultural societies that they had formed before World War I. The

Muslim-Christian Associations were the most influential bodies, which brought together political, commercial, and religious leaders of the two faiths for their common national purpose. Palestinians held demonstrations as early as 1920 to protest the Balfour Declaration and Jewish immigration.

Protests sometimes became violent, notably when Arabs attacked Jews in the Old City of Jerusalem in 1920. Jewish-Arab clashes in 1921 in the port city of Jaffa included an attack on a hostel for Jewish immigrants. In 1929 the most serious interreligious crisis resulted from conflicting claims at the Western (Wailing) Wall, which was legally Muslim property but was venerated by Jews as the only remnant of the Temple destroyed by the Romans. Jewish militants staged political demonstrations at the Wall where they sang the Zionist national anthem and raised their movement's flag. Muslim demonstrators the next day damaged the Jewish prayer area and attacked Jews in Jerusalem, Hebron, and Safad. They killed dozens of Jews in Hebron, where religious Jews had lived for centuries near the burial site of the patriarch Abraham. Adding religion to the volatile political mix dangerously inflamed feelings on both sides.

The Palestinian elite tried to form institutions that would counter the impact of the Zionist movement and would present their case to the international community. An Arab congress elected an Arab Executive in late 1920 to coordinate protests. The Executive sent several delegations to London that lobbied unsuccessfully to cancel the Balfour Declaration and win Palestine's independence.

In the early 1930s, radicalized young people and labor activists goaded the elite to use strikes and violence to confront the British and Zionists. By then, Arabs were giving up on the possibility of persuading Britain to change its policies. The British ignored their calls for equal treatment and for the formation of a legislative council with an Arab majority. As Jewish immigration swelled, Palestinians launched a general strike in 1936 that they sustained for an unprecedented six months. The strike was followed by a widespread rural revolt that lasted nearly three years. The rebellion encompassed unemployed workers and displaced peasants as well as villagers who feared that they would lose their land to Jewish immigrants. Many merchants and professionals in the towns helped to fund the uprising because their livelihoods and future were also at stake. The fervor generated among Palestinians was expressed by the poet Abd al-Rahim Mahmoud, an Arabic teacher at a nationalist school in Nablus, who participated in the 1936 revolt and died fighting in 1948:

Call of the Motherland

The slain motherland called for our struggle
and my heart leapt with joy.
I raced the winds, but did not boast.
Isn't it my simple duty to redeem my country? . . .

People of my country, our days of sacrifice have arrived;
they shine, radiant, across the hills of this holy land.
Redeemed by our young men too proud
to endure oppression.[10]

The political elite formed the Arab Higher Committee in 1936, which replaced the Arab Executive and was headed by al-Hajj Amin al-Husseini, Mufti of Jerusalem and head of the Supreme Muslim Council. Despite his standing as a Muslim religious leader, the Committee did not seek a religious-based state. Moreover, the Committee included members from the three principal Christian denominations in Palestine: Greek Orthodox, Catholic, and Protestant.

Reaction to Partition

In July 1937 the British proposed the territorial partition of Palestine, according to the Jewish state a third of the land, including Galilee, which was almost entirely Arab in population. The Arab portion would be linked to Transjordan, thereby denying the Palestinians national self-determination on even a part of their homeland. (See Document 4.) That British Royal Commission argued that the "irrepressible conflict" between the two nationalist movements could only be resolved by each nation achieving political independence on part of its land. That Solomonic judgment partially satisfied the Zionist movement, which accepted its terms in principle, but the judgment infuriated Palestinians. Even though the British jailed Palestinian political activists and banned the Arab Higher Committee, the rebellion escalated and encompassed most of the country.

British forces crushed the uprising by 1939, but the revolt persuaded London to withdraw the plan for territorial partition. Britain's policy at this time was largely shaped by the rapidly growing threat of war in Europe, which heightened London's awareness of the value of Arab friendship. Thus, the British government issued a White Paper in 1939 that placed limits on Jewish immigration and land purchases, and proposed that Arabs and Jews share power in an independent, unitary state. That formula assumed that it would be possible to create a civic nationalism that would link the

Arab and Jewish communities in a common loyalty to the same territory. By 1939 that form of territorial nationalism was almost certainly unattainable in Palestine, given the intensity of the Zionist demand for independence and the strength of the Arab community's insistence on their majority rights.

With the decapitation of the Palestinian national movement and forcible suppression of the revolt, the Palestinians had no coherent organizations or skilled leaders that could confront the Zionist movement in its final drive for statehood in the 1940s. Moreover, al-Hajj Amin al-Husseini, who fled Palestine to avoid arrest in 1937, was discredited for supporting Hitler during World War II. Nonetheless, Palestinians continued to demand their independence in a state that would reflect the reality of an Arab majority.

However, the Palestinians lacked sufficient political cohesion and military force to ward off partition in 1947–1948. Their scattered volunteer forces in villages and towns were no match for the Haganah, which routed Palestinians from their homes. Moreover, although Arab rulers denounced partition, they hesitated to commit their armed forces to fight Israel. When they finally did so, they were defeated by the Haganah, which had transformed itself into the Israeli Defense Forces. Sixty percent of the Palestinians became refugees, and they lost three-quarters of the land. The Palestinian national movement was crushed in the process of creating the Jewish state.

ASSESSMENT

The military defeat in Palestine, the establishment of a Jewish state, and the flight of the Palestinians traumatized the Arab world. Many Arabs blamed the British and French for carving up the Arab provinces of the Ottoman Empire and thereby undermining the unity of the Arabic-speaking peoples. They also blamed their own rulers for not fighting effectively on behalf of the Palestinians. Some Arab politicians concluded that only Arab unity under radical regimes would solve their problem. A cohesive, militant Arab bloc was essential to ward off the threat from Israel.

As for the Palestinians themselves, the shock of defeat, dispersal, and dispossession was a blow from which Palestinian nationalism required time to recover. Not until the 1960s did Palestinian nationalism again become visibly active. As discussed in Chapter 4, Fatah emerged as the dominant actor espousing Palestinian national ideals. These initially crystallized in the demand for Israel's destruction and the creation of Palestine as a secular, Arab state, thus reflecting the same civic-territorial form of nationalism that characterized the Palestinian community prior to 1948. However, by the late 1980s an ethnic Palestinian nationalism, in the form of militant fundamentalist Islamist movements, began to attract increasing numbers of followers. Despite this development, the predominant nationalist orientation among Palestinians has remained civic-territorial, and its leading organization, the PLO, has agreed to accept Israel's legitimacy and work toward a peaceful solution to the Arab-Israeli conflict.

As for the Israelis, their sense of Jewish nationalism solidified and strengthened through their confrontation with the Palestinians and the Arab states. Their determination to rule themselves and to provide a haven for Jews throughout the world was deepened immeasurably by the horror of the Holocaust. They thought that offering Palestinians a state on part of the land had been sufficient, and they argued that the Palestinians, by rejecting partition, had forfeited their rights to that solution. Israeli leaders accepted no responsibility for the Palestinian refugee problem and expected the Arab world to absorb the refugees and to recognize the legitimacy of the Jewish state. If not, Israel would maintain the military strength necessary to secure its own survival. Only in recent years has the possibility of peace with the Arabs—and especially with the Palestinians—begun to alter the assumption of unremitting confrontation. The effort to build the Israeli state and society and the ongoing tensions with its Arab neighbors are detailed in the next chapter.

NOTES

1. Excerpts from Arthur Hertzberg, ed., *The Zionist Idea* (New York: Doubleday and Company, 1959; reprint, Westport, CT: Greenwood, 1970), 209, 220, 222 (page citations are to the reprint edition).

2. Quoted in Hertzberg, ed., *The Zionist Idea*, 429.

3. Excerpts from Institute for Palestine Studies, *The Palestinian-Israeli Peace Agreement: A Documentary Record*, 2nd ed. (Washington, DC: Institute for Palestine Studies, 1994), 27–28.

4. Quoted by David Ben-Gurion in *My Talks with Arab Leaders* (New York: Third Press, 1973), 2.

5. Quoted in Sami Hadawi, *Bitter Harvest: Palestine 1914–1969* (Delmar, NY: Caravan Books, rev. ed. 1979), 215.

6. Quoted in Ann Lesch, *Arab Politics in Palestine* (Ithaca, NY: Cornell University Press, 1979), 43–44.

7. Statement during a debate in the Yishuv's executive council, June 1919, quoted by Neil Caplan, *Palestine Jewry and the Arab Question, 1917–1925* (London: Frank Cass, 1978), 42.

8. Speech to the Mapai political committee, July 6, 1938, quoted in Simha Flapan, *Zionism and the Palestinians* (New York: Barnes and Noble, 1979), 141.

9. Flapan, *Zionism*, 25, 39.

10. Excerpt from Salma Khadra Jayyusi, ed., *Anthology of Modern Palestinian Literature* (New York: Columbia University Press, 1992), 210–11.

3

The Israelis

Israel faced two interrelated challenges at its birth: building a state and building a nation. The former required establishing the foundations of sovereign Jewish existence, including the institutions and processes through which the state would function. Israelis made good use of the Yishuv's experience under the British mandate. The level of communal organization reached by Palestine's Jewish settlers prior to 1948 gave the new state a structure and a pool of skilled officials. The Yishuv's tradition of participatory politics and widespread interest in public affairs ensured that Israel would have a vibrant domestic political life.

Constructing a nation was a task of a different order. Although the Yishuv had experience in absorbing immigrants during the decades prior to Israel's creation in 1948, little in its past could serve as a model for what faced the newly proclaimed Jewish state. Primarily impelled by commitment to the Zionist cause, fewer than four hundred thousand Jews reached Palestine between 1920 and the outbreak of World War II. Moreover, those early immigrants were overwhelmingly from eastern Europe and therefore shared a degree of cultural similarity. Their process of acculturation was described in the autobiography of Leah Rabin, widow of assassinated Prime Minister Yitzhak Rabin. She was five years old when her wealthy family fled Hitler's Germany and arrived in Palestine. Her recollections of that early experience offer insights into the challenges that faced Jewish immigrants and the processes that helped promote national consciousness within the Yishuv:

It took the adults such a long time to master the language. . . . Conversing in Hebrew was easier for my father than my mother. . . . My father's determination paid off in slow, hard-earned stages. First mastery of a Hebrew newspaper. Then classics. . . . But most of all, it was my father's commitment to converse with others in Hebrew that gave him his skill. . . . My mother—for all her virtues and charm—could never really master a single spoken sentence.

School jump-started my own Hebrew skills enormously. . . . School meant more than just skills and rudiments, it also nurtured the beginnings of political and social awareness for me among my peers. . . . I joined HaShomer HaTzair (a socialist Zionist youth movement) in the eighth grade. I embraced its uniform of . . . shorts with blue blouses. We had compulsory meetings twice during the week and on Friday and Saturday evenings. We hiked throughout Palestine. . . . We savored the history of labor movements, monumental revolutions, and—of course—Zionism. And on Friday . . . we sang together, often deep into the night.[1]

The waves of immigration that poured into Israel immediately after its establishment were far greater than anything witnessed under the British mandate. The country's Jewish population doubled in only four years, rising from 650,000 in 1948 to over 1.3 million in 1952. Many of the new immigrants arrived not so much because of ideological conviction but rather because no other option existed. The scathing experience of Hitler's genocidal campaign generally made it impossible for Holocaust survivors to consider rebuilding their lives in Europe, but strong legal barriers to immigration to other parts of the world, including the United States and Canada, severely restricted where they might go in search of a new start. The initial post-1948 immigration of Jews from European displaced persons camps and British detention centers on Cyprus (where unauthorized would-be immigrants to Palestine were interned by British authorities during the final years of the mandate) was immediately succeeded by massive arrivals from the Middle East. The deeply rooted Jewish communities in the Arab world suffered political persecution arising from the passions unleashed by the Palestine problem and suddenly found it difficult to remain in Arab lands.

By the end of 1951, some 200,000 immigrants had arrived from Yemen and Iraq. The influx of "oriental Jews," known as Mizrahim, was sustained throughout the 1950s and into the 1960s. During that period, immigrants from North African and other Arab and Middle Eastern states continued to outnumber others. With the beginning of large-scale immigration from the Soviet Union in the 1970s, European Jews (Ashkenazim) again solidly predominated. Between 1968 and 1990, just under 280,000 Soviet Jews, the vast majority of whom were Ashkenazi, reached Israel. European Soviet

Jewry formed most of the nearly 430,000 immigrants who poured into the country betwen 1991 and 1995.

NATION-BUILDING

Such massive immigration generated enormous problems, for the new-comers generally arrived with few resources of their own and with little, if any, knowledge of modern Hebrew. Moreover, the successful absorption of immigrants required more than just meeting their immediate material needs and helping them function in an Israeli context. Nation-building essentially demanded that immigrants identify fully with the Israeli collective.

Israel's nation-building efforts have been remarkably successful. Most of the state's citizens, who now number some 5.5 million, have internalized a strong commitment to Israeli national identity. This has been no small achievement, given the varied backgrounds of Israel's population. It is of course true—and important—that Israel is a Jewish state and that Judaism has therefore been a strong bond. Under Israel's 1950 Law of Return, Jews may be granted citizenship immediately upon reaching the country. However, the essence of Jewishness is not seen in the same way by all Israelis. For some, as was true of most of the leaders of the Zionist movement and founding fathers of modern Israel, it is primarily a secular, historical, ethnic identity with regard to which religious observance or non-observance is relatively immaterial. To others, the practice of Judaism as a religion is a central element of Jewishness. Yet, even here differences exist, for different strands of Judaism interpret differently the role and requirements of religious practice in the context of the state.

Thus, religion has consistently been a factor in Israeli politics. Israelis have generally managed to strike compromises that satisfy both the secular and various Judaic inclinations of the public. It was, for example, in this spirit that Israel's Declaration of Independence made no specific reference to a deity but did refer to the "Rock of Israel," a biblically acceptable term for God. Yet, religious-secularist tensions have continued to be a part of Israel's domestic political scene. Among issues that periodically cause intense political controversy are questions such as whether the state should permit public transport on the Jewish weekly holy day (Shabbat), or allow autopsies, or recognize the eligibility of certain individuals to marry or be recognized as Jewish. The controversy over "Who is a Jew?" flared up in 1986 when the interior ministry refused to recognize as Jewish an American immigrant who had converted to reform Judaism in the United States, on the grounds that conversions must follow Halacha (religious law). This is a highly sensitive issue for American Jews, whose vigorous reform and conservative movements resent the orthodox's monopoly of religious authority inside Israel.

For reasons discussed later, the political weight of religiously motivated groups has not only been disproportionate to their numbers within the Israeli body politic but has also grown considerably in the past two decades. This has allowed religious fervor to mold public policies in directions that affect daily life in Israel in a variety of ways. In the main, however, even secularists admit that religiously rooted laws do not seriously limit individual freedom. Moreover, although three-quarters of Israeli Jews consider themselves non- or minimally observant, half of the public maintain that the government should ensure that public life is conducted in accordance with Jewish religious tradition.[2] That does not mean that those citizens support the political aims of religious groups. In fact, many secularists view with alarm those groups' rising political strength, particularly when that is linked to staking maximalist claims over the West Bank on theological grounds.

Israel is also divided along ethnic/socioeconomic lines. The influx of Mizrahi Jews during the 1950s and 1960s led to cleavages that have had much political importance. Settling in a Jewish state that was created and led by Jews of European origin, Mizrahim were handicapped by lower levels of education and by cultural traits that set them apart from their Ashkenazi countrymen. Many of them began to resent what they perceived as an unfriendly ruling establishment controlled by the Mapai-dominated Labor government. By the late 1970s, such feelings led them to support the opposition, headed by Menachem Begin's (Revisionist) Likud Bloc. Though the Likud was also led by Ashkenazim, many Mizrahi believed the Labor Alignment was responsible for their problems.

In view of Israeli society's multiple divisions, how do we explain the apparent paradox of a cohesive Israeli national identity? Three broad and interrelated reasons stand out. First, the common denominator of Judaism brought Jews together. Whether secular or religiously inclined, the bulk of Israelis recognize the Jewish people's subjection to oppression and violence at the hands of non-Jews. The Holocaust was an extreme example of a pattern that had become all too familiar in Jewish history. In this light, most Israelis perceived Arab hostility to the Jewish state as yet another instance of non-Jewish antagonism toward Jews. Thus, Arab threats against the Jewish state have constituted a second major factor promoting national cohesion. Determined that the Holocaust will never again be repeated, Israelis have tended to give priority to internal cooperation rather than to differences. Related to this is the fact that virtually all Israelis are subject to compulsory military service and therefore share an intense socializing experience right after high school. Finally, Israel's success in providing most of its citizens with a high standard of living fosters Israelis' commitment to the state. Israel's economy, a main support of which, as noted in Chapter 5, has been public and private U.S. aid, places the country among the world's developed states.

In short, most Israelis find solid reasons to be strongly committed to their state, with its Jewish nationalist basis. However, not all Israeli citizens are satisfied with the state, particularly Israel's Arab community, whose second-class status is discussed later in this chapter.

GOVERNMENT AND POLITICAL SYSTEM

Local government in Israel provides much opportunity for grass-roots involvement in helping to shape public services. At the national level, Israel has a parliamentary system. The head of government is the prime minister. The head of state is a president, elected for five years by the Knesset, as Israel's parliament is called. Real executive power is located in the cabinet, especially in the office of prime minister. A change in Israel's law made the prime ministry a directly elected office as of 1996.

Israel's cabinet-governments have, at least in theory, a virtually free hand to rule as they wish. In practice, because no single political party has ever won a majority of seats in the Knesset, the leading party must form a coalition with smaller parties to claim a majority of seats and thereby form a government. Those coalitions are often unstable, however, because the coalition partners may not agree on socioeconomic or foreign policies and continually jockey for greater influence within the government.

The Knesset is composed of 120 members elected for terms of four years. Israel is not subdivided into electoral districts. There is only one, national constituency. The electoral system is based on proportional representation, with candidates appearing in order of priority on party lists. The public does not vote for individual candidates but for lists of candidates that are compiled by each party. The number of representatives each party sends to the Knesset is based on the proportion of overall votes won by that party. In other words, if a party wins twenty seats, then the first twenty names on its list become its Knesset members. If a party receives less than 1 percent of the overall vote, none of its candidates gains a seat in the Knesset.

The third branch of Israel's government is the judiciary, which is comprised of religious and civil courts. The religious courts are divided into courts that deal with personal status issues—divorce and inheritance, for example—for each of Israel's major religious groups: Jewish, Muslim, Christian, and Druze. Civil courts, on the other hand, rule on the applicability and interpretation of legal statutes and administrative decisions. The judiciary has won a reputation for preserving its independence and for sustaining a high degree of professionalism. Nonetheless, the high court has consistently deferred to the security services in, for example, rejecting petitions to order the secret police to stop torturing Arab suspects.

Parties are the heart of Israel's political system. The major political groupings go back to pre-State organizations and range across the ideological spectrum, falling into three broad categories: leftist-socialist parties, religious parties, and rightist parties. Though political organizations calling for Israel's dissolution are illegal, non-Zionist parties—those opposed to the state's Jewish nationalist character but not to the state itself—are allowed. As discussed later, such parties have become particularly relevant to the Israeli Arab community. Since Israelis began to conduct separate—but simultaneous—elections for the Knesset and the prime minister, it is possible that smaller parties will progressively gain strength at the expense of the country's larger parties. This is because a voter can choose the candidate from the largest parties for prime minister while voting according to ideological or religious inclination for the Knesset. If this happens, all smaller parties—even non-Zionist parties—may find themselves with better chances of participating in ruling coalitions. It may also lead to a more fractured parliament, in which ideological differences are even more pronounced.

Overall, Israeli politics have been long dominated by the division between Mapai (the Labor Alignment), religious parties, and the Herut party (Likud bloc). Mapai, led by David Ben-Gurion, called for a largely socialist economy in which the Histadrut would play the leading role. Mapai was also pragmatic in its approach to statehood, accepting territorial partition in order to consolidate the Jewish state on at least part of the land. Mapai led the coalition governments from independence until 1977, generally in alliances of leftist parties and with certain religious groups. Since 1968, one such bloc—the Labor Alignment—has been a major force in Israeli politics.

Israel's religious parties have played an important role in the country's affairs. The National Religious party (NRP) holds right-wing, strongly nationalistic positions and was the most prominent religious group for a long time. By the late 1980s it was replaced in that role by Shas, an ultra-Orthodox party that drew support from the Mizrahi community and espoused a less rigidly nationalist program. Israel's 1996 elections saw the political power of religious parties reach new heights, with three such groups acquiring an unprecedented total of 23 percent of the Knesset's seats. Even in past years, when religious parties were less represented in the Knesset, at least one of them participated in every ruling coalition since

Israel's birth. The reason for this was the failure of larger parties on the left and right to achieve clear majorities. This generally allowed religious parties to hold the balance of parliamentary power. Thus, they gained a degree of political influence disproportionate to their popular support.

The core element of Israel's right-wing parties has been the Herut party, which emerged from the Revisionist Zionist Movement that, by the closing years of the British mandate, was led by Menachem Begin. The Revisionists sought to conquer the entire land of Palestine, rather than to accept partition, and generally supported an economy that would be led by private enterprise rather than the government or the Labor-controlled Histadrut. The intense Mapai-Revisionist rivalry led to a deadly clash between the Israeli army and the Revisionists' militia, the Irgun, in the midst of the war of independence. The army killed members of the Irgun when they attempted to unload weapons near Tel Aviv from the ship *Altalena*. Ben-Gurion feared that the arms were intended, not to fight the Arabs, but to mount a putsch against his government.

Over the years, Herut combined with other rightist parties, and since the mid-1970s the rightist standard bearer has been known as the Likud. The rightist position is more conservative on economic issues—favoring private enterprise and less government regulation—than the socialist parties and has sought to break the political power of Histadrut. The Likud is also more intensely nationalistic, demanding the retention of the West Bank, Gaza Strip, and Golan Heights on both historical and strategic grounds. Only in 1977 did the Labor Alignment's unbroken string of electoral victories end and Israel's first Likud government take power. Since then, Likud and the Labor Alignment have alternated in power and even shared power in coalition governments.

Other parties in Israel include smaller organizations, such as the Communist party and various Arab parties. After the 1967 Arab-Israeli War, ultranationalist groups developed to the right of the Likud party. Perhaps the most extreme among these was Kach, a racist organization that demanded the expulsion of Arabs from Israel and the Occupied Territories. In 1988 Kach was denied the right to participate in Israel's national elections because of its racism, and in 1994 it was legally banned on the grounds that it was a terrorist organization.

The post-1967 period also saw the growth of other political groups concerned with the final disposition of the Occupied Territories. Peace Now, a leftist-liberal group calling for greater flexibility in the search for peace with Palestinians and the Arab world, is one such movement. Another far more influential group—the Gush Emunim (Bloc of the Faithful)—espouses an expansionist, messianic nationalism in support of settlement activity in the Occupied Territories and retains close ties to religious and rightist parties. The platform of Gush Emunim states explicitly:

The whole of this country is ours. . . . It is the inheritance of our father Abraham, "To thy seed will I give this land" (Exodus 12, 7).

Therefore there can once and for all be no possible doubt that there are no Arab territories and Arab lands here, only Jewish lands, the eternal inheritance of our forefathers, on which others came and built without our permission or presence. And we never left or were separated from the inheritance of our forefathers, we everlastingly continued . . . to protest against their cruel and artificial control of the land. So we are commanded to liberate our lands and never to relinquish them.

This whole land, according to all the Biblical borders, belongs to and comes under the rule of the people of Israel.[3]

Overall, the rivalry between the country's two leading political blocs has steadily intensified, with small political groups clustering around each bloc. As discussed later, Labor and Likud differ significantly over both the substance and style of policies toward the Arab states and Palestinians, with Labor advocating a trade-off of land for peace and Likud generally insisting on the retention of lands captured in 1967. Their mutual antagonism was heightened by Prime Minister Yitzhak Rabin's tragic assassination in late 1995 at the hands of a young Jewish Israeli who felt that the Oslo accords and subsequent movement toward Palestinian-Israeli peace constituted treason against the Jewish state and its holy land.

ISRAELI ARABS

Arab citizens comprise approximately 20 percent of Israel's population. Of these, about 790,000 are Muslims, 160,000 are Christians, and 80,000 are Druze. From the time of the establishment of the Jewish state in 1948, Israeli Arabs were relegated to a special, and inferior, status. They were initially governed by a military administration. Although Israel suspended this practice in 1966, emergency laws continue to allow security measures such as curfews and detentions to be leveled against Arab citizens. Israeli Arabs are not completely equal citizens under the law in other ways as well. For example, citizenship requirements for Jews are different (and much more easily met) than for Arabs, and the vast majority of Arabs are exempted from national military service, an experience that remains central to Israeli identity. The exception to this limitation on Arab military service is Israel's Druze community. Although the religious creed of the Druze is an offshoot of Islam and they are ethnically and linguistically Arab, their beliefs evolved into a distinct religion. The Druze are officially treated in Israel as a minority distinct from Arab citizens and are required to serve in the Israeli armed forces.

Apart from official differences in the implications of citizenship for Arab and Jewish Israelis, the two communities are divided by social realities and informal, but well-understood, practices. Israeli Arabs have generally remained at the bottom of the country's socioeconomic ladder. Lower levels of education and lack of economic resources have made most Arabs less upwardly mobile than members of the Jewish community. Arabs complain that this has not resulted from lack of effort on their part but rather from obstacles placed in their way by the Jewish state. In this vein, they bitterly recall that many of them were temporarily displaced by the fighting in 1948 and then not allowed to reclaim their homes and lands. They also point out that Israeli laws allowed the state to confiscate over half of the country's Arab-owned land by 1985. Such practices severely undermined the Arab community's economic base.[4]

Israeli Arabs complain that they are barred from the higher levels of Israel's government bureaucracy as well as from those in the private sector. Polls reveal that most Jewish Israelis feel that preference should be given to Jewish citizens in matters related to employment, higher education, and responsible positions in government. They also show that Israeli Arabs feel that unstated, but effective, government policies are designed to ensure the continuation of their inferior status and that this stems from an underlying Israeli disdain for Arabs and Arab culture. Whether or not this is true, there is no doubt that most Israeli Arabs and Jews perceive one another through negatively stereotyped lenses. The poems by Tawfiq Zayyad, the recently deceased mayor of Nazareth (the largest Palestinian town inside Israel) and a long-term activist in the Israeli Communist party, express the sense of loss and longing of a Palestinian living in Israel:

All I Have

I never carried a rifle
on my shoulder
or pulled a trigger.
All I have is a lute's melody
a brush to paint my dreams,
a bottle of ink.

All I have
is unshakeable faith
and an infinite love
for my people in pain.[5]

Israeli Arabs have tried to improve their situation by participating in the country's political processes. Granted the right to vote at the time of Israel's creation, Arab citizens found that major parties competed for their support. Although minor Arab parties were launched over the years, most Israeli Arabs tended to back the dominant Mapai/Labor party by voting for lists of Arab Knesset candidates affiliated with, but not part of, that party. By carefully including on such affiliated lists local notables and leaders of important family networks in Arab-populated areas, Labor developed a functional patron-client relationship through which it gained a reservoir of votes. In return, local Arab communities could hope for practical benefits.

In the 1970s and 1980s, however, Israeli Arabs split their votes among Labor and other established Zionist parties and, on the other hand, growing non-Zionist, predominantly Arab parties. Of the latter, the Democratic Front for Peace and Equality (DFPE) emerged as the strongest. Efforts to overcome inter-Arab competition in order to weld the Arab electorate, who now comprise 21 percent of total Israeli voters, into a strong single bloc have been unsuccessful. In the 1996 elections, the DFPE and other Arab parties split over 60 percent of the Arab votes while Zionist parties won more than 30 percent.

Although Israeli Arabs have become increasingly organized as participants in Israel's national life, Arab parties are still not included in the country's active coalition politics. Mainstream Israeli political parties continue to discount the possibility of seeking parliamentary control by including Arab parties in ruling coalitions. It remains true, as one observer noted nearly two decades ago, that Israeli Arabs lack "effective access to those institutions and organizations that dominate the life of the state."[6]

National authorities have been far more ready to allow Arab citizens to engage in effective politics at local levels, an opening to which they have enthusiastically responded. However, Israeli Arabs have increasingly demanded full participation in Israel's national political life. It is notable that the living standard of most Israeli Arabs has improved markedly since 1948. Because a majority of Israeli Arabs show no eagerness to relocate to a Palestinian state if such an entity arises on the West Bank and Gaza Strip, it appears that they see their futures as tied to the state of Israel. This seems to underline their rootedness in their historic homeland as well as their increasingly visible desire for full political participation in Israel.[7]

Time will tell whether that hope is realistic. For the past fifty years, most Israeli Jews have been more concerned about Arabs beyond the state's limits than about the state's Arab citizens. However, as the quality of life of Israel's Arab minority continues to improve, demands for more equitable political, social, and economic treatment can be expected to grow. If Israel and the Arab world beyond its borders arrive at a lasting peace, Israeli governments will almost certainly have to grant higher priority to dealing with the needs of the country's Arab citizens.

ISRAEL AND THE ARAB WORLD

Israeli governments have had two main objectives when considering the Arab world: to win official Arab acceptance of Israel's legitimacy and to maintain a regional balance of power that ensures the country's security regardless of Arab attitudes. The virtually uninterrupted hostility between Israel and the Arab world led Israel's leaders to place increasing emphasis on guaranteeing security through military means. Israel secretly embarked on a militarily significant nuclear research program in the late 1950s. By the 1970s, it was common knowledge that Israel possessed nuclear arms.

However, Israeli governments continued to give priority to achieving security through a favorable conventional military balance. In the wake of the 1967 war, one of the factors that initially fueled expansionist sentiment in Israel was the improved strategic situation that resulted from control over the Sinai Peninsula, the Golan Heights, and the West Bank. During the first few years after the 1967 war, most of the peace plans suggested by individual Israeli leaders (but not by Israel's government, which avoided specifying territorial demands) called for retention of much of the Sinai peninsula, all or most of the Golan Heights, and all or much of the West Bank. Yet, it is notable that once sustained Egyptian-Israeli contacts began after 1974, Israeli governments (both Labor and Likud) found it possible to modify such views of strategic necessity by accepting the land-for-peace formula that lay at the heart of the 1979 Egypt-Israel Peace Treaty (Document 8). In effect—at least in terms of Israel's borders with Egypt—Israeli leaders concluded that territorial space was not as essential to security as political arrangements that promised full peace.

King Hussein's renunciation of claims to the West Bank in 1988 allowed Israel and Jordan to negotiate their 1994 peace without having to overcome competing territorial claims. Although Israeli troops still effectively occupy a portion of Lebanon, Israel has not made any claims to that area, and it would appear that Lebanon's territorial integrity would not be compromised by a peace treaty. However, such an eventuality must await a settlement between Israel and Syria. The Golan again raises difficult questions regarding the relationship between territorial control and security—and therefore the validity of the land-for-peace peacemaking strategy.

As noted in Chapter 1, Israelis are divided over how to proceed in the search for peace with Syria. This was particularly evident in the aftermath of the apparent progress made during the 1995–1996 talks between the two sides at the Wye Plantation. The basic difference between the Labor government's willingness to apply the land-for-peace formula to the Golan and the Likud government's subsequent reversal of that position have led to a deadlock on the Syrian-Israeli track. Israeli Prime Minister Benjamin Netanyahu campaigned on a platform of "secure peace." He held that a Syrian presence in the Golan was incompatible with Israel's strategic needs and that the Golan's water resources were vital to Israel's welfare. Thus, according to the guidelines of the government in June 1996, which were approved by all political parties in the cabinet headed by Netanyahu: "The Government views the Golan Heights as essential to the security of the state and its water resources. Retaining Israeli sovereignty over the Golan will be the basis for an arrangement with Syria" (see Document 14). Nonetheless, Netanyahu has continued to express interest in negotiating with Syria. Damascus has declined because, in its view, to return to the negotiating table on the basis of what has so far been offered by Israel's Likud government would go back to "square one."

The Likud government's hard-line stance was not limited to Syria. By the spring of 1997, its steps on the West Bank and in Jerusalem were seen by Palestinians and the Arab world in general as backtracking on earlier Israeli commitments and on the spirit of mutual accommodation inherent in the peace accords. Those steps included delaying the handing over of additional territory to the Palestinian Authority (PA), blocking Palestinian economic development through frequent closures of the West Bank and Gaza, expanding Jewish settlements, and making unilateral changes in the still-contested areas of Jerusalem. Although neither Egypt nor Jordan—nor, for that matter, the Palestinian Authority under Yasir Arafat—showed any willingness to undermine the existing formal state of peace with Israel, their relations with the Israeli government became markedly strained.

So too did Israel's budding relations with other Arab states when the Arab League, meeting in Cairo at the end of March 1997, called on members to stop normalizing relations with the Jewish state and resume the economic boycott of Israel. The Arab League also asked member states to suspend participation in multilateral working groups related to refugees, the environment, water resources, economic development, and arms control and regional security, which had met sporadically since 1992.

ASSESSMENT

Zionist immigrants to Palestine succeeded in building a state and a nation. Israel's governing institutions for the most part serve its Jewish public well. The state is active and strong, helping the Jewish citizens to enjoy a productive life in full knowledge that the state has sufficient military power to meet any possible current threat. Most Jewish Israelis have come to share a strong sense of common national identity, despite the variety of origins that helped produce their society. The combination of strong, participatory governing institutions and solidly rooted national identity that characterizes Israel gives hope that the country will overcome the challenges it faces.

The importance of such challenges should not be minimized. Some are internal: They arise from, and must be confronted within, Israeli society. Others are external: They relate primarily to Israel's interactions with other groups.

Internally, the bulk of Israeli society must continue to seek to overcome the divisive effects of secular-religious controversies, quarrels over the nature and requirements of Judaism, and tensions generated by socioeconomic-cultural differences between Ashkenazim and Mizrahim. Even more important, however, is the need for Israeli society to reduce the divide between Israeli Jews and Israeli Arabs. So long as Israeli Arabs are not fully equal citizens and remain marginalized from the most important avenues of full participation in public affairs, both the tasks of state-building and nation-building will be incomplete.

Israel has always had to pay special attention to external challenges, and this remains as true today as it was fifty years ago. However, today's challenges differ from early ones. In the past, Israel faced military challenges from its neighbors. Those were successfully met by the growth of Israel's own military power. Israel is now increasingly challenged politically by its neighbors, who hold out the prospect of arriving at mutually acceptable compromises that will ensure peace and security for Arabs and Israelis alike.

Although Israel has been partly successful in dealing with this change in the Arab position—making peace with Egypt, the PLO, and Jordan—its public is deeply divided over how to proceed with the peace process. Voting patterns indicate that very few Israelis are willing to consider a land-for-peace formula that would lead to a fully independent state on the West Bank and Gaza Strip for the Palestinians and that would restore full sovereignty for Syria over the Golan Heights. A larger number, who tend to vote for the Labor bloc, are willing to relinquish Israeli control over a significant part of those territories in the context of demilitarization, the retention of most Israeli settlements, and other limitations on Palestinian and Syrian sovereignty. A slightly larger number of Israelis, who vote for Likud and parties to its right, reject the idea of trading territory on the Golan Heights and the West Bank, and seek to establish Israeli sovereignty over those areas in the context of limited autonomy for the Palestinians.

Thus, Israel is currently deeply divided by two questions whose answers will profoundly affect future relations with its neighbors. The first relates to security. Will the application of the land-for-peace formula to the Golan, West Bank, and Gaza undermine or strengthen Israel's security in the long run? Though answers to this question may be debatable, the issue can at least be discussed on the basis of data regarding levels of military capability and possible political arrangements.

The second question, however, is more complex: Are territorial withdrawal from occupied territories and the creation of a Palestinian state in the West Bank and Gaza compatible with Israel's fundamental purpose as a state? In the final analysis, this question will be answered through actions that reflect Zionism's basic values.

Differences among Israelis over how best to proceed with the peace process are therefore ultimately over different visions of Zionism's true meaning. For some, the ideology is sufficiently flexible to allow for territorial compromise; for others, it is not. Eventually, Israel's response to the political challenges of peacemaking will redefine Zionism. The clearest touchstone will be found in Israel's final response to Palestinian nationalism.

NOTES

1. Leah Rabin, *Rabin: Our Life, His Legacy* (New York: G. P. Putnam's Sons, 1997), 50–51.

2. Polls from 1962 to 1988, cited in Asher Arian, *Politics in Israel* (Chatham, NJ: Chatham House Publishers, 1989), 237. Discussion of "Who is a Jew?" on 240–41.

3. Extract from Rabbi Zvi Yehuda Kook, *LeNetivot Yisrael* (*For the Paths of Israel*), published just after the 1967 war.

4. Sammy Smooha, "Existing and Alternative Policies towards the Arabs in Israel," in Ernest Krausz and David Glanz (eds.), *Politics and Society in Israel*, Vol. III (New Brunswick and Oxford: Israel Sociological Society, 1985), 342.

5. Salma Khadra Jayyusi, ed., *Anthology of Modern Palestinian Literature* (New York: Columbia University Press, 1992), 331.

6. Ian Lustick, *Arabs in the Jewish State* (Austin: University of Texas Press, 1980), 116.

7. Majid al-Haj, "The Changing Strategies of Mobilization among Arabs in Israel: Parliamentary Politics, Local Politics, and National Organizations," in Efraim Ben-Zadok (ed.), *Local Communities and the Israeli Polity* (Albany: State University of New York, 1993), 72.

Palestinian stamp issued by the national movement in 1938 during the revolt, showing the Church of the Holy Sepulcher and the Dome of the Rock in Jerusalem with the Arabic names of Palestinian towns superimposed on a map of Palestine. Walid Khalid, ed., *Before Their Diaspora: A Photographic History of the Palestinians, 1876–1948* (Washington, DC: The Institute For Palestine Studies, 1984). Courtesy of The Institute For Palestine Studies

ארגון צבאי לאומי

IRGUN ZWAÏ LËUMI BE-EREZ JISRAËL

ORGANISATION MILITAIRE NATIONALE JUIVE D'EREZ JISRAËL

JEWISH NATIONAL MILITARY ORGANISATION OF EREZ JISRAËL

An Irgun poster for distribution in Central Europe.

Poster of the Irgun printed in 1946, proclaiming that the establishment of a Jewish state throughout Palestine and Transjordan by force was "the sole solution." Walid Khalidi, ed., *Before Their Diaspora: A Photographic History of the Palestinians, 1876–1948* (Washington, DC: The Institute For Palestine Studies, 1984). Courtesy of The Institute For Palestine Studies

Ship with Jewish immigrants arriving at Haifa port in the summer of 1946 despite the British ban on Jewish immigration to Palestine. The banner reads: "We survived Hitler. Death is no stranger to us. Nothing will keep us from our Jewish homeland. The blood is on your head if you fire on this unarmed ship." Walid Khalidi, ed., *Before Their Diaspora: A Photographic History of the Palestinians, 1876–1948* (Washington, DC: The Institute For Palestine Studies, 1984). Courtesy of The Institute For Palestine Studies

David Ben-Gurion, prime minister of Israel, in his office on March 3, 1958. Library of Congress

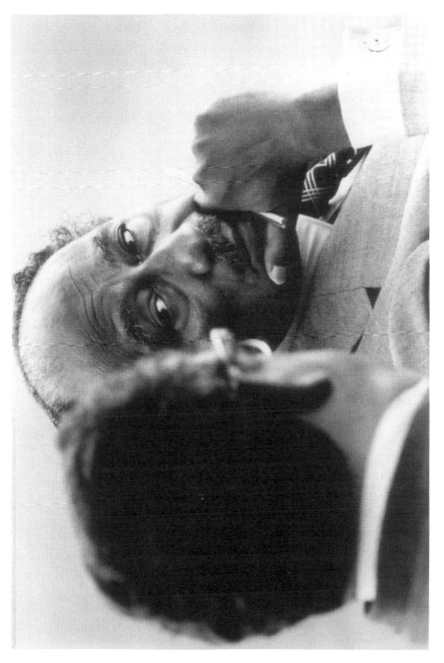

Egyptian President Anwar Sadat looking toward U.S. Secretary of State Henry Henry Kissinger on August 31, 1975, while they finalized the second Egypt-Israel accord on disengagement in the Sinai peninsula. Library of Congress

Yasir Arafat, Shimon Peres, and Yitzhak Rabin displaying their copies of the Nobel Peace Prize in Oslo, December 9, 1994. http://www.israel-mfa.gov.il/images/nobel3.jpg

New apartment blocs in Ma'ale Adumim, an Israeli settlement midway between Jerusalem and Jericho, August 2, 1995. Photo by Ann Lesch

Palestinian boys protesting Israeli policies by burning car tires in Nuseirat refugee camp, Gaza Strip, September 26, 1996. Courtesy of Taroub Abdul Hadi

Israeli border police on patrol in the Muslim quarter of the Old City of Jerusalem, October 5, 1996. Courtesy of Taroub Abdul Hadi

4

The Palestinians

The Palestinians are central players in the Arab-Israeli drama. Indeed, the core issue in the Arab-Israeli conflict involves the conflicting claims to the same piece of land made by Israeli Jews and Palestinian Arabs. Palestinians claim that they have the right to the land, based on their long-standing presence there. They also believe that the Jewish community treated them unjustly in asserting its claim to the same territory.

This chapter covers the period since 1948, during which Palestinian institutions and political objectives changed significantly. Palestinian political aims shifted from a determination to regain all of Palestine to acceptance of the idea of territorial partition and the establishment of a Palestinian state alongside Israel. The concept of partition remains controversial among Palestinians, but they increasingly view it as the only way to ensure their national survival and meet their basic political needs.

During those decades, Palestinians engaged in both the primary conflict with Israel and side conflicts with Arab governments. Although Arab governments felt a moral obligation toward the Palestinian cause, they gave priority to their own national interests in developing their policies toward Israel. When Palestinian priorities clashed with those of an Arab state, Palestinian interests suffered. Moreover, Arab governments sought to control the Palestinian national movement. This dual conflict—with Israel and the Arab states—complicated the Palestinian quest.

FRAGMENTATION IN EXILE

The Israeli war for independence in 1948 shattered the Palestinian community. More than 750,000 Arabs fled from the area that became Israel. Only 40 percent of the Palestinians remained in their own homes inside Israel, on the West Bank (annexed by Jordan), or in the Gaza Strip (administered by Egypt). (See Table 4.1.) The flight into exile had an overwhelming impact on them. Previously, their society was largely rural, with a small landed aristocracy and a substantial class of urban merchants. When they became refugees, they lost their livelihoods and property. Moreover, they lived under Arab governments that restricted their political activities and generally did not offer them citizenship. Palestinians were fragmented and silenced.

Table 4.1
Places Where Palestinians Lived in 1950[1]

Israel:	150,000	
West Bank:	800,000	(350,000 refugees)
Gaza Strip:	280,000	(200,000 refugees)
Lebanon:	100,000	
Syria:	80,000	
Elsewhere:	50,000	
Total:	1,460,000	

The situation facing Palestinians in each country varied considerably. However, there were certain common elements in the political realm, in their psychological reactions, and in the attitudes of the host countries toward them.

At the political level, the landed and professional political elites lost their credibility because the public blamed them for the defeat. Only village structures remained partly intact, because clan, local, and religious institutions helped to organize life in the refugee camps. However, they lacked agricultural land and did not own their homes, which caused severe distortions in the social structure.

The refugees underwent profound psychological transformations. At first they felt lost, disoriented, and torn from familiar ways of life. The humiliation of being landless contributed to their sense of alienation. The older generation succumbed to an ever-lengthening wait to return home.

The ambivalence of host countries toward the refugees increased that sense of alienation. Although the Arab states sought the commercial and professional skills of the Palestinian middle class, they could not absorb the mass of displaced farmers. Moreover, Palestinians resisted attempts to cancel their refugee status because they feared that this would deny them the right to reclaim their homes. Their anguish and longing were expressed by Abu Salma, the pseudonym for Abd al-Karim al-Karmi, a lawyer and poet from Haifa, who fled to Lebanon in 1948 and then lived in exile in Damascus, Syria. A segment of his poem follows:

We Shall Return

Beloved Palestine, how can I live
away from your plains and hills?
The valleys call me and the shores
cry out, echoing in the ears of time!
Even fountains weep as they trickle, estranged.
Your cities and villages echo the cries.
Will there be a return, my comrades ask,
a return after such long absence?
Yes, we'll return and kiss the moist ground,
love flowering on our lips. . . .

We'll return with raging storms,
holy lightning and fire,
winged hope and songs,
soaring eagles,
the dawn smiling on the deserts.[2]

The controls imposed by host countries took different forms. In Israel, Arabs gained citizenship but lived under military rule until 1966. The government regulated the movement of Arab residents, restricted access to education and employment, and curtailed political activities.

In the Gaza Strip, the Egyptian military government maintained tight control over the restive Palestinian population, which was composed mostly of refugees. Nonetheless, Egypt established a largely elected national assembly in the late 1950s as a political safety-valve for the residents.

Palestinians living in Syria had the same access to jobs and schools as Syrian citizens, which enabled them to normalize their lives considerably. In contrast, Lebanese authorities were highly restrictive, because they feared that the presence of the largely Sunni Muslim Palestinian refugees would upset the delicate religious balance in that country. Lebanon denied Palestinians the right to study in public schools or to obtain permanent employment. Soldiers entered the refugee camps at will to arrest residents.

Life was least disrupted on the West Bank, where most Palestinians remained in their original homes and all the Palestinians gained Jordanian citizenship. Despite this, they lost trade outlets through the Mediterranean ports that Israel took over and lost valuable agricultural land to Israel. Because Jordan had a small and poorly educated population, Palestinians staffed much of the administrative and educational systems in Jordan and developed many of its commercial enterprises. Nonetheless, the Jordanian government tended to favor the East Bank in its industrial and agricultural development plans, and the monarchy never trusted Palestinians with senior posts in sensitive ministries and the armed forces.

During the 1950s, Palestinians were attracted to various forms of pan-Arabism that asserted that regaining Palestine required Arab political and military unity. But the idea of Arab unity received a blow in 1961 when Syria ended its union with Egypt, called the United Arab Republic, after less than three years. Faith in Arab military prowess was destroyed in June 1967 when the Israeli army defeated the combined Arab forces in a lightning strike and seized control of the Golan Heights (Syria), West Bank, Gaza Strip, and Sinai peninsula (Egypt).

That disillusionment accelerated processes that were already underway among the Palestinians. The sense of being discriminated against by fellow Arabs and disappointment with Arab regimes led many Palestinians to stop being passive. They sought to transform their situation through their own actions, rather than wait for Arab governments to rescue them. Small underground guerrilla cells sprang up in the early 1960s. Fatah, founded in Kuwait in 1959 by a young engineer, Yasir Arafat, and several professional colleagues, launched its first raid into Israel in 1965. The *fidayiin* (guerrillas) had a two-fold strategy: to assert that self-reliance was the route to liberation, as Algerians had just demonstrated in their successful eight-year war against the French, and to stir popular mobilization that would shame Arab rulers into fighting Israel.

EVOLUTION OF THE PLO

The growing discontent among Palestinians worried Arab governments, who sought to channel that alienation by forming the Palestine Liberation Organization (PLO) in 1964. Egypt appointed the PLO leaders, whose support was drawn from professional, business, and government circles in the Arab world. Even though it was controlled by Arab governments, the PLO's existence represented a critical step toward reestablishing political structures to represent the Palestinians.

The PLO convened the first Palestine National Council (PNC) in East Jerusalem in May 1964. The equivalent of a parliament-in-exile, the PNC adopted an uncompromising political charter that refused to accept Israel's existence. The charter called for a return to the situation as it was before 1948 so that the refugees could reclaim their homes.

The 1967 defeat discredited the Arab states and their armed forces. When Fatah and other guerrilla groups escalated their military and terrorist attacks after the war, Arabs widely praised the fidayiin for defying Israeli power more bravely than the Arab states' heavily armed troops. Volunteers rushed to join the guerrillas, especially after Fatah withstood an Israeli attack on Karameh (Jordan) in March 1968. In 1969 the guerrilla organizations became dominant in the PLO and elected Arafat to chair the PLO Executive Committee.

By then, the PNC amended the charter to reflect the new power of the fidayiin. The amendments emphasized popular armed struggle, rejected Zionism and the partition of Palestine, termed Judaism "a religion . . . not an independent nationality" (Article 20), and called for "the total liberation of Palestine" (Article 21). The charter upheld Arab unity, but emphasized that just as the PLO would "not interfere in the internal affairs of any Arab state" (Article 27), it rejected control by Arab regimes (Article 28). The charter could only be amended by a two-thirds vote of the more than four hundred members of the PNC.

The PLO included not only Fatah but also many small guerrilla groups. The most important were

1. The Popular Front for the Liberation of Palestine, led by Greek Orthodox physician Dr. George Habash, which called for the overthrow of Arab monarchies and the establishment of Arab unity before the liberation of Palestine, and which hijacked European and Israeli civilian airplanes in a bid to call international attention to the Palestinian plight;

2. The Democratic Front for the Liberation of Palestine, led by the Jordanian Naif Hawatmeh, which was the first Palestinian group to recognize that Jews were a people, not only a religious community;

3. The Popular Front-General Command under Ahmad Jabril, a former officer in the Syrian army, which Syria supported and which engaged in terror and hijackings;

4. Sa'iqa, sponsored by the Syrian Baath party; and

5. The Arab Liberation Front, sponsored by Baathist Iraq.

The PLO began to revise its goals in the mid-1970s. This was partly in response to the major setback the movement had experienced in 1970–1971 when the Jordanian army cracked down on its presence in the country and forced the guerrillas to flee to Lebanon. That confrontation reflected the clash between the interests of Arab states and Palestinian interests: The Jordanian army and politicians could not tolerate the presence of an armed Palestinian state-within-a-state because that provoked Israeli military retaliation on Jordanian soil and challenged the authority of the Jordanian government.

In Lebanon, where the government denied Palestinians access to public schools and to government jobs, the PLO developed a sophisticated organizational structure to meet educational, employment, and social needs. The PLO provided medical services in the refugee camps and promoted light industries to employ refugees. Affiliated organizations such as the unions of workers, engineers, writers, journalists, teachers, students, and women extended their activities to Palestinian communities throughout the Middle East. The Palestine National Fund relied heavily on contributions from Palestinians working in Kuwait, Abu Dhabi, Saudi Arabia, and other Gulf countries. Those Palestinians, often professionally and financially successful, nonetheless remained insecure: They could be deported at any moment and could not remain in those countries after their work contracts ended. They therefore yearned for a political home that would offer them diplomatic protection and economic security, and eagerly contributed to the revival of Palestinian nationalism through the PLO. Thus, the PLO galvanized and structured the political activities of Palestinians throughout the Arab world.

THE SITUATION UNDER ISRAELI OCCUPATION

Meanwhile, Palestinians living on the West Bank and the Gaza Strip lived through very different experiences after Israel seized those territories in 1967. They became aware of the reality and strength of Israel and began to seek strategies to end Israel's occupation.

In June 1967 Israel established a military government to control the West Bank and Gaza Strip, which meant that army officers ran all of the health and educational services, set economic policy, and expropriated land for Jewish settlements and military installations. The military government arrested people at will, and Israeli military courts handled criminal and security cases. Most Palestinian lawyers boycotted the courts and protested the military orders that transformed the legal status of the territories.

Teachers protested Israeli control over the public school system, which enabled Israeli officers to hire and fire teachers and to select curricula and textbooks. The military government did not construct new public schools or provide in-service training for teachers. This resulted in a marked deterioration of the educational environment and serious overcrowding in the schools. Palestinians controlled their own university-level education, however, because those colleges were private.

The military government also restricted economic life in the occupied territories. Although Israel allowed Palestinians to export agricultural produce to Jordan, it usually banned them from selling goods to Israel in order to protect Israeli farmers and businesses from competition. Palestinian farmers had to get a permit from the military government to plant fruit and citrus trees and even to plant vegetables in the occupied territories. Similarly, Israel controlled permits for operating factories and for industrial exports, which meant that Palestinian industry stagnated. In contrast to these heavy restrictions on Palestinians, Israeli agricultural produce and industrial goods could be sold freely in the West Bank and Gaza Strip.

This constricted economy forced most Palestinian men to seek employment abroad—either in the oil-rich Gulf states or inside Israel. By the 1980s a third of the West Bank and Gaza's labor force worked inside Israel in agriculture, construction, factories, or restaurants. Even women and children worked in Israeli factories and fields in low-wage jobs that lacked security or health benefits. This exacerbated the Palestinians' economic dependence on Israel and compounded the unhealthy imbalance between the two economies.

Palestinians protested the legal and educational changes as well as the expropriation of land for Jewish settlements from private owners, tenant farmers, and absent refugees. That expropriation escalated in the 1970s and 1980s. Even though there were only 150,000 Jewish settlers on the West Bank and 5,000 in the Gaza Strip in 1997—as against two million Palestinians—the Israeli government had expropriated 40 percent of the Gaza Strip and 60 percent of the West Bank for exclusive use by Israelis for settlements or military sites. Settlers also had access to nine times the quantity of water that the Israeli authorities permitted neighboring Palestinian villagers to use. The military government capped village wells to limit the water flow and refused to give permission to dig new wells in order to limit the expansion of agricultural production. These policies led to stark contrasts: Village women carried water in cans from springs to their homes whereas settlers enjoyed swimming pools and virtually unlimited running water.

Palestinians protested the merger of East Jerusalem into the Israeli municipality in June 1967, which was reinforced by a Knesset resolution of August 1980 that declared unified Jerusalem the eternal capital of Israel. Israel deported to Jordan the former Arab mayor of East Jerusalem, introduced Israeli social services, and altered the curricula of the Arab schools. The Israeli government expanded the area of East Jerusalem to incorporate land from neighboring villages, and constructed large apartment complexes for exclusively Jewish use. By 1996 the Jewish population in East Jerusalem exceeded the Arab population, as a result of this deliberate settlement policy. However, the two peoples had virtually no social or economic contact, and the Palestinians continued to insist that East Jerusalem should become the capital of an independent Palestinian state.

The Israeli army clamped down on all forms of resistance. The military government deported mayors, religious leaders, teachers, lawyers, and doctors who articulated residents' grievances and organized strikes. It also banned all political meetings and political parties and censored the press extensively. Palestinians who joined political organizations or engaged in violence received lengthy prison terms. Some political leaders were held for years under administrative detention, which meant that no charges were filed against them and no trials were held. Most Palestinian protests were nonviolent, but some groups attacked Israeli civilians and soldiers with bombs and homemade Molotov cocktails. Moreover, a full-scale rebellion engulfed the Gaza Strip in the late 1960s. Gaza's huge refugee camps and dense citrus groves provided shelter for the guerrilla fighters, who attacked Israeli patrols.

CHANGES IN THE PLO'S OBJECTIVES

The PLO began to change its political aims in the early 1970s. A meeting of the PNC in January 1973 secretly resolved to form an umbrella political organization in the occupied territories called the Palestine National Front (PNF). The PNF sought "independence and self-determination" and the end to Israeli occupation through political action rather than force. The PNF encompassed all political groups that accepted the concept of a Palestinian state alongside Israel. Fatah and the Communist party were its leading members. Communists had supported a two-state solution since 1947, when Moscow endorsed the UN partition plan. Politicians who supported the PNF swept the elections for municipal councils on the West Bank in 1976, which indicated broad public support for negotiating an end to Israeli rule.

The Arab-Israeli war of October 1973 also encouraged Palestinians to moderate their attitudes. In June 1974 the PNC hinted that the PLO would negotiate to regain part of the land when the members passed a resolution that advocated establishing "the independent combatant national authority . . . over every part of Palestinian territory that is liberated." Even though Arafat claimed that he would not give up the struggle against Israel, hard-line groups such as the Popular Front withdrew from the PLO's

Executive Committee, accusing Arafat of granting *de facto* recognition to Israel.

The PLO's shift toward a negotiating strategy helped to consolidate its standing in the Arab world. In October 1974 an Arab summit conference in Rabat (Morocco) affirmed "the right of the Palestinian people to establish an independent national authority under the command of the Palestine Liberation Organization, the sole legitimate representative of the Palestinian people, in any Palestinian territory that is liberated."[3] The PLO's international role was further enhanced in November 1974 when, following Arafat's address to the UN General Assembly, the PLO secured observer status at the UN.

This shift crystallized at the PNC's meeting in March 1977, which stressed the Palestinians' "right to establish their independent national state on their own land." This pointed to the PLO's strategic shift away from the goal of reclaiming all Palestine toward the goal of forming a state alongside Israel. However, its impact internationally was muted because Egyptian President Anwar Sadat soon initiated bilateral negotiations with Israel that distracted attention from the Palestinian issue. Moreover, the civil war in Lebanon and Israeli invasions of Lebanon in 1978 and 1982 further disrupted and disoriented the Palestinian national movement.

The PLO was seriously weakened by the 1982 Israeli invasion of Lebanon and the forced removal of its offices from Beirut to Tunis. At that time Israel also fired most of the mayors on the West Bank and Gaza Strip and closed the municipal councils, thereby stripping the Palestinians of even local self-rule. Palestinians responded by developing grass-roots institutions to provide rudimentary services in the occupied territories. Medical, agricultural, and women's committees became particularly active. Medical programs focused on the deteriorating quality of health services and the lack of clinics in the villages. They introduced basic preventive measures, including improved hygiene and prenatal care. Agricultural committees provided seeds, loans, and technical advice to farmers in the absence of an agricultural bank or an effective government agricultural extension program. Women's committees organized literacy programs and day care for working mothers. Associations of journalists, writers, and artists promoted exhibits and symposia. Politically oriented theatrical troupes also became active.

The Israeli military government cracked down on overt expressions of Palestinian nationalism and tried to create or support alternative political groups in order to weaken the nationalist movement—with mixed success. The army, for example, raided Palestinian art exhibits, banned public lectures, and censored theatrical performances. The Israeli government refused to recognize that labor and professional unions had the authority to maintain professional standards and protect group interests. Instead, the military government promoted alternative structures, such as the Village Leagues and the Muslim Brotherhood, in order to sow discord among Palestinians.

Israel financed and armed the Village Leagues, which claimed to represent the rural areas. They had no credibility because everyone knew that Israel paid their members' salaries and because they acted as armed vigilantes on behalf of the Israeli military and security forces. Moreover, the escalating land expropriations for Israeli settlements during the 1980s angered villagers and destroyed the Village Leagues' claim that cooperation with Israel could benefit Palestinians.

The members of the Muslim Brotherhood, a long-established religious movement, viewed Israeli rule as a tribulation brought on the Palestinians by their failure to be sufficiently religious. Palestinians must return to personal piety before any political change could occur. The Muslim Brothers strongly opposed the PLO's secular orientation and the active role played by Palestinian Communists in political and cultural life. The military government allowed the Brotherhood to establish charities, clinics, and educational programs. When Muslim Brothers physically attacked nationalists and leftists, the Israeli army did not stop the violence—even though the army quickly suppressed all other protests.

THE INTIFADA

Palestinians appeared divided and demoralized in the 1980s. Nonetheless, a profound transformation took place at the grass-roots level that reinvigorated the national movement. The local committees that tried to solve economic and social problems linked urban professionals to refugees, villagers, and the urban poor. Many Palestinians realized that, even though they could not force the Israeli government out of the occupied territories, this popular mobilization might shift the political advantage to their side.

The *intifada* (uprising) that swept the West Bank and Gaza Strip in 1988–1990 differed significantly from previous protests. Previously, the urban elite—mayors and intellectuals—led the political movement. But Israel had deported many of them, forced others out of office, and banned most institutions that expressed nationalist views. In contrast, the leaders of the intifada remained anonymous so that they could avoid arrest and emphasize that the intifada was a mass movement rather than one run by the political elite. Committees in neighborhoods helped residents survive the pressures of curfews, arrests, and diminished income. Grass-roots networks of medical, agricultural, educational, and women's committees also sustained those efforts. Overall, the intifada represented a sustained effort to prove to Israelis—and the outside world—that military occupation had denied the Palestinians their basic rights and that the people would use their moral force to win their independence.

The Israeli army responded massively to the intifada. Defense Minister Yitzhak Rabin initially thought he could crush the uprising by force. But the diffuse nature of the protests made that impossible. Teenagers played cat-and-mouse games with soldiers, throwing stones at them and then dashing away when the soldiers shot rubber-coated bullets and tear gas. Israel dampened protests by imposing curfews that sometimes lasted for weeks. Those actions hurt Israel's image abroad and reinforced the perception that the Israeli-Palestinian conflict required a political, rather than a military, solution.

The pervasive bitterness at the behavior of the Israeli army was exemplified in the poem by Hanan Mikha'il Ashrawi, later spokesperson for the Palestinian negotiators in 1991 and one of five women who won seats in the Palestinian legislature in January 1996. Ashrawi, who holds a Ph.D. from the University of Virginia and taught literature at Bir Zeit University on the West Bank, became minister of higher education in the Palestinian Authority in 1996. Her poem imagines the feelings of Rasha Houshiyya, a young girl who lost one eye when an Israeli soldier shot at her in March 1988:

From the Diary of an Almost-Four-Year-Old

Tomorrow, the bandages
will come off. I wonder
will I see half an orange,
half an apple, half my
mother's face
with my one remaining eye?

I did not see the bullet
but felt its pain
exploding in my head.
His image did not
vanish, the soldier
with a big gun, unsteady
hands, and a look in
his eyes
I could not understand.

. . .

I hear a nine-month-old
has also lost an eye,
I wonder if my soldier
shot her too—a soldier
looking for little girls who
look him in the eye—
I'm old enough, almost four,
I've seen enough of life,
but she's just a baby
who didn't know any better.[4]

The intifada's goals evolved rapidly during the first year. Initially, activists wanted to ameliorate the conditions of life under occupation. But they soon began to talk about ending the occupation itself and creating an independent state alongside Israel. That shift reflected their growing confidence that they could sustain the protests. They realized that the uprising had compelled Washington to turn its attention to the Middle East, and they hoped to capitalize on that attention. They supported convening an international peace conference, in which the PLO could represent their interests.

The PLO leaders responded to the opportunity offered by the uprising. In November 1988 the PNC officially called for an independent Palestinian state on the West Bank and the Gaza Strip, with its capital in East Jerusalem. For the first time, the PNC accepted UN resolutions that called for territorial partition and that recognized Israel (Document 10). In a press conference soon after, Arafat explicitly renounced terrorism and affirmed his commitment to reach a peace agreement with the Jewish state (Document 11). As discussed in Chapter 5, the U.S. administration finally responded positively and opened a dialogue with the PLO. The Israeli government, caught off guard by the shifts in the American and Palestinian positions, rejected contact with the PLO.

THE GULF CRISIS

Neither the intifada nor the PNC resolutions proved sufficient to change the situation on the ground. Israel's basic reluctance to consider the PLO as anything but a terrorist organization, and its equally strong reluctance to concede the principle that Palestinian national rights existed, helped prevent any movement toward negotiations. Israel's Likud government accelerated the construction of settlements in the Occupied Territories, and some cabinet members even advocated expelling Palestinians *en masse* from the territories. That proposal evoked painful memories among survivors of the Holocaust, as expressed in this poem by the Israeli writer Dan Almagor:

Voluntary Transfer

Lately there is talk about "voluntary transfer,"
Entirely voluntary, of course.
My grandparents (on both sides) boarded trucks,
Entirely voluntarily.
It must be true; there is no evidence that they resisted
or cried out:
And I never had the opportunity to meet them
In order to ask them why not.[5]

Meanwhile, the PLO's hope that the dialogue with the United States would produce diplomatic results was dashed when the United States suspended contact in June 1990 after a radical, anti-Arafat Palestinian group tried to land speedboats on Israel's coast. Feeling desperate at the setbacks on the diplomatic front and the deterioration on the West Bank, Palestinians turned to Iraqi President Saddam Hussein for support. Although they criticized his seizure of Kuwait on August 2, 1990, they welcomed his declaration that Israel must withdraw from the West Bank and Gaza before he would consider leaving Kuwait. Palestinian support for Iraq reached fever pitch in January 1991, when Iraqi SCUD missiles hit Israeli cities during the war that forced Iraqi troops out of Kuwait.

Iraq's defeat left the PLO isolated and weakened, because Saudi Arabia and Kuwait—angered by the PLO's pro-Iraqi stance—cut financial aid. Kuwaitis wreaked vengeance on Palestinian residents, whom they accused—often unfairly—of collaborating with Iraq. Within a year, only twenty-five thousand of the previous four hundred thousand Palestinians remained in Kuwait. Moreover, the disintegration of the Soviet Union removed an important diplomatic counterweight to the United States.

Nonetheless, the Gulf war generated demands for international attention to the Arab-Israeli conflict. The following chapter discusses how the United States responded to this challenge by convening the Madrid Peace Conference in October 1991. Palestinians from the West Bank and Gaza Strip participated in the negotiations, but Israel refused to negotiate with either East Jerusalem residents or PLO officials. However, the Palestinian negotiators maintained constant contact with Arafat, headquartered in Tunis.

Negotiations focused on establishing a five-year period of self-rule, with the final status left for later negotiations. The Palestinians pushed for an interim period that would lead to the establishment of a Palestinian state alongside Israel. Their proposal stressed that "all the territories [occupied in 1967], the land, natural resources and water" and "all the Palestinian inhabitants" must come under the jurisdiction of the interim self-govern-ment, whose legislative assembly would be elected by Palestinian residents. This contrasted with the Israeli concept of limited communal self-rule that would leave Israel in control of land, water, and security.

As talks dragged on, Palestinian disillusionment deepened and violence escalated. Palestinian militants attacked settlers and soldiers in the territo-ries and civilians inside Israel. Moreover, Islamic groups challenged the secular nationalists' authority in the Occupied Territories. Particularly active in this respect was Hamas, a militant Islamist organization that had developed in 1988 as an outgrowth of the Muslim Brotherhood. Hamas denounced negotiations with Israel on the grounds that the entire land was holy and all of Palestine must become an Islamic state. According to the Hamas charter, "no one has the right to give away any part of Palestine." (This viewpoint represented the mirror image of Israel's Gush Emunim, whose covenant—described in the previous chapter—claimed that all the land was holy to Jews.) Although the Israeli army initially tolerated attacks by Hamas on Fatah in the summer of 1992, it reacted strongly when Hamas operatives killed Israelis. In December 1992, Israel deported more than four hundred alleged leaders of Hamas, who became stranded in no-man's-land on the Lebanese border after the Beirut government refused to admit them. The UN General Assembly condemned Israel for the expulsions, and the PLO sought to mend fences within the Palestinian community by rallying behind the expellees. Palestinian negotiators withdrew in protest from the ongoing talks in Washington, D.C.

BREAKTHROUGH

It was in this tense atmosphere that a secret track of PLO-Israeli talks suddenly reached a dramatic conclusion. Meeting in Oslo under Norwegian auspices since the spring of 1993, the two sides hammered out a Declaration of Principles that Israel and the PLO signed in Washington on September 13, 1993 (Document 12). The historic document contained the two sides' mutual recognition of political legitimacy. Arafat and Rabin both realized that they could lose power if they failed to conclude an accord. If Arafat could not gain self-rule, Palestinians based in the Occupied Territories might assume the leading roles in the national movement or uncompromis-ing Islamists might overwhelm the secular nationalists. If Rabin could not build a more secure and prosperous Israel through negotiations, public support might shift to the hard-line annexationists. Moreover, Israeli offi-cials finally concluded that excluding the PLO from negotiations guaran-teed that talks would fail: Only the PLO could deliver.

The impetus was not merely negative. Both sides perceived the need to overcome hatred and mistrust and to place their relationship on a new basis. During the signing ceremony, Israeli Foreign Minister Shimon Peres spoke of the need for a fundamental "healing" between the two peoples with their "two parallel tragedies." Arafat stated that his people hope "that this agreement . . . marks the beginning of the end of a chapter of pain and suffering . . . [and ushers] in an age of peace, coexistence and equal rights." Indeed, the preamble of the accord stressed the importance of this "historic reconciliation."

The agreement called for Palestinian self-rule in the Gaza Strip and Jericho (see Map 5), followed by the establishment of Palestinian civil administration over the entire West Bank for a five-year interim period. After lengthy negotiations, Israel and the PLO signed an accord on May 4, 1994, that enabled Arafat to become *ra'is* (president) of the Palestinian Authority. Arafat and PLO officials returned to Gaza and Jericho in July 1994—for the first time since 1967. After another agreement in September 1995, Israeli troops redeployed from most Palestinian towns on the West Bank and the Palestinians held elections for their president and the eighty-eight–seat legislative council in January 1996. Palestinians participated enthusiastically in those elections, which was the first time they ever had the opportunity to choose their political representatives.

Nonetheless, many Palestinians were disappointed that executive power remained concentrated in the hands of Arafat, the newly elected president, and polls indicated that the public overwhelmingly expected Arafat to implement laws and resolutions passed by the legislature. In practice, Arafat ignored most legislative acts and even jammed the airwaves to prevent its sessions from being broadcast live by radio. When polled in late 1996, nearly a quarter of the respondents had a negative view about the status of human rights under the Palestinian Authority.[6]

The Palestinian Authority controlled police forces needed for internal security and operated the educational, health, social welfare, and tax systems. The tax base was too limited, however, to cover the cost of those expensive services, which had deteriorated markedly during the thirty years of Israeli rule. Moreover, per capita Gross National Product fell by nearly a quarter on the West Bank and Gaza Strip between 1992 and 1996. With the unemployment rate reaching 39 percent in the Gaza Strip and 24 percent on the West Bank in mid-1996, leading UN analysts concluded that the drop in wages meant that even those laborers who were employed could cover barely two-thirds of their family's daily needs.[7] Israel's continued forced separation of the West Bank and Gaza Strip, its closure of Jerusalem to

Map 5
The Gaza Strip, 1994

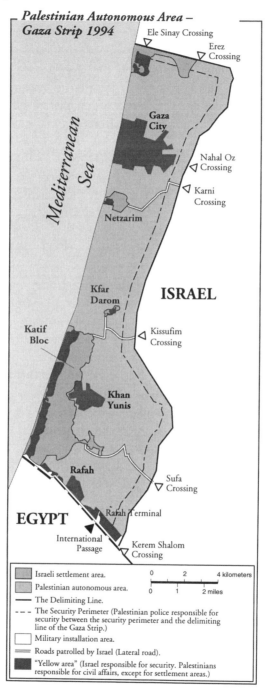

Palestinian Autonomous Area –
Gaza Strip 1994

Ele Sinay Crossing

Erez
Crossing

Gaza
City

Nahal Oz
Crossing

Karni
Crossing

Netzarim

Mediterranean Sea

ISRAEL

Kfar
Darom

Katif
Bloc

Kissufim
Crossing

Khan
Yunis

Rafah

Sufa
Crossing

EGYPT

Rafah Terminal

International
Passage

Kerem Shalom
Crossing

Israeli settlement area.

Palestinian autonomous area.

The Delimiting Line.

The Security Perimeter (Palestinian police responsible for security between the security perimeter and the delimiting line of the Gaza Strip.)

Military installation area.

Roads patrolled by Israel (Lateral road).

"Yellow area" (Israel responsible for security. Palestinians responsible for civil affairs, except for settlement areas.)

0   2   4 kilometers

0   1   2 miles

Source: Foundation for Middle East Peace, *Report on Israeli Settlement in the Occupied Territories,* November 1996, 5. Used by permission of the Foundation for Middle East Peace. By Andy Hemstreet.

nonresident Palestinians, its severe limitation on the number of Palestinians who could work inside Israel, and its restrictions on trade with Jordan were the prime causes of that economic crisis.

In addition, Israel's redeployment remained limited under the terms of the agreement signed in September 1995. The area of the West Bank under exclusive Palestinian control—known as Area A—totalled only 3 percent, which comprised eight cities. (According to a supplementary agreement reached in January 1997, the town of Hebron remained divided, with the Palestinian Authority controlling 80 percent of the town and Israel ruling 20 percent that included Jewish settlements and religious sites.) Another 20 percent—Area B—fell under Palestinian civil and administrative control, but the Israeli army still operated freely within that zone. More than three-quarters of the West Bank and a third of the Gaza Strip remained under exclusive Israeli control—called Area C—including areas with Jewish settlements and military bases. (See Map 6.)

Hamas boycotted the Palestinian legislative council elections and challenged the meager results of the negotiations. In the spring of 1996 Hamas and the more militant Islamic Jihad bombed buses and markets in Jerusalem and Tel Aviv, killing more than sixty Israelis. Recognizing that the terror attacks undermined the accords, Arafat ordered Palestinian security forces to clamp down on the Islamists. Nonetheless, Israelis reacted by electing a security-oriented Likud government in May 1996, led by Benjamin Netanyahu. Tensions escalated throughout the following year as Palestinians became increasingly disillusioned with Israel's implementation of the accords and fearful that they would never gain independence. By early 1997, as Israel continued to expand settlements on the West Bank and establish Jewish suburbs in East Jerusalem, disappointment erupted into angry protests and violent confrontations. Renewed terrorism by Islamist militants, whose suicide bombers killed Israelis in Tel Aviv and Jerusalem during the summer, again inflamed the political atmosphere.

ASSESSMENT

The Palestine problem has been transformed over the past century. Palestinians composed the majority of the population until 1948, when most of them fled into exile. Nearly two decades passed before Palestinians in the diaspora reestablished their political institutions and reinvigorated their national will. They then confronted the challenges of Israel's power, the reluctance of Arab regimes to tolerate an independent Palestinian movement, and—as will be seen in the following chapter—the unwillingness of major international actors to perceive Palestinians as political participants

Map 6
The West Bank, 1994

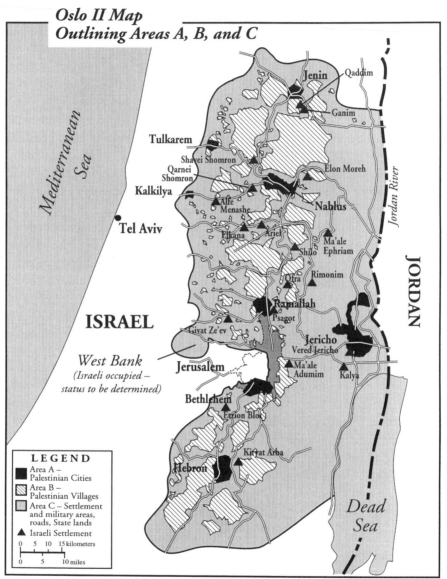

Oslo II Map
Outlining Areas A, B, and C

Mediterranean Sea

Jordan River

JORDAN

Jenin
Qaddim

Ganim

Tulkarem

Shavei Shomron
Qarnei
Shomron

Elon Moreh

Kalkilya

Alfe
Menashe

Nablus

Tel Aviv

Elkana
Ariel

Ma'ale
Ephriam

Shilo

Rimonim

Ofra

Ramallah
Psagot

ISRAEL

Givat Ze'ev

Jericho
Vered Jericho

West Bank
(Israeli occupied –
status to be determined)

Jerusalem

Ma'ale
Adumim

Kalya

Bethlehem

Etzion Bloc

LEGEND
◼ Area A –
Palestinian Cities
▨ Area B –
Palestinian Villages
▢ Area C – Settlement
and military areas,
roads, State lands
▲ Israeli Settlement
0 5 10 15 kilometers
0   5   10 miles

Kiryat Arba

Hebron

Dead
Sea

Source: Foundation for Middle East Peace, *Report on Israeli Settlement in the Occupied Territories*, November 1996, 4. Used by permission of the Foundation for Middle East Peace. By Andy Hemstreet.

rather than as passive refugees. Palestinians had to fight on all fronts. Nonetheless, a deeply rooted national identity expressed through autonomous political institutions has reemerged in the thirty years since 1967.

Palestinians have now restructured their political objectives. They continue to believe that they were wronged and that complete justice would require the restoration of the refugees to their homes and the reconstitution of the entire land as a Palestinian state. However, most Palestinians have concluded that the counterclaims of Israeli Jews cannot be ignored and that the only feasible solution is a Palestinian state alongside Israel. In that manner, they argue, both peoples will achieve their national aims and the contradiction between them will be removed. Tension between the Palestinians and the Arab governments will decrease, because their political status will be normalized.

Polls show that three-quarters of the Palestinians on the West Bank and Gaza Strip still support the peace process. Nonetheless, that strong support is shrinking as Israel continues to construct settlements, and the economic situation worsens.[8] Dissident groups that reject compromise with Israel can play on that disappointment by resorting to violence to protest the terms of the peace accords. Even as the interim accord is being implemented, Palestinians increasingly doubt that their minimal aspirations will be achieved. Negotiations on final-status issues including Jerusalem, settlements, and refugees were supposed to begin by March 1996, but—as of early 1998—had not yet been launched.

The lives of Palestinians in the territories and in exile are still insecure. Untangling the Israeli-Palestinian conflict remains difficult, with many pitfalls along the way. Nonetheless, for the first time in a long time there is hope that Palestinian-Israeli relations may become firmly based on mutual accommodation. Movement toward this end will do much to ease Israel's outstanding tensions with Arab states, thereby furthering chances of a definitive resolution of the Arab-Israeli conflict. However, much will depend on the policies pursued in the Middle East by external states, and particularly by the United States.

NOTES

1. Figures compiled by Ann Lesch from various sources. Detailed comparative figures on Palestinians by location through 1987 can be found in *Middle East Report*, 146 (May–June 1987), 10.

2. Excerpts from Salma Khadra Jayyusi, ed., *Anthology of Modern Palestinian Literature* (New York: Columbia University Press, 1992), 96–97.

3. Text in *Arab-Israeli Conflict and Conciliation*, ed. Bernard Reich (West-port, CT: Praeger, 1995), 130.

4. Excerpt from Jayyusi, ed., *Anthology of Modern Palestinian Literature*, 340–41.

5. Almagor had written popular songs for the Israeli army and first publicly criticized Israeli policies when he read this poem at a peace demonstration on December 10, 1988, commemorating the first anniversary of the intifada and international human rights day. Translation published in *Middle East Report*, 157 (March–April 1989), 4.

6. Twenty-two percent of 1,327 male and female respondents on the West Bank and Gaza Strip, polled December 26–28, 1996, by the Center for Palestine Research and Studies, Nablus. The percent is particularly significant when one considers that 32 percent said that they were afraid to criticize the PA. *Journal of Palestine Studies*, 26, 3 (Spring 1997): 116.

7. Quarterly reports of the United Nations Special Coordinator in the Occupied Territories: October 1996 report cited in *News from Within* XIII, 1 (January 1997): 20; April 1997 report cited in the Jerusalem Media and Communication Centre, *Palestine Report*, 2, 45 (April 18, 1997).

8. A poll of 1,200 Palestinians from the West Bank, East Jerusalem, and Gaza Strip on April 3–4, 1997, indicated that 72.9 percent support the peace process, but 70.1 percent believe that the economy has been harmed by that process. The percent opposing the peace process had increased from 18.1 percent to 23.1 percent in the three weeks since the previous poll, largely due to the Israeli construction of a new settlement in East Jerusalem. JMCC, *Palestine Report*, 2, 44 (April 11, 1997).

5

The United States and the
Arab-Israeli Conflict

The search for a definitive settlement to the Arab-Israeli conflict became a major U.S. foreign policy priority only after the 1967 Arab-Israeli war. Previously, Washington had called for an end to the conflict and occasionally sought to interest the Arab states and Israel in cooperative development plans that could only be launched in the context of a peaceful settlement. But the real thrust of U.S. policy during the 1950s and most of the 1960s aimed at containing the conflict—at preventing the outbreak of further warfare at a time when the United States was preoccupied with the Cold War.

The basis of the policy through which the United States sought this goal was support of the principle of "territorial integrity" for all states in the Middle East. By impartially upholding this generally recognized international principle, the United States served notice to all parties in the Middle East that an aggressor would be punished, whereas a victim of aggression could expect support.

Washington's pre-1967 approach resulted from the original considerations that in the 1940s caused the U.S. government to seek as impartial a stance as possible toward the Arab-Zionist conflict in Palestine. The strategic and economic importance of the Middle East and its oil had been made clear by World War II. The Middle East's importance was enhanced even more as U.S.-Soviet relations developed into the Cold War in the late 1940s. Preventing the growth of Soviet influence in the Arab world therefore became a key U.S. foreign policy objective. However, during those same years, the Holocaust caused articulate U.S. public opinion to sympathize strongly with the Zionist cause. This sentiment was channeled by organized pro-Zionist pressure groups into an effective domestic political force. Foreign policy planners in the State Department and the Pentagon tended to stress strategic and economic reasons for sustaining friendly ties with the Arab world. Congress, however, generally responded to mobilized public opinion. The White House inevitably became the focal point of these conflicting pressures.

Both Presidents Franklin D. Roosevelt (1933–1945) and Harry Truman (1945–1953) tried to guide U.S. policy toward Palestine without giving in totally to either of the contending views. Yet, U.S. policy did affect events in Palestine. As noted in Chapter 1, the overall impact of U.S. policy toward Palestine helped exacerbate Arab-Jewish tensions.

Once Israel was a reality, support for territorial integrity lent a degree of consistency and purpose to the U.S. approach to the Arab-Israeli conflict. Washington tried to cultivate good relations with Israel and the Arab states. The United States became the leading contributor to international efforts to alleviate the plight of Palestinian refugees and, despite recurring tensions, developed a functional relationship with the regime of Egypt's Gamal Abdel Nasser. U.S.-Israeli relations also grew close, despite occasional differences—as after the 1956 Suez War, when the United States pressured Israel, Britain, and France to withdraw from Egypt.

U.S. aid to Israel became a very significant feature of relations between the two states. Total official American aid in the years between Israel's creation and the 1967 war came to just under $1 billion. Although modest in comparison with later U.S. support, this was vitally important for Israel during its initial period of consolidation. Following the 1967 war, U.S. aid skyrocketed. A congressional research report put total official American aid going to Israel between 1948 and 1995 at $77.7 billion.[1] Private aid, in the form of donations and bond purchases from American Jews, was also significant, coming to $1.5 billion annually by the 1990s. Until 1968, Congress regularly appropriated about 1 percent of all foreign aid to Israel. After 1967, this percentage rose. By the 1990s, Israel received $3 billion per year in U.S. aid, approximately one-third of total annual U.S. external aid.

At the same time, the proportion of aid dedicated to military support increased. Not until 1962 did Washington agree to a limited direct transfer of U.S. arms to Israel. In the years after 1967, however, military support accounted for about 60 percent of U.S. aid to Israel. By the 1980s, Egypt emerged, after Israel, as the second principal recipient of U.S. foreign aid, reflecting how important the Middle East had become to Washington's global concerns.

These developments had their roots in Washington's reaction to the 1967 war in the Middle East. That war showed that Arab-Israeli tensions had deepened rather than abated with the passage of time. A second obvious point was that the deterrent effect of a stand in favor of territorial integrity was not reliable, for it required that an act of territorial violation be clearly identifiable. In 1967 it depended on one's perspective whether Israel's strike against Egypt on June 5 was to be termed "aggression" or "pre-emptive defense." Finally, the 1967 war showed that the Soviet Union had emerged as the Arabs' chief international advocate. American sympathies over-whelmingly sided with Israel, whereas Moscow assumed the role of pro-tector of Arab interests.

Washington concluded that U.S. interests demanded a resolution of the Arab-Israeli conflict. Israel's victory in the 1967 war seemed to provide an obvious mechanism for attaining that end: the return of Arab lands occupied by Israel during the war in exchange for a clear commitment to peace by the Arab states. As the rest of this chapter shows, this did not necessarily lend consistency to U.S. policy after 1967, for administrations differed in the urgency they assigned to the search for Middle East peace as well as in the strategies they employed.

EARLY PEACEMAKING: THE NOT-SO-SIMPLE LAND-FOR-PEACE FORMULA

On June 19, 1967, President Lyndon B. Johnson announced five princi-ples for peace in the Middle East. Although Johnson pointed to the need for the territorial integrity of all states to be respected, the United States was no longer committed to the post-1948 territorial boundaries between Israel and its neighbors. The president referred to these as "only fragile and violated truce lines."[2] The United States saw the essence of a peaceful resolution as lying in the hands of Israel and the Arab states. The president referred to the Palestinians only indirectly, noting that peace required "justice for the refugees." In the administration's view, Israel's occupation of Arab territories offered the prospect of a relatively straightforward exchange of land for political concessions that would end the Arab-Israeli conflict. Those principles asserted:

1. Every nation in the area has a right to live and have this right respected by its neighbors.

2. Justice for the refugees.

3. Maritime rights must be respected.

4. Curtailing the arms race in the Middle East.

5. Respect for the political independence and political integrity of all states in the area.[3]

Initial optimism that Israel could be persuaded to enter into an indirect bargaining process soon faded. Israel would not agree to indirect negotiations with the Arabs. The Arabs would not agree to direct negotiations with Israel, arguing that such a forum would imply recognition of the Jewish state. Moreover, they wanted an Israeli commitment, at least in principle, to withdraw from the Occupied Territories. Washington uneasily watched the growth of Moscow's role in the Arab world.

Although election years have typically heightened the sensitivity of U.S. policymakers to the views of pro-Israel domestic pressure groups and public opinion, the Johnson administration tried to pressure Israel into indirect negotiations throughout much of 1968, which was an election year. It did this by delaying action on an Israeli request for Phantom warplanes. In September, Johnson—who had announced in March that he would not seek reelection—issued his first major statement on the Middle East since the "Five Principles" speech of June 1967. This time, the president urged the parties to "begin exchanging views on hard issues through some agreed procedure." He added that final boundaries between Israel and its neighbors "cannot and should not reflect the weight of conquest."[4] However, the pressure did not work and Israel remained unmoved. In October 1968, a month before the elections, the Johnson administration finally agreed to Israel's request.

Domestic considerations played a role in the decision. All presidential candidates, including Hubert Humphrey, the nominee of Johnson's Democratic party, by then strongly supported Israel in its controversy with the White House. However, political dynamics in the Middle East were probably an even greater factor in the president's final decision. This was because the United States faced a dilemma in the Middle East. On the one hand, Israel could not be persuaded to engage in an indirect search for peace with its neighbors. On the other hand, a U.S. effort to pressure Israel into taking that path would probably not only reinforce hard-line Arab tendencies but also be seen by the Arabs as confirming the value of Soviet support. Washington therefore saw little option but to meet Israel's request for weapons. However, with the Soviets continuing to funnel arms to the principal Arab states, there was a danger that Washington would find itself locked into an open-ended regional arms race that would progressively enhance Soviet influence in the Arab world.[5]

In an effort to escape this situation, the Johnson administration used its final months in office to develop a dialogue with the Soviet Union. The underlying logic was that if Washington and Moscow could agree on the outlines of a Middle East peace settlement, they would each be in a better position to influence the contending parties.

The new administration of Richard Nixon initially pursued the course charted by its predecessor. U.S.-Soviet talks on the Middle East, together with four-power (U.S.-Soviet-British-French) talks were undertaken with a view to producing a peace plan. There was, however, a fundamental split in the administration's ranks. The two-power/four-power approach was supported by the State Department, under the leadership of Secretary of State William P. Rogers. Yet, Nixon's National Security Advisor, Henry Kissinger, did not agree with this strategy. Nixon, as the final arbiter of U.S. foreign policy, tended to vacillate.

Rogers' views reflected the basic element of traditional U.S. political calculations related to the Arab-Israeli conflict: U.S. support for Israel had to be limited lest it drive the Arab world into the arms of the Soviet Union. The post-1967 diplomatic stalemate was seen as threatening because it might have the same effect. Kissinger, however, saw the stalemate as an opportunity virtually to eliminate Moscow's political influence in the Arab world. The United States, he argued, should extend full support to Israel and prove to the Arabs that Soviet backing could not help them recover the territories lost in 1967. The Arabs, in short, would have to learn that only Washington could help them. In his memoir *The White House Years*, Kissinger states:

I thought delay was on the whole in our interest because it enabled us to demonstrate even to radical Arabs that we were indispensable to *any* progress and that it could not be extorted from us by Soviet pressure. The State Department wanted to fuel the process of negotiations by accepting at least some of the Soviet ideas. . . . I wanted to frustrate the radicals . . . by demonstrating that in the Middle East friendship with the United States was the precondition to diplomatic success. When I [said] that we did not *want* a quick success in the Four-Power consultations . . . I was speaking a language that ran counter to all the convictions of [the] Department.[6]

Rogers and the State Department initially guided the administration's policy. By the end of 1969, this led to the Rogers Plan discussed in Chapter 1, which still stands as the most explicit and comprehensive vision of an Arab-Israeli peace ever presented by the United States. Its fate, however, was a quick death. Several factors contributed to this result, among which were divisions within the U.S. government. Neither Nixon nor Kissinger supported the plan. The plan was greeted by a storm of opposition in

Congress. Nor was it treated much better abroad. Only Jordan's King Hussein spoke out in its favor.

After the Rogers Plan collapsed, the United States abandoned attempts to devise specific peace plans. The "war of attrition" along the Suez Canal became the focus of more limited efforts to stabilize the potentially explosive Middle East, leading to the Rogers Initiative and the cease-fire that were discussed in Chapter 1. At the same time, Kissinger's belief that the Arab-Israeli stalemate would provide an opportunity to undermine the Soviet Union's presence in the region increasingly shaped the official U.S. outlook. A strong boost to Kissinger's position was provided by Israel's role in protecting Jordan from Syria's radical regime when King Hussein took up arms against Palestinian guerrillas in 1970. The United States began to support Israel more strongly. In October 1970 the White House approved a $90 million arms transfer to Israel. This was followed in January 1971 by the extension of $500 million in credits for Israeli arms purchases. By the end of its first term, the Nixon administration had authorized some $1.5 billion in military and economic aid to Israel. On the other hand, Washington did not act on attempts that Nasser's successor, Anwar Sadat, made to rekindle diplomatic movement in the Middle East between 1971 and 1973.

SEARCHING FOR PEACE
WITHOUT THE PALESTINIANS

The aftermath of the October 1973 war partly upheld Henry Kissinger's political calculations. Although Syria and other radical Arab states continued to appear unwilling to participate in a peace process unless it comprehensively addressed all Arab demands, including those related to the Palestinians, Sadat was anxious for a settlement. Largely impelled by his country's growing economic difficulties, he distanced Egypt from the Soviet Union and invited the United States to become a full partner in the search for Middle East peace.

Kissinger's efforts were vital in producing initial agreements disengaging the opposing forces on the Egyptian and Syrian fronts after the October War. But only Egypt offered an opportunity for more significant progress. This, of course, was because Sadat's eagerness to resolve his country's conflict with Israel tended to be balanced by the value that Israel saw in removing Egypt from the ranks of its enemies. Chapter 1 indicated how the United States promoted two Egyptian-Israeli agreements within a period of twenty-three months. The last of these, the 1975 Sinai II Agreement, solidified Washington's central role in (and the Soviet Union's exclusion from) the peace process. Although post-1973 war diplomatic activity in the Middle East had been inaugurated by a symbolic one-day Peace Conference in Geneva under joint U.S.-U.S.S.R. chairmanship, Moscow did not participate in the process that led to Sinai II.

The political gain for the United States was great but came at a cost. Fiscal year 1976 saw the United States commit $2.2 billion in economic and military assistance to Israel and $1 billion to Egypt. By the time the administration of Gerald Ford, who became president after Nixon's 1974 resignation, left office in 1977, total U.S. aid to Israel since Nixon first occupied the White House amounted to $8.8 billion, while Egypt had received some $2.3 billion. Politically, Washington entered into a significantly enhanced relationship with Israel as a result of Sinai II, one that has been aptly described as "a virtual alliance in all but name."[7] The thrust of this unstated alliance lay in U.S. commitments to support Israel militarily, economically, and diplomatically. Of particular importance in this last category was the secret American promise not to negotiate with or recognize the PLO until it accepted Israel's right to exist and Security Council Resolutions 242 and 338.

Jimmy Carter's election in 1976 produced the first U.S. administration that attempted to incorporate the Palestinian national movement into efforts to bring peace to the Middle East. Carter's administration broke new ground by conceding that Palestinians had "legitimate political rights" that should be upheld by a Middle East peace settlement. Various statements by Carter and his assistants revealed key elements of their view of a peace settlement. These included: Israel's withdrawal to lines reflecting its pre-1967 boundaries, within a context of full peace and normal interstate relations with its neighbors; steps to strengthen Israel's security, including minor modifications of pre-1967 boundaries and the establishment of demilitarized zones; Palestinian participation in the formulation of a final peace and the creation of a Palestinian political entity, preferably in association with Jordan; and direct negotiations between the parties to the conflict within the framework of the Geneva Peace Conference—which technically had been in a state of suspension since its symbolic meeting after the 1973 war.

Carter and his advisers believed that these goals could most effectively be pursued during the administration's first year in office—before the approach of biennial congressional elections, which typically made members of both political parties more reluctant to displease pro-Israeli public opinion. The administration chose the Geneva format because it believed that the involvement of the Soviet Union—still technically cochair of the

Geneva Conference—was necessary if Syria was to support the peace process.

President Carter and Secretary of State Cyrus Vance had extensive contacts with Middle East leaders. However, the administration's plans collapsed by early fall for several reasons. The Carter administration failed to obtain the PLO's unconditional recognition of Israel's right to exist and was therefore unable to negotiate with that body. Thus, the issue of Palestinian participation in the conference remained unresolved. On the other hand, the Israelis—though not rejecting the notion of a peace conference outright—increasingly distrusted the Carter administration and the proposed Geneva forum. They also rejected PLO participation in a peace conference. The election of a Likud government under Menachem Begin in May 1977 heightened Israel's hostility to Washington's policy. At the same time, domestic opposition to the administration's approach mounted as Israel's supporters found common cause with those in the United States who felt that the Soviets were being given too great a role in the Middle East. By November 1977 Sadat concluded that Geneva was not the forum in which to pursue his own drive for peace with Israel. He then made his historic trip to Jerusalem.

Although the Carter administration doubted that a separate Egyptian-Israeli settlement would lead to overall regional peace, it saw little choice but to go along with the course set by Sadat. Chapter 1 indicated how the Carter administration's efforts, and particularly the president's personal intervention at Camp David in 1978, helped bring to fruition the process that led to the 1979 Egypt-Israel Peace Treaty.

Despite the credit that Carter won for negotiating that peace treaty, he lost the election for a second term in the fall of 1980. Iranian students had seized the U.S. embassy in Tehran in November 1979, following the ouster of U.S.-backed Shah Muhammad Reza Pahlavi in January and the transformation of Iran into an Islamic republic. The students were supported by the new regime in their demand that the Shah return to stand trial. Carter severed diplomatic relations, froze Iranian assets in U.S. banks, imposed trade sanctions, and even attempted a risky rescue mission. But the failure of that operation and Carter's evident frustration at his inability to end the stalemate contributed to a drop in public confidence. The sixty-six hostages, detained for 444 days, were released just as Ronald Reagan took office in January 1981.

Reagan and his Secretary of State Alexander Haig felt that U.S. policy had been distracted by "the Palestinian issue" from more pressing problems in the Middle East and that friendly Arab states, particularly Egypt and the Gulf oil producers, were eager for a reassertion of U.S. leadership against the growth of Soviet-backed radical forces. This view accorded Israel a prominent role as a strategic asset for the United States, a status that was institutionalized some months after Reagan took office when the two states signed a Memorandum of Understanding on strategic cooperation. In the meantime, the administration had worked hard to forge a "strategic consensus" among the countries of the Middle East. The goal was not to bring them into a formal defense treaty but rather to foster a tacit understanding, particularly among Israel, Jordan, Egypt, and Saudi Arabia, that radicalism, Islamic fundamentalism, and the Soviet Union were the major threats to regional political stability.

The Reagan administration soon discovered that it could not convince the parties in the Middle East to share this view. Only Sadat seemed to agree with the administration's arguments. Other Arab leaders, including the kings of Jordan and Saudi Arabia, insisted that Israel presented the greatest strategic threat to the Arab world. On the other hand, Israeli leaders strongly opposed the implication that moderate Arab countries should receive American arms in order to defend the region against the threats that Washington deemed paramount.

During the first year of Reagan's presidency, events related to the Arab-Israeli conflict repeatedly forced policymakers to alter their priorities. In the spring of 1981, violence flared up in Lebanon, causing overt hostilities between Israel and Syrian and PLO forces. The crisis was temporarily resolved when the United States mediated a cease-fire. Coming at almost the same time, Israel's bombing of an Iraqi nuclear reactor forced Washington to deal with another sudden Middle East crisis. In late 1981, Israel's annexation of the Golan Heights sparked a third crisis and led to U.S. support of a Security Council resolution declaring the step "illegal" and "null and void." However, when Israel failed to rescind its action, the United States vetoed another resolution calling for the imposition of sanctions. By then, it was clear that the Reagan administration's attempt to promote a U.S.-dominated anti-Soviet consensus in the Middle East had failed. And yet there was still no indication that Washington had any plan for dealing with the pressing issues of the Arab-Israeli conflict and the languishing peace process.

Israel's Likud government filled this vacuum in the summer of 1982 by invading Lebanon in a bid to crush the PLO. The Reagan administration appeared to give tacit approval to this step as a useful strike against radical forces in the Middle East. After Beirut's bloody ten-week siege caused the evacuation and dispersal of PLO troops, and a few days prior to the massacres at Sabra and Shatila, Washington announced its intention to revive the peace process. The Reagan Initiative called for renewed movement toward the goal of "self-government by the Palestinians of the West Bank and Gaza in association with Jordan."[8] Israeli Prime Minister Menachem Begin immediately demonstrated that Israel had not expelled the PLO from Lebanon in order to promote any form of Palestinian self-government. He pronounced Reagan's initiative "a lifeless stillborn."[9]

Begin's assessment was almost completely correct. During the remaining six years of Reagan's presidency, Washington virtually abandoned all effort to promote the 1982 initiative. Instead, the Sabra and Shatila massacres led to U.S. entanglement in Lebanon's civil war and, as mentioned in Chapter 1, Washington's ill-fated effort to promote a peace treaty between Israel and Lebanon. American forces finally withdrew from Lebanon in 1984, after the loss of 241 Marines to a terrorist attack. Following that disaster, the Reagan administration was reluctant to promote the search for a Middle East settlement.

On the other hand, the Reagan initiative led to several years of intense political activity in the Middle East as Arabs groped to find a means of exploring whether the Reagan initiative might provide a starting point for moderate Arab states and the PLO to work toward a settlement with Israel. This began with the 1982 Fez Plan (Document 9) and continued throughout most of the 1980s as the PLO, Jordan, and a variety of other Arab actors sought to promote a diplomatic peacemaking process. Although the effort failed, it provided the context within which more flexible outlooks progressively dominated the PLO. The outbreak of the intifada in 1987 increased the sense of urgency among all parties, including the Palestinian leadership, over the need to revive the quest for peace.

The Reagan administration proved extremely reluctant to take seriously the mounting signs of a fundamental change in the PLO's policy toward Israel. Neither that body's renunciation of terrorism nor the Palestine National Council's adoption in November 1988 of resolutions that amounted to an acceptance of Security Council Resolutions 242 and 338, as well as of Israel's right to exist, convinced Washington that its conditions for a dialogue with the PLO had been met. By the end of the year, however, rising international pressure and continued PLO affirmations of its new approach forced Washington's hand. The outgoing Reagan administration grudgingly agreed to a direct dialogue with the PLO.

SEARCHING FOR PEACE WITH THE PALESTINIANS

Contacts between the administration of President George Bush and the PLO did not initially lead to any significant change in the Middle East equation. Washington remained firmly opposed to the PLO's primary objective—the establishment of a Palestinian state—and continued to distrust the organization's commitment to political means of resolving the conflict. The desultory dialogue was suspended, as explained in Chapter 1, in June 1990.

Iraq's invasion of Kuwait in the summer of 1990 set the stage for what eventually proved to be a major breakthrough in the peace process. The crisis generated by Iraqi President Saddam Hussein was an inter-Arab affair, but it threatened vital Western interests in the region and quickly inflamed Arab-Israeli tensions. The Soviet Union—by then on the verge of collapse—supported the U.S.-led international campaign to restore Kuwait's sovereignty. Arab participation in the effort was necessary, whereas Israel's strategic utility in the crisis was virtually nil. Fearful that any Israeli involvement would shatter Arab support for the anti-Saddam international coalition, the United States successfully urged Israel to keep a low profile, even when Iraq attempted to provoke the Jewish state by launching deadly missile strikes upon its territory.

With the Soviet Union well on its way to disappearing into history and Washington proclaiming the arrival of a New World Order in which international law would prevail, the Bush administration decided that a renewed effort to settle the Arab-Israeli conflict was warranted. Underlying this decision was a basic lesson drawn from the crisis that Saddam Hussein had created: The Palestine issue continued to be so centrally important to political dynamics in the Arab world that it was a constant potential threat to regional stability. The U.S.-inspired 1991 Madrid Conference initiated the series of steps, discussed in Chapter 2, that in 1993 led to the Oslo accords, through which Israel and the PLO recognized each other as legitimate partners in the search for a negotiated peace. There followed the establishment of the Palestinian Authority (PA) in part of the West Bank and in Gaza in 1994 and the process of continuing—although acrimonious—negotiations between the PA and Israel.

The U.S. role in promoting the post-Oslo peace process has been essential. Washington recruited a wide array of donors who pledged large-scale international funding to support Palestinian development efforts in the West Bank and Gaza. U.S. diplomats worked hard to sustain movement in Palestinian-Israeli negotiations. Jordan and Israel paid tribute to U.S. sponsorship of the peace process when they signed the treaty ending the state of war between them on October 30, 1994. Although the U.S. contribution to the Jordanian-Israeli peace primarily amounted to having spearheaded renewed interest in the Middle East peace process, Washington's efforts

were instrumental in fueling the far more difficult Syrian-Israeli negotiations. President Bill Clinton and Secretary of State Warren Christopher
began serious efforts to promote talks between the two sides in 1993. These
culminated when Israeli and Syrian representatives met for secluded talks
in the winter of 1995–1996 at the Wye Plantation in Maryland. The Likud
government's subsequent undermining of the progress made at the Wye
Plantation talks was discussed earlier. The ensuing stalemate in Israeli-Syrian relations remains a source of concern for Washington. Because war
between Syria and Israel would not only complicate U.S. relations with
friendly Arab states but might also have unforeseeable consequences for
what the peace process has achieved so far, rekindling diplomatic activity
between those two states is a major challenge for the United States. Urgency
on this front seems to be required because of Lebanon, in which both
countries maintain a presence that increases the chances of a confrontation
between them.

Despite the importance of U.S. contributions to the peace process, there
have developed increasing doubts that Washington can continue to play a
useful role without taking more purposeful stands on key remaining issues.
Chief among these are the problems of Jerusalem and Israeli settlement
construction in occupied territories. Although the United States is officially
on record as holding that East Jerusalem is occupied territory and that the
construction of Israeli settlements in such territories is illegal, it is also on
record maintaining that the final status of all occupied lands must be worked
out through negotiations between Arabs and Israelis. By 1997 Arabs were
unanimously arguing that Washington's increasing emphasis on the latter
position amounted to turning a blind eye to unilateral Israeli activities that,
if not stopped, would irrevocably bind East Jerusalem and most of the
occupied lands to Israel, leaving little—if anything—to be negotiated. In
the spring of 1997, the Clinton administration's veto of two UN Security
Council resolutions condemning Israeli settlement construction in East
Jerusalem left the post-Oslo peace process in a state of crisis from which
no exit was readily apparent. The situation also left many observers won-
dering whether, or to what extent, the United States could continue to
promote peace without taking clearer and firmer positions on the difficult
questions that still divide Arabs and Israelis.

ASSESSMENT OF THE U.S. ROLE

Related to, but distinct from, speculation about how Washington can best
promote peace in its future policy toward the Arab-Israeli conflict is the

problem of assessing the U.S. impact on that conflict's development since the 1967 war. This complex issue remains a matter of controversy, with serious scholars differing deeply in their conclusions.

Some argue that the United States, particularly since the 1967 Arab-Israeli war, has followed shortsighted policies that caused it to miss several opportunities that might have helped end the conflict years ago. Proponents of this view point to several features of past U.S. policy. Among others, these include the Nixon administration's failure to pursue the Rogers Plan with consistency and firmness, Henry Kissinger's apparently complacent certainty that the Arab world would not go to war in order to break the 1967–1973 diplomatic stalemate, and Washington's refusal to negotiate with the PLO between 1975 and 1988. Such examples of alleged missed opportunities for productive U.S.–Middle East peacemaking are frequently explained as having primarily resulted from two factors: first, the priority Washington gave to competing with the Soviet Union in the Middle East and, second, a basic U.S. bias in favor of Israel. The former is generally attributed to the global Cold War framework within which U.S.-Soviet relations were conducted. Allegations that an unduly pro-Israeli bias has shaped U.S. policy point to the effectiveness of pro-Israeli pressure groups in lobbying Congress and in mobilizing sympathy for Israel among the broader American public.

Other students of the conflict arrive at very different conclusions. In their view, the most significant impact of U.S. policy has been double-edged: First, it managed to contain, or at least limit the frequency and intensity of, outbreaks of war between Arabs and Israelis. Second, U.S. policy was responsible for conditions that eventually led to the Egypt-Israel, PLO-Israel, and Jordan-Israel peace agreements as well as to negotiations between Syria and Israel and the recognition of Israel's legitimacy by most of the Arab world. In support of their analyses, these students also point to a variety of links between U.S. policy and events in the Middle East. Among others, these include Anwar Sadat's conclusion that Egypt's best interest lay in turning to the United States and making peace with Israel, Israel's acceptance of the principles of returning territory for peace and Palestinian participation in the peace process, and PLO acceptance in 1988 of Israel's legitimacy as a sovereign state. Each of these developments, goes the argument, largely resulted from two outstanding characteristics of U.S. policy. The first of these was Washington's unwavering support of Israel's right to exist and the practical expression of this stand through U.S. financial, political, and military aid. The second was Washington's steady, though usually undramatic, insistence that Israel not yield to the temptation to impose its full will upon its Arab neighbors, including the Palestinians.

Such interpretations generally attribute Washington's policy-making to a combination of clear-sighted self-interest and commitment to liberal democratic principles. Proponents of this view argue that U.S. power was put to good use by supporting Israel, the sole functioning democratic system in the Middle East. It was the consistency of this stand that showed the Arab states and the PLO that Soviet support was of little value and that it was hopeless to seek Israel's destruction. This realization brought the Arab world to accept the necessity of dealing with the Jewish state while relying upon the United States to promote a fair peace.

It is easy to see why both sides in the debate over the U.S. role in the Arab-Israeli conflict make strong arguments. Even a superficial glance at the recent history of U.S. involvement in the Middle East shows that Washington's actions have impacted differently, at different times, on the region. U.S. involvement at the highest levels in the Arab-Israeli conflict furthered key moves in the peace process; Kissinger's shuttle diplomacy and Carter's efforts at Camp David are examples. On the other hand, U.S. policy at times exacerbated the Arab-Israeli conflict: Washington's promotion of a diplomatic stalemate in the early 1970s led to the 1973 war, and its implicit consent helped produce Israel's invasion of Lebanon in the early 1980s. Finally, it must be noted that some very important milestones in the peace process—Sadat's trip to Jerusalem and the Israeli-PLO Oslo agreement, for example—took place without U.S. involvement. Such considerations appear to make it certain that debate over the impact and sources of U.S. policy toward the Arab-Israeli conflict will continue for a long time.

NOTES

1. Congressional Research Service, "Israel: U.S. Foreign Assistance," August 30, 1995, compiled by Clyde Mark. Cited by Stephen Zunes, "The Strategic Functions of U.S. Aid to Israel," *Middle East Policy*, IV, 4 (October 1996): 90.

2. U.S. Department of State, *Department of State Bulletin*, LVII, 1463 (July 10, 1967): 33–34.

3. U.S. Department of State, *Department of State Bulletin*, LVII, 1463 (July 10, 1967): 33–34.

4. U.S. Office of the Federal Register, *Weekly Compilation of Presidential Documents*, IV, 37 (September 16, 1968): 1342.

5. Dan Tschirgi, *The American Search for Mideast Peace* (New York: Praeger Publishers, 1989), 47–51.

6. Henry Kissinger, *White House Years* (Boston: Little, Brown and Co., 1979), 354. Original emphasis.

7. Nadav Safran, *Israel: The Embattled Ally* (Cambridge, MA: Belknap Press, 1978), 593.

8. " 'United States Policy for Peace in the Middle East,' Address to the Nation, September 1, 1982," *Weekly Compilation of Presidential Documents: Administration of Ronald Reagan* (Washington, DC: U.S. Government Press Office, September 6, 1982), 1081–85.

9. *The New York Times*, September 3, 1982, 6.

6

Conclusion

This book opened with the observation that many analysts have viewed the Arab-Israeli conflict as so deep-rooted, intense, and multifaceted that a comprehensive resolution of the issues is virtually impossible. Such analysts cite the historic depth of the conflict between Israeli Jews and Palestinian Arabs that dates back to the late nineteenth century and their bitter contest for the same national territory. They argue that it was impossible for Jewish and Arab ethnic nationalisms to accommodate each other by establishing one territorial nationalist state, but it is also impossible for the two nations to reach a mutually acceptable accommodation concerning a territorial division that would enable each to have a stable and secure state of its own.

Other analysts, however, look at the series of diplomatic accords that have been signed since the mid-1970s and argue that ideologically and ethnically rooted policies are in the process of giving way to pragmatically motivated approaches on the part of both Israel and the Arabs. Arab governments, these analysts argue, recognize that their national interest impels them to recognize—and deal with—Israel. Otherwise they cannot hope to have economic development and security. Similarly, many Israelis are said to realize that they must address the fears and interests of their Arab neighbors in order to hope to live in the region on a peaceful basis, rather than in a continual state of alert and mobilization.

The tension between political pragmatism and ideological rigidity remains crucial today. The tension is not only between Israel and its Arab neighbors but also within both the Israeli and Arab communities.

Israelis are polarized over their relationship with the Palestinians, as the 1996 elections indicated. Their outcome made clear that nearly half of the Jewish voters prefer to apply Israeli sovereignty to the West Bank and Gaza Strip, leaving Palestinians with limited self-rule among a growing population of Jewish settlers. A slightly smaller number would accept a Palestinian state within about half of the West Bank and Gaza Strip—under stringent conditions. It must be demilitarized, must exclude East Jerusalem, and must enable most of the settlers to remain in their homes. This basic division within Israel has resulted in contradictory policies. Thus, although Rabin and Peres signed accords with the PLO that enabled Arafat to reestablish the Palestinian political center in the West Bank and Gaza and the Labor party indicated that it would not oppose the formation of a Palestinian state in those territories, Netanyahu acted rapidly to empty the accords of their content, in line with Likud's goals of promoting Jewish settlement in and subsequently annexing those territories. Because Israel retains direct control over most of that land, Netanyahu can carry out those policies despite the protests of other Israelis and the anger of Palestinians.

Arabs are also divided, but their divisions have less immediate consequences on the ground. Many Palestinians retain their dream of going home. Some actively oppose the concessions that the PLO has made to gain limited self-rule on part of their national territory. A minority of Palestinians seek to transform their homeland into an Islamic state in which Jews and Christians would play secondary roles. At present, those rejectionist and Islamic trends are limited in their political strength because they cannot provide a clear alternative to the current course and cannot mobilize large numbers behind them. Nonetheless, their resort to terror against Israelis can—at least temporarily—derail the peace process, and this gives credence to the arguments of Israeli hard-liners that Israeli efforts to achieve peace will be met by Arab violence rather than enhanced security.

Other Arabs are also divided on the principle and practices of peace with Israel. Some argue that unless—and until—Palestinians gain their statehood, Arabs should not normalize their relations with Israel. Trade ties, cultural exchanges, and tourism should be contingent on Israel adopting policies that meet the Palestinians' need for full self-determination. Other Arabs go further to argue that no peaceful relations are possible with Israel so long as it retains its Jewish nationalist essence. Such views reflect the minority at present, but their emotional appeal remains strong.

External actors can play an important role in bolstering intransigence or encouraging pragmatic accommodation. Efforts to provide incentives to promote diplomatic contact and to overcome ideological divisions can be crucial in furthering accords. Actions that fuel the Arab-Israeli arms race or tilt toward one side at the expense of the other can promote intransigence and tension.

Negotiations have begun to shift the balance of incentives toward peaceful accommodation. However, vital issues remain to be resolved. These issues involve Israel and Syria, Israel and Lebanon, and Israel and the Palestinian Authority.

Negotiations between Israel and Syria focus on the Golan Heights, the 450-square-mile territory that Israel captured in 1967 and retained after the fighting in 1973. Labor Alignment governments have come close to reaching accords with Syria that would restore Syrian political control on the Golan in return for the demilitarization of the territory and withdrawal of Israeli settlements. Israel and Syria would establish diplomatic relations in the context of full peace accords. The two sides have not agreed on whether Israel could retain early-warning stations on hills on the Golan or how Israel's withdrawal would be phased in relation to Syria's opening up its country to Israeli diplomats, tourists, and businessmen. But the principle of land-for-peace has been accepted by both Syria and the Labor Alignment as the basis for a long-lasting accord. In contrast, the Likud maintains that Israel must not withdraw militarily from the Golan in order to achieve peace: Syria should make peace with Israel without Israel's making any territorial concessions. If Syria will not agree to those terms, it is better to continue with the current situation in which Israel has the military upper hand. Likud's approach virtually shuts the door to negotiations. It might lead to either an escalation of the arms race between the two countries (which Syria cannot afford economically) or to Syria's increased effort to exert pressure on Israel via the back door of Lebanon. The latter possibility could produce a spiraling confrontation between Israel and Syria.

That leads to the second set of issues still to be resolved, relations between Israel and Lebanon. Although Israel retains a "security zone" in south Lebanon that covers about 10 percent of Lebanese territory, Israel does not have territorial claims toward Lebanon. The Israel-Lebanon treaty of May 1983, which called for full diplomatic relations, was abrogated by Lebanon. That treaty provided for Israel to retain a security presence in the south. The Lebanese government argues that the presence of Israeli forces in the south exacerbates tension and fosters the very instability that Israel claims it wants to contain. Lebanese officials assert that they cannot finalize a peace treaty until Israel withdraws totally from Lebanese soil. Once Israel withdraws, the Lebanese army will be accountable for maintaining security and ensuring that guerrilla forces not attack Israel. When Labor came to power in 1992, one official maintained that "we believe that the security provided by peace treaties is preferable to security enforced by troops."[1] The Likud is more likely to insist on Israel having the right to retaliate against attacks from Lebanon. Nonetheless, Israel and Lebanon are not divided by issues of principle. A pragmatic accommodation that ensures the security of both Israelis and Lebanese is feasible. However, negotiations are on hold (at the time this book is being written) basically because of the freeze in talks between Israel and Syria. Syria, whose army dominates central Lebanon, will only countenance an Israeli-Lebanese accord if Syria comes to an acceptable arrangement with Israel over the Golan Heights. Thus, the territorial issues of south Lebanon and the Golan are linked diplomatically. A Syrian-Israeli accord would open the way quickly to Israeli-Lebanese peace.

The third set of issues involves Israel and the Palestinian Authority. Those issues remain complex and difficult to resolve. There are still questions related to the current interim period that have not been resolved. For example, the creation of an open passage for transit between the West Bank and Gaza, the opening of the Gaza airport, the construction of an adequate port in Gaza, and the release of Palestinian political prisoners were agreed upon in principle in Israeli-Palestinian accords, but Netanyahu has reopened negotiations on those issues. Even the return of Palestinians who had fled the West Bank and Gaza during and just after the war in 1967, which was provided for in Oslo, remains largely unimplemented. Similarly, although the PLO rescinded in April 1996 the clauses in the PLO charter that call for the elimination of Israel, it has neither formulated new clauses that would embody the spirit of the Oslo accords nor cancelled the charter as a whole. Territorial issues also remain unresolved: The exact extent of Israeli military redeployment in the West Bank is uncertain, dependent upon Israel's assessment of the security situation and thereby also hostage to Israel's political ambitions.

The delays in carrying out those provisions of the Oslo accords make Israelis and Palestinians increasingly suspicious of each other. That suspicion is compounded, on the Israeli side, by terror attacks by Hamas and Islamic Jihad against Israeli civilians and, on the Palestinian side, by Israeli actions—such as building settlements and changing Jerusalem's demographics—that prejudge the outcome of final-status talks.

In addition to those tensions over the interim accords, no start has been made to negotiating final-status issues. Those negotiations were supposed to begin in 1996 but have been continually postponed due to security or political crises between the two parties. Final-status issues include the refugees, Jerusalem, settlements, borders, and Palestinian statehood. Each of those issues evokes deep feelings on the part of both peoples.

On the issue of refugees, Israel adheres to a consistent position that the Palestinians who became refugees in 1948 must be resettled abroad. They must never be allowed to return to their original homes, which have been lived in for decades by Israeli Jews. Palestinian thinking has shifted from the principle that the refugees must return to their original homes to the idea that they can "return" to the land controlled by the Palestinian Authority and the future Palestinian state. Financial compensation would be needed, both as material recompense for their lost lands, businesses, and bank accounts and as a way to begin healing the psychological wounds. The Oslo accords opened up the possibility that some refugees would settle in the areas controlled by the Palestinian Authority, if Israel agreed. But discussions in the multilateral refugee working group, initiated in the context of the Madrid talks, failed to reach even minimal agreement on that contentious issue. Then when the Likud government was elected in 1996, it asserted its opposition to settling refugees even in those Palestinian-administered lands and failed to attend the multilateral working group meeting in December 1996.

The future of Jerusalem is supposed to be negotiated in final-status talks. (See Map 7.) Israelis overwhelmingly insist on retaining control over all of Jerusalem, in part because they remember bitterly that they could not pray at the Western (Wailing) Wall when Jordan ruled East Jerusalem and a physical barrier divided the city. Both Muslim and Christian Palestinians also attribute deep religious significance to the city. They call for the capital of the future Palestinian state to be located in East Jerusalem, but they agree with Israelis that the city should remain physically united, with no barriers dividing people living in the Jewish and Arab sectors. Israeli demographic policies have reduced the proportion of Arabs residing in the city. Arabs now constitute 27 percent of the total population and slightly less than half of the residents in East Jerusalem. Those Palestinians live on only 13 percent of East Jerusalem land, and vague promises of government-subsidized housing for Arabs have not been carried out. Moreover, since March 1993, barriers to traveling between East Jerusalem and the West Bank have isolated Arab residents from their economic and cultural hinterland. The start in constructing a settlement at Har Homa (Jebel Abu Ghneim) between East Jerusalem and Bethlehem in March 1997 helps complete that separation of Arab areas from the West Bank as well as deny the Palestinian residents vitally needed land for their own residential construction. When the construction of Har Homa is coupled with the demolition of Arab houses

Map 7
Jerusalem After 1967

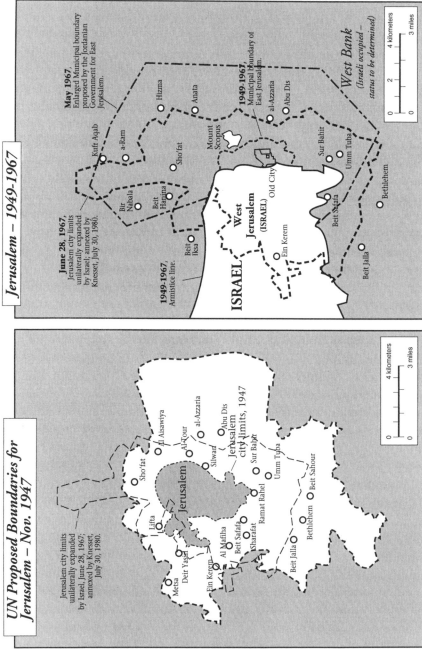

Source: Foundation for Middle East Peace, *Report on Israeli Settlement in the Occupied Territories*, March 1997, 5. Used by permission of the Foundation for Middle East Peace. By Andy Hemstreet.

in East Jerusalem and plans for additional housing for Jewish Israelis within East Jerusalem, the outcome of final-status negotiations is clearly prejudged by these Israeli actions.

The overall number of Israeli Jews living in settlements outside East Jerusalem currently totals about 150,000 on the West Bank and 5,000 in the Gaza Strip. Although their numbers are insignificant in relation to the two million Palestinians in those territories, the settlers control the bulk of the land on the West Bank and sizable enclaves in the Gaza Strip. Most importantly, their political goals are diametrically opposed to those of the Palestinians, because the settlers seek to ensure that the West Bank and Gaza will eventually be absorbed into Israel. Their presence is an explicit effort to preclude the formation of a territorially unified Palestinian state in the Occupied Territories.

The settlers have a major impact on two other final-status issues—borders and Palestinian statehood—because the continued presence of settlers means that the Palestinians would be able to control only half, or less, of the West Bank and 60 percent of Gaza. Settlement patterns, along with Israeli concerns about access to water and maintaining external security, are the major determinants of Israel's proposals for permanent borders. Israel seeks to control the underground aquifers on the West Bank, which supply water to northern Israel and to settlements in the Jordan Valley.

Moreover, Israel insists on maintaining long-term military deployments within the West Bank and Gaza Strip in order to ensure its security against external aggressors. That means retaining control along the border with Jordan in the Jordan Valley, placing early-warning stations on the heights of the West Bank to alert the armed forces to air raids, and guarding the south end of the Gaza Strip that borders on Egyptian Sinai. Israeli forces would also protect those Israeli settlements that would remain on the West Bank and Gaza Strip, thereby placing them in the heart of Palestinian areas.

Palestinians, however, insist that they must control the aquifers so that they can use a fair share of the water, rather than merely a fraction of that allocated to Jewish settlers, and also because control of resources should be the sovereign prerogative of a people with full self-determination. They try to assure Israelis that they will not attempt to divert water from Israeli territory. Palestinians also argue that Israeli troops must withdraw entirely from the West Bank and Gaza Strip, where their continued presence would be politically provocative and would deny the Palestinians their sovereignty. Noting the specific limitations in armaments in the Oslo accords, they maintain that a demilitarized Palestinian area could not threaten Israel and would serve as a buffer zone for Israel. The governments of Jordan and

Egypt also point out that the peace treaties have altered Israel's strategic context. In the era of peace, they argue, Israel need not militarily dominate either the Jordan Valley or Palestinian areas adjacent to Sinai, which is monitored by international forces and largely demilitarized.

The issue of Palestinian statehood is also a major point of contention. Palestinians insist that the interim period should lead to the implementation of their right to self-determination, which they view as meaning the creation of an independent state on the West Bank and Gaza Strip, with its capital in East Jerusalem. Statehood might be followed by the formation of a confederation with Jordan, but that decision must be made by the free will of the Palestinian and Jordanian governments and peoples. As noted above, election results demonstrate that Israelis are deeply divided on this issue: A significant number accept the concept of a conditional Palestinian independence, but a slightly larger number strongly object to Palestinian statehood and seek to establish Israeli sovereignty over the West Bank and Gaza as well as East Jerusalem.

The outcome of negotiations on this deeply felt issue will serve as a litmus test. If the two parties can reach an accommodation based on the principle that both nations have the right to independence and that one should not rule the other, then a stable, mutually respectful relationship will become possible. Jewish nationalism will achieve the recognition that its proponents have long sought, and Palestinian nationalism will finally be embodied in a sovereign state. Other issues—refugees, settlements, security, and even Jerusalem—will be more amenable to negotiation once the basic nationalist clash is defused.

The Arab-Israeli conflict has always unfolded within a political context largely shaped by the policies of external powers. For the past two decades, the United States has been the leading outside power influencing the peace process. This remains true today and seems likely to be true in the foreseeable future.

What can the United States do to help promote chances for comprehensive, enduring peace between Israel and all Arab actors? In some ways, the history of U.S. involvement in the conflict since 1967 helps provide an answer. Active and sustained American efforts to encourage the parties to "keep talking" even in periods of great stress have at times prevented the peace process from crumbling. So too has the clear commitment of the United States to Israel's security and welfare, a stand that has helped ease Israeli fears of the peace process. By the same token, the United States has taken positions that have encouraged Arabs to see hope in the process. Cases in point were Lyndon Johnson's affirmations that final boundaries between Israel and its neighbors "cannot and should not reflect the weight of conquest" and Jimmy Carter's support for the idea of a "Palestinian homeland."

Washington has sought to project itself as an honest broker whose interest is to facilitate agreement between Arabs and Israelis, not to impose its own view of a settlement on one side or another. There is merit in that position, for any lasting agreement must have its true roots in the parties who are directly involved.

Yet, it is clear that the parties themselves are internally divided between moderates, who have faith in the wisdom of practical compromise, and those who take inflexible ideological stances precluding anything less than total realization of their objectives. If Arab and Israeli moderates are to find a solid middle ground of agreement upon which enduring peace can grow, they must each be supported against the extremists in their own camps. Perhaps the strongest and fairest role the United States can play in the peace process is to help Arab and Israeli moderates by basing its own actions clearly upon enduring American principles favoring the right of states to enjoy security, territorial integrity and peace, and the right of peoples to self-determination.

NOTE

1. Deputy Foreign Minister Yossi Beilin, "op ed" in *The New York Times*, August 31, 1992.

Biographies: The Personalities Behind the Arab-Israeli Conflict

Abdullah ibn Hussein (1882–1951)

The first king of Jordan, Abdullah was born in Mecca in 1882. He was the second son of Sharif Hussein ibn Ali. Abdullah fought on the side of the British against the Ottoman Empire during World War I. The British had promised the Arabs independence in Syria and Arabia as the reward for their support (the Hussein-McMahon Correspondence) but had also promised the French a special role in Lebanon and Syria (Sykes-Picot Agreement). When Abdullah's older brother Faisal proclaimed Syria an independent state in March 1920, French troops invaded in July 1920 and seized direct control of Syria and Lebanon. In response, Abdullah marched north from Mecca through Transjordan. His plan to attack Damascus was deflected by the British government, which offered him the throne in Transjordan in March 1921.

Abdullah consolidated his power in Transjordan despite the opposition of many local notables and of the World Zionist Organization, which wanted to extend the Jewish National Home to Transjordan. He served as emir from 1921 to 1946, technically under a British mandate, and then became king of independent Transjordan. Abdullah was unhappy with the small size and limited resources of his kingdom and sought to extend his rule over Palestine as well. The British partition plan of 1937 (Peel Commission) accorded him the right to rule the areas designated for an Arab state in Palestine, even though most Palestinians preferred independence under their own leaders.

Prior to the Arab-Israeli war of 1948–1949, Abdullah reached a tacit agreement with the Zionist leadership that he could control the central mountains of the West Bank. However, they could not agree on how to divide or share Jerusalem. Therefore fighting was most intense in Jerusalem, where Abdullah's forces held onto the Old City. Palestinians resented the king's failure to prosecute the war strongly in other sectors, his failure to defend vital towns such as Ramla and Lydda, and his willingness to relinquish Palestinian farmland near Tulkarm and Qalqilya to Israel during the armistice negotiations.

Abdullah annexed the West Bank to Transjordan in 1950, renaming the combined state the Hashemite Kingdom of Jordan. He quietly pursued negotiations with Israel but could not reach an agreement on the thorny issue of the return of Palestinian refugees to their homes. Abdullah was assassinated by a Palestinian on July 20, 1951, as he left al-Aqsa mosque in Jerusalem, with his grandson Hussein at his side. Hussein became king in 1953.

Al-Asad, Hafiz (1930–)

The president of Syria was born in the port town of Latakia in 1930 to a poor family of the Alawi religious minority in Syria. Asad joined the armed forces as the most effective career route. He became a leader of the Baath party, which supported social reform internally and pan-Arabism internationally. In 1965 Asad became defense minister in the Baath government, but he criticized the radicalism and adventurism that led the regime to support Fatah's raids into Israel in 1965–1966, engage in war with Israel in June 1967, and support the PLO in its showdown with the Jordanian army in September 1970.

Asad engineered a *coup d'état* in November 1970 and became president in March 1971. He cautiously built up Syria's alliances with conservative Saudi Arabia and coordinated with Egypt an attack on the Israeli-controlled Golan Heights and Sinai in October 1973. Although Syrian troops were pushed back by Israeli forces, he achieved a disengagement agreement with Israel in May 1974 that enabled Syria to regain the symbolically important town of Qunaitra on the Golan Heights and to restore diplomatic relations with the United States. He sent Syrian troops into Lebanon in 1976 to quell the civil war and protect Syria's western flank against possible Israeli attack.

Due to his long-standing rivalry with Baath-ruled Iraq, he aligned with Iran in the Iran-Iraq war (1980–1988) and supported the United States in the Gulf war against Iraq (1990–1991). Although Asad began direct negotiations with Israel in 1991, the two sides have not yet reached an accord on the terms for Israel's returning the Golan Heights to Syria and for Syria's recognizing Israel diplomatically. Tensions between Syria and Israel continue to flare up in southern Lebanon, but the Golan Heights have remained calm since 1974.

Internally, Asad rules through the armed forces, security services, and Baath party. Although the Alawi minority is dominant politically, Asad gains support from the Sunni merchant class, from farmers who benefit from land reform, and from Christians who welcome the regime's secularism and fear the rise of the Muslim Brotherhood, with whom Asad's regime had a bloody showdown in Hama and other cities in 1982. Asad's rule was challenged by his brother Rifaat in 1984, but he has recently clamped down on his relatives' corrupt business practices and political machinations. He is grooming his son Bashar, an ophthalmologist, to succeed him as president. Bashar al-Asad became the anointed heir when his brother Basil died in an auto accident in 1994. Observers question whether Bashar has the ability and will to rule and expect a struggle for power should Asad die soon.

Al-Husseini, Al-Hajj Amin (1895–1974)

A key Palestinian leader during the British mandate period, Al-Hajj Amin al-Husseini came from an aristocratic landowning family in Palestine which traced its lineage to the prophet Muhammad and held prominent religious positions in Jerusalem. Born in Jerusalem in 1895, Husseini studied briefly at al-Azhar University in Cairo (1912–1913). After serving in the Ottoman army, he became an active Arab nationalist during World War I. From 1918 to 1920, Husseini supported the unification of Palestine with Syria as a step toward a pan-Arab state. He fled from Jerusalem to Damascus in April 1920 after leading violent protests against the Balfour Declaration.

Husseini became a powerful figure when the British not only pardoned him but appointed him Mufti of Jerusalem (May 1921) and president of the Supreme Muslim Council (January 1922). Husseini apparently pledged to maintain order, and the British hoped that the move would pacify the Palestinian elite. His effort to maintain calm while pressing for political concessions from the British became difficult to maintain in the wake of the Wailing Wall crisis (1928–1929) and soaring Jewish immigration in the 1930s.

Husseini headed a delegation to London (January 1930) that called for the formation of a Palestine government with an Arab majority. He also organized the General Islamic Congress in Jerusalem (December 1931) to galvanize support for the Palestinian cause in the Muslim world. The failure of those initiatives encouraged anti-British radicals to challenge Husseini's influence. They also criticized his efforts as president of the Arab Higher Committee to limit the scope of the general strike that began in April 1936.

Husseini broke decisively with the British when the Royal Commission called for territorial partition in 1937. He escaped to Lebanon in October 1937. He supported an anti-British political movement in Iraq (October 1939 to May 1941) and then fled via Iran to Italy and Germany. Husseini tried to get Hitler to pledge support for Arab independence and appealed over Mussolini's radio station for Arabs and Muslims to support the Axis. At the end of World War II, Husseini escaped to France (May 1945) and then to Cairo (May 1946). He bitterly opposed the partition of Palestine in 1948. He lived in exile in Egypt and Beirut until his death in 1974.

Husseini remains a controversial figure. He galvanized support for the Palestinian nationalist cause, but his endorsement of the Axis made Zionist and British leaders view him as the embodiment of fanaticism and intransigence.

Arafat, Yasir (1929–)

The chair of the PLO and president of the Palestinian Authority, Arafat was born in Cairo on August 24, 1929, but witnessed the Palestinian revolt firsthand when he spent 1936–1937 with relatives in Jerusalem. His subsequent experience as a volunteer fighting in Palestine in 1948 led him to criticize the Egyptian regime for lack of determination in the struggle against Israel.

Arafat became the first president of the Palestinian Student Union in Egypt while he studied engineering at Cairo University. He worked as an engineer in Kuwait from 1956 to 1964, where he founded the nationalist-oriented group called Fatah in 1959. Arafat criticized pan-Arabism for failing to unify the Arab states against Israel. He urged Palestinians to follow the example of Algeria by organizing their own liberation movement. Arafat gained support from the Syrian government, which enabled Fatah to mount its first raid into Israel on January 1, 1965.

After Israel defeated the Arab armies in June 1967, Fatah won credibility for its daring forays into Israel. Arafat emerged as a charismatic leader after the battle of Karameh in March 1968, in which Fatah held off an Israeli counterattack across the Jordan River. He was elected chair of the Executive Committee of the Palestine Liberation Organization in February 1969, thereby consolidating the guerrilla movement's control over the Palestinians' nascent political institutions. The PLO suffered a major setback in September 1970, when the Jordanian army attacked its bases, and suffered further setbacks when it became enmeshed in the Lebanese civil war that broke out in 1975. The Israeli bombardment of Beirut in 1982 compelled Arafat and the PLO to evacuate to Tunis.

Arafat addressed the UN General Assembly in November 1974: He wore military fatigues with an empty holster but waved an olive branch in his hand and appealed for peace. Nonetheless, Arafat condemned the separate peace treaty between Egypt and Israel in 1979 and did not recognize UN Security Council Resolution 242 and the existence of Israel as a Jewish state until 1988.

Despite the PLO's loss of financial aid and support from most Arab states when it tilted toward Iraq in the Gulf crisis (1990–1991) and despite the exclusion of the PLO from the Arab-Israeli talks that began in Madrid in 1991, Arafat played a key role behind the scenes. Secret meetings with Israeli diplomats in Oslo (Norway) led to the PLO-Israel Declaration of Principles in 1993 and to Arafat's return to the West Bank and Gaza Strip in July 1994. He shared the 1994 Nobel Peace Prize with Israeli Prime Minister Yitzhak Rabin and Foreign Minister Shimon Peres. In January 1996 Arafat was elected president (*ra'is*) of the Palestinian Authority, using his authority to consolidate his control over the executive branch of government, maintain his dominance of the PLO, and sideline the elected legislative council. Although his personalistic style of rule angers many Palestinians and many Israelis continue to assert that he is a terrorist, Arafat has managed to retain his central role in the negotiations as well as in Palestinian political life.

Begin, Menachem (1913–1992)

The leader of the Irgun prior to Israel's independence and Israel's prime minister at the time of the peace treaty with Egypt was born on August 16, 1913, in Brest Litovsk (Poland) on the eve of World War I. When a teenager, Begin became active in Betar, the Revisionist youth movement. Betar members criticized the Labor Zionists for insufficient militancy and for not demanding the immediate formation of an independent Jewish state throughout Palestine. After Begin completed his law studies at Warsaw University in the 1930s, he headed Betar in Poland (1939). The Soviets shipped him to Siberia because of his Zionist activism, but then they released him so that he could fight in the Polish army against Nazi Germany.

Begin immigrated to Palestine in 1942, where he quickly took over the command of the Irgun, which aimed to force out the British and establish a Jewish state in the entire area of Palestine and Transjordan. That Jewish underground movement attacked both British soldiers and Arab markets and villages. Its operatives bombed the British headquarters in the King David Hotel in Jerusalem in 1946 and killed villagers in Deir Yassin in 1948. Irgun's shelling of the Arab port of Jaffa precipitated the Arabs' flight from that vital city adjoining all-Jewish Tel Aviv. After a showdown with the Israeli army in mid-1948, when Begin tried to import arms on the *Altalena*, the Irgun was forced to disband.

Begin then founded the Herut party, whose platform called for a Jewish state in all of Israel and Jordan and rejected territorial partition. The Herut led the opposition to the Labor governments from 1948 to 1977. Begin served in the national unity government established just before the June 1967 war, but resigned in the summer of 1970 in protest against the Rogers Initiative's principle that Israel should restore land to the Arab states in return for gaining peace.

Following elections in May 1977, Begin became prime minister and accelerated the construction of Jewish settlements on the West Bank. Despite his hard-line reputation, he welcomed Egyptian President Anwar Sadat to Jerusalem in November 1977 and negotiated the Camp David accords of September 1978 and the peace treaty with Egypt, which was signed in March 1979. Those agreements led to the withdrawal of Israeli forces and settlers from Sinai by May 1982, a year after Begin was reelected to office. Begin and Sadat received the Nobel Peace Prize in 1978.

In June 1982 Begin's government, at the urging of his militant defense minister Ariel Sharon, invaded Lebanon. The three-month campaign besieged and shelled Beirut and destroyed the PLO military infrastructure in south Lebanon. Sharon's alliance with a Lebanese militia enabled those Maronite forces to enter the Palestinian refugee camps of Sabra and Shatila in September 1982, where they killed hundreds of civilians. Begin felt wounded personally—as well as politically — by the war in Lebanon, which many Israelis sharply criticized. He resigned in 1983 and lived in virtual seclusion until his death in 1992.

Ben-Gurion, David (1886–1973)

The first prime minister of Israel was born David Gruen on December 16, 1886, in Plonsk, a town near Warsaw in Russian-ruled Poland. His family was active in the Lovers of Zion movement. Ben-Gurion immigrated to Palestine in 1906. He became a leader of Poalei Zion, a party that upheld the rights of workers and the importance of laboring on the land. He returned briefly to Russia in 1908 to enlist in the army. He later studied law in Istanbul in 1912. Ben-Gurion spent most of World War I in the United States and then joined the Jewish Legion in 1918, a unit that aided the British campaign in the Middle East. He returned to Tel Aviv in 1918, where he helped found the Histadrut (the Jewish labor federation) and participated in the first elected assembly of the Jewish community (*Yishuv*) in Palestine.

As general secretary of the Histadrut (1921–1935), chair of the Executive Committee of the Jewish Agency (1935–1948), and head of the Mapai party (1930–1965), Ben-Gurion played a pivotal role in organizing the ingathering of Jews, pressuring Jewish employers to hire only Jewish labor in agriculture and industry, developing the underground Haganah armed forces, and consolidating the Yishuv's political authority. He endorsed negotiations with neighboring Arab rulers, in the hope of gaining their support for Jewish statehood, but rejected negotiations with Palestinian Arab leaders. Nonetheless, he accepted the concept of territorial partition in 1937 and 1947 in order to gain Jewish political independence in at least part of the desired territory.

Ben-Gurion read Israel's Declaration of Independence to cheering crowds in Tel Aviv on May 14, 1948, as he was sworn in as Israel's first prime minister and defense minister. He held those posts from 1948 to 1953 and from 1955 to 1963. Ben-Gurion helped to organize the emigration of Jews from Europe and the Arab world to Palestine, while rejecting the return of Palestinian refugees. He adopted a militant policy toward Egypt in the mid-1950s, which led him to order the attacks on the Gaza Strip in 1955 and the invasion of Sinai in October 1956. Following the 1967 war, however, he supported the land-for-peace formula and argued that Israel should not try to absorb the newly conquered territories.

After attempting political comebacks in the late 1960s, Ben-Gurion retired from the Knesset in 1970, at the age of 84. He died three years later on Kibbutz Sde Boker in the Negev.

Faisal I (Faisal ibn Hussein) (1885–1933)

Faisal served as commander of the Arab armies in the revolt against the Ottoman Empire in 1916–1918. The British promised his father, Sharif Hussein of Mecca, they would grant the Arabs independence in Arabia and Syria. However, when the Syrians proclaimed their independence in March 1920 with Faisal as their king, the French government asserted its counterclaim to rule Syria. The French army, marching from Beirut, defeated Faisal's forces in July 1920 and forced him to flee the country.

The British government compensated Faisal by installing him as king of Iraq in 1921, which he ruled until his death in 1933. During that time, he sought to integrate the diverse peoples in that territory and to work out viable self-rule arrangements with the Kurds in the oil-rich north. Iraq gained its independence from Britain in 1932, although the British continued to have the dominant influence militarily and economically until the monarchy was overthrown in 1958.

Faisal was revered as an Arab patriot and skillful ruler. Born in Mecca in 1885, he was buried near al-Aqsa mosque on al-Haram al-Sharif in Jerusalem in 1933.

Gemayel, Bashir (1947–1982)

The militant Maronite politician Bashir Gemayel was the youngest child of a leading Lebanese Maronite politician, Pierre Gemayel. His father founded the Phalange party in 1936, modeled on the Fascist movements in Germany, Italy, and Spain, and based his power in the family's mountain stronghold in Bikfaya village. Bashir Gemayel, who was born in 1947, studied law at the Jesuit Saint Joseph University in Beirut and briefly in the United States before working his way up the party ranks of his father's Phalange party. He became the military commander of the Phalange in July 1976, when he was only twenty-nine years old.

Gemayel swiftly and ruthlessly consolidated his control over the Maronite militias, which he renamed the Lebanese Forces. He orchestrated power plays against rivals and did not hesitate to plot the assassination of rivals, notably Tony Franjieh (son of President Suleiman Franjieh) and his family in 1978 and followers of Danny Chamoun (son of former president Camille Chamoun) in 1980. The Phalange received arms from Israel to fight against the PLO, Muslim and leftist Lebanese forces, and the Syrian army. In a showdown in Zahle (eastern Lebanon) in April 1981, Israeli bombers even attacked Syrian positions on behalf of the Lebanese Forces.

When the Israeli army occupied the southern third of Lebanon in June 1982, Prime Minister Menachem Begin and Defense Minister Ariel Sharon openly supported Gemayel's candidacy for the presidency of Lebanon. He gained the presidency on August 13 and was immediately pressured by Begin to sign a peace treaty that would accord full diplomatic recognition to Israel. Gemayel had not yet consolidated his power sufficiently to attempt such a bold move and so he hesitated to comply. He was assassinated by a powerful bomb in the Phalange party headquarters in East Beirut on September 14, 1982, which may have been detonated by a supporter of the Syrians.

As soon as Gemayel died, the Israeli army seized West Beirut and allowed the Lebanese Forces to enter Sabra and Shatila refugee camps, where they killed hundreds of Palestinian civilians in revenge for their leader's death. On September 20, 1982, Bashir's elder brother Amin became president. The urbane Amin Gemayel never acquired Bashir's authority, which was based on his role as the tough head of the toughest militia. He signed a U.S.-brokered peace treaty with Israel in May 1983, but the parliament never ratified the treaty because it was strongly opposed by Syria and by the majority of the political groups inside Lebanon.

Hussein ibn Ali (Sharif Hussein) (1854–1931)

The leader of the Arab revolt during World War I, Hussein ibn Ali was born in Mecca in 1854. A descendant of the Prophet Muhammad, Hussein served as guardian of the holy cities of Mecca and Medina from 1908 to 1916 and then as king of the Hijaz until 1924. During World War I he corresponded with British officials in order to arrange for an Arab uprising against the Ottoman Empire on the most advantageous terms. Known as the Hussein-McMahon Correspondence, that exchange led to a British promise of Arab independence in the Arabian peninsula and Syria, with the exception of such places as the British colony in Aden, the protectorates on the Persian Gulf, and coastal Lebanon, where France had its own claims. Hussein's sons Faisal, Abdullah, and Ali led the fighting in 1916 to 1918 along the Hijaz railway line, which was immortalized by the film *Lawrence of Arabia*.

When Britain promised a Jewish National Home in Palestine and allowed French troops to seize Damascus in July 1920 and depose Faisal, Hussein was deeply embittered against the British. Faisal and Abdullah were mollified when the British appointed them to rule Iraq and Transjordan, respectively. However, Hussein refused to recognize the British and French mandatory regimes that the League of Nations imposed on the Arab territories. He also did not accept the application of the Balfour Declaration to Palestine, arguing that Palestine was included in the area promised independence in the Hussein-McMahon Correspondence.

Hussein and his son Ali were ousted from Mecca and Medina in 1923–1924 by the rival army of Ibn Saud, whose base of power was in central Arabia. Hussein died in 1931, an exile on Cyprus. Ibn Saud later created the kingdom of Saudi Arabia, which included the Hejaz.

Hussein ibn Talal (1935–)

The king of Jordan, Hussein was born in Amman in 1935, the son of Prince Talal. Hussein was seventeen years old when he was crowned king of Jordan on May 2, 1953. Educated at the Royal Military Academy in Sandhurst (England), he was present when his grandfather, King Abdullah, was assassinated in Jerusalem in 1951. His father Talal then ruled for two years, but was declared mentally ill and unfit to continue as monarch.

In 1955–1956, during the height of Pan-Arabist and anti–Cold War neutralist movements in the Arab world, King Hussein responded to popular demands by refusing to join the Baghdad Pact, allowing multiparty elections for the parliament, firing the British commander of Jordan's army (General John Glubb), and annulling the British-Jordanian treaty. However, in April 1957, he cracked down on pan-Arab political forces in Jordan. With the strong support of the armed forces, the king ousted the pan-Arab government, banned political parties, and tamed the parliament. He also endorsed the Eisenhower Doctrine, which offered American aid to countries in the Middle East that sought to ward off Communist subversion.

When King Hussein lost control over the West Bank and East Jerusalem to Israel in June 1967, he initially accommodated the angry Palestinians by allowing the PLO to operate from Jordanian soil. But the creation of a virtual state-within-a-state by the PLO led him to unleash the army against the Palestinian guerrillas in September 1970. Tensions remained high within the country, and the king suspended parliament in 1974. He ruled without any semblance of representative government for the next decade.

In July 1988 King Hussein renounced his claim to rule the West Bank, and in November 1989, following widespread riots against the worsening economic situation, he allowed parliamentary elections on a nonparty basis. The next round of elections in 1993, in which parties were allowed to compete, deepened the democratization process. Nonetheless, decision-making remained firmly in King Hussein's hands. Caught between Israel and Iraq, he tilted toward Iraq during the Gulf crisis of 1990–1991. Nonetheless, King Hussein subsequently played a crucial role in promoting negotiations with Israel. Jordan signed a comprehensive peace treaty with Israel in 1994. Since then King Hussein has worked hard to find ways for the Israelis and Palestinians to bridge their differences, because the stability of the Israeli-Jordanian peace depends upon the success of the Israeli-Palestinian accords.

King Hussein has suffered from cancer, which has caused speculation about the future of the monarchy and the stability of the political system. The royal family has instituted a succession process that makes his brother Crown Prince Hassan the heir, with the probability that King Hussein's elder son would subsequently become king. Crown Prince Hassan already plays a central role in fostering economic and social development and strengthening Jordan's relations with international organizations, but he lacks the charisma and personal touch for which the king is noted.

Hussein, Saddam (1937–   )

The president of Iraq was born in 1937 into a Sunni Muslim peasant family in the village of Tikrit in north-central Iraq. Hussein was raised by his strict stepfather and sent to Baghdad for schooling as a teenager. He was rejected by the military academy, a slight that he resented deeply. In 1955 Hussein joined the Baath party, one of several underground groups that sought to overthrow the autocratic monarchy and that opposed Iraq's membership in the pro-West Baghdad Pact. When military officers deposed King Faisal II in July 1958, tensions increased among the radical groups. The pan-Arab Baath clashed with the Communist party and with Kurdish nationalists.

Hussein participated in a plot to kill President Abd al-Karim Qasim in 1959 and then fled to Egypt. He returned to Baghdad during the short-lived Baath regime of 1963–1964 and quickly strengthened his personal power when the pro-Baath General Ahmad Hasan al-Bakr seized power in 1968. The next year Bakr appointed Hussein vice president. Through his grip on the security apparatus and the Republican Guard, Hussein consolidated his power base inside the party and the governing apparatus. Hussein negotiated a treaty with Iran in 1975 that accorded Iran rights in the Shatt al-Arab waterway in return for ending Iran's support for Kurdish rebels. Hussein welcomed the opportunity to quell the Kurdish revolt but resented making concessions to Iran on that vital waterway.

Hussein became president in July 1979 and quickly purged his rivals within the Baath party. In September 1980 he attacked Iran, seeking to gain exclusive control over the Shatt al-Arab. But the war dragged on until August 1988, resulting in hundreds of thousands of casualties and draining the economic resources of the country. Two years after the war ended, Hussein attacked and annexed Kuwait, seeking its oil riches as well as strategic control over the north end of the Persian Gulf. His defeat in February 1991 by a U.S.-led international coalition triggered uprisings inside Iraq. The continued deadlock between Hussein and the UN has resulted in the impoverishment of the Iraqi people and exacerbated economic and political problems in the Kurdish areas of northern Iraq.

Meir, Golda (1898–1978)

Prime minister of Israel at the time of the October 1973 war, Golda Meir was born Golda Mabovitch in 1898 in Kiev, the capital of Ukraine (then part of Russia). Her family moved to Milwaukee, Wisconsin, in 1906, when she was eight years old. She became active in the Zionist labor movement and emigrated to Palestine with her husband Morris Myerson in 1921, just as the British mandate was being consolidated. She initially lived on kibbutz Merhavia but moved to Jerusalem in 1924, where she became active in the workers' political movement called Ahdut Haavoda. Her leadership abilities were evident in her swift ascension from the post of secretary of the Women Workers' Council in 1928 to the pivotal position of secretary of the Executive Committee of the labor federation, Histadrut, in 1934 and head of its Political Department in 1939. She was also a founding member of the Mapai party (1930).

After World War II, Meir served as a high-ranking official in the Jewish Agency, including head of its Political Department from 1946 to 1948. She met secretly with King Abdullah of Transjordan to arrange a division of territory between the two countries. After briefly serving as Israel's first ambassador to the Soviet Union (1948–1949), she became minister of labor and national insurance from 1949 to 1956 and then foreign minister until 1966. In that capacity, she played a key role in the diplomatic struggles during and after the Suez crisis, in promoting cordial relations with newly independent African countries, and in establishing diplomatic relations with West Germay. She also handled the secret transfer of Adolf Eichmann from Argentina to Israel in 1960, where he stood trial as a Nazi war criminal.

Meir retired in 1966 but remained secretary general of Mapai and guided the negotiations in 1967–1968 to form the Labor party out of three political factions. She suddenly became prime minister on March 17, 1969, when Prime Minister Levi Eshkol died of a heart attack. This was a critical period, marked by the "war of attrition" with Egypt and the PLO guerrilla raids from Jordan. Although Meir accepted the Rogers Initiative of 1970, she argued in favor of retaining most of the territories occupied in June 1967 and would not acknowledge Palestinian nationalism. Meir resigned in April 1974, assuming responsibility for the failure in October 1973 of the armed forces to preempt and block the Egyptian assault across the Suez Canal and the Syrian attack on the Golan Heights.

Nonetheless, Meir remained a respected figure in Israeli politics. She was the first dignitary whom Anwar Sadat greeted when he landed in Israel in November 1977 on his quest for peace. She died a year later, in 1978.

Mubarak, Hosni (1928–)

The president of Egypt, Hosni Mubarak was born in 1928 in Shibin al-Kum, a town in the Delta. The son of a provincial civil servant, Mubarak graduated from the military and air force academies shortly before the Egyptian Free Officers' *coup d'état* in July 1952. Mubarak pursued a military career that included command of Egyptian squadrons in Yemen in 1962 and then command of a key airbase near Cairo.

In the wake of Egypt's defeat by Israel in June 1967, Nasser elevated Mubarak to be director-general of the Air Force Academy. Mubarak used that position to work to restore morale and upgrade training. Two years later, Nasser appointed him chief of staff of the air force. He remained in that post under Sadat and directed the air force's operations during the October war in 1973. Sadat's selection of Mubarak for vice president in 1975 reflected the improved image of the military following that conflict. His entire career until then had been that of a cautious military bureaucrat and tactician.

Mubarak's own views on political issues were unknown until he suddenly became president of Egypt following the assassination of Sadat on October 6, 1981. Mubarak gained credit for releasing political prisoners, opening up the political system, and working toward systematic economic reform. However, he soon reverted to the repression of outspoken political opponents, questionable practices during elections, and crackdowns on Islamist groups whether or not they used violence against the regime. He was reelected unopposed for a third six-year term in 1993.

Mubarak played a mediating role in Arab politics. He guided Egypt back into the Arab League in 1989, orchestrated Arab opposition to Iraq's invasion of Kuwait in 1990, and helped to mediate Palestinian-Israeli tensions. He maintained correct but cool relations with Israel, which enabled Egypt to regain all of the Sinai peninsula without seeming to endorse Israeli policies in Lebanon and on the West Bank.

Nasser, Gamal Abdel (1918–1970)

The leader of the 1952 Egyptian revolution and president of Egypt, Nasser was born on January 15, 1918, in the port city of Alexandria, a year before the nationalist uprising of 1919. The son of a postal clerk, Nasser was active in student demonstrations against the British in 1935. When the Anglo-Egyptian treaty of 1936 enabled middle-class Egyptians to become officers, Nasser joined the Military Academy. He formed close relationships with fellow students who similarly chafed at the British presence, the monarchy, and the landed elite. They began to organize the Free Officers movement during World War II, particularly at the time that Nasser taught in the Military Academy. They resented the poor equipment and lack of training given to soldiers when they fought against Israel in 1948–1949. Nasser was one of the few war heroes to emerge from those battles.

The Free Officers deposed King Farouk in July 1952 and formed a Revolutionary Command Council (RCC). The RCC banned the parliament and political parties, and undertook extensive social programs and efforts at land reform. Nasser became president in 1954, after he had weakened the power of alternative political forces such as the Communist party and the Muslim Brotherhood.

Nasser did not become a popular and charismatic leader until the Suez Crisis of 1956, when he nationalized the Suez Canal and won a political victory against Britain, France, and Israel. Later, however, his foreign policies backfired: The union with Syria failed to last (1958–1961), Egyptian troops became bogged down in Yemen (1962–1967), and Egypt engaged in a debilitating cold war with Saudi Arabia. Nasser was pressured by Syria to confront Israel in 1967, which led to his demand for the withdrawal of UN forces from Sinai and triggered Israel's attack in June 1967. As a result, Egypt lost the Sinai peninsula, the revenue from the Suez Canal, and the valuable oil fields in the Gulf of Suez.

The economic crisis after the war caused Nasser's programs to redistribute land, improve medical care, and enhance access to education to falter. Public discontent with the pervasive security structures deepened. The one bright spot was that the construction of the Aswan High Dam, whose first phase had been completed before the war, stabilized the flow of the Nile River and provided valuable hydroelectric power.

Nasser mediated a cease-fire on September 27, 1970, between Jordan and the PLO that temporarily halted their bitter fighting during that month. A few hours later, he died of a heart attack. Despite his military and political failings, Nasser was eulogized as the first ruler of Egypt who came from Egyptian stock and who fought for his country's independence and dignity.

Netanyahu, Benjamin ("Bibi") (1949–   )*

The Israeli prime minister since 1996, Benjamin Netanyahu was born in Tel Aviv on October 21, 1949, a few months after the end of Israel's war for independence. His father was a professor of Jewish history who supported the Revisionist movement that had opposed partition and sought to form a Jewish state in all of Palestine. As a teenager, Netanyahu lived in Philadelphia, but he returned to Israel on the eve of the June 1967 war and enlisted in an elite antiterrorist unit that summer. His team blew up civilian planes at the Beirut airport in 1968 and foiled hijackers who had landed a Sabena Airlines jet in the Israeli airport near Tel Aviv.

In 1972 Netanyahu returned to the United States, where he studied architecture and business management at the Massachusetts Institute of Technology and worked for a consulting firm in Boston. In October 1973 he returned home briefly to fight in the October war. He returned permanently in July 1976, after his elder brother, Yonatan (Jonathan), died while

*Source: Adapted from Current Biography Yearbook, pp. 399–403. New York: The H. W. Wilson Company, 1996.

leading the Israeli commando raid on Palestinian hijackers at the airport in Entebbe, Uganda. Netanyahu's preoccupation with terrorism merged with his wish to memorialize his brother when he founded the Jonathan Institute in Israel and organized international conferences on terrorism.

Netanyahu ventured into diplomacy in 1982, becoming deputy to Israel's ambassador in Washington. Two years later he became the Israeli ambassador to the United Nations (1984–1988). Netanyahu's defense of Likud policies often irritated U.S. diplomats and angered dovish Israeli politicians. Nonetheless, he had an impact on U.S. antiterrorist strategies during the 1980s.

Netanyahu entered Israeli politics directly in 1988 and won a Knesset seat. In March 1993, he became leader of the Likud, the youngest person to head an Israeli party.

While deputy foreign minister and then deputy minister in the office of the prime minister in 1991–1992, Netanyahu rejected contact with the PLO and opposed making territorial concessions to the Palestinians. He therefore strongly opposed the 1993 Declaration of Principles between Israel and the PLO. He also became increasingly intense in his personal criticism of Prime Minister Yitzhak Rabin for subsequent accords with the PLO and for indicating that Israel might relinquish the Golan Heights as a result of negotiations with Syria. Some Israelis blamed Netanyahu's hot rhetoric for creating an extremist atmosphere that led to Rabin's assassination by a young Israeli. Rabin's widow Leah even refused to shake Netanyahu's hand at her husband's funeral.

Netanyahu led Likud to victory in May 1996, being elected prime minister by 50.4 percent of the vote. Likud formed a coalition government that stated its determination to resume constructing Jewish settlements on the West Bank, retain the Golan Heights, and prevent the formation of a Palestinian state. Likud had benefited politically from terrorist attacks by Palestinian Islamist groups in February and March 1996, which made Israelis fear that peace had not brought them personal security. Netanyahu's youthful vigor also contrasted with aging and weary Shimon Peres, who had succeeded Rabin as head of Labor.

As prime minister, Netanyahu discovered that Israeli actions such as opening a tunnel near Muslim holy sites in Jerusalem and expanding Jewish settlements in Jerusalem triggered violent protests by bitter and disillusioned Palestinians. His only concession was to move Israeli troops from 80 percent of Hebron, leaving Israel in control of the holy places and enclaves with Jewish settlers in that West Bank town. That action angered his right-wing supporters but did not mollify Palestinians or those Israelis who sought territorial and political separation between the Palestinian entity and Israel.

Peres, Shimon (1923–   )

The architect of the Israeli-Palestinian peace accords, Shimon Peres was born in Vishinev, Poland, in 1923 and immigrated to Palestine in 1934, where he quickly became active in youth groups associated with the labor movement. A protégé of David Ben-Gurion, he purchased arms for Haganah in 1947 and then headed the navy. At the end of the war for independence Peres served in the ministry of defense, rising to be director general from 1953 to 1959 and deputy minister of defense from 1959 to 1965. He developed close ties with the French government, which sold sophisticated weapons to Israel and helped Israel develop its nuclear weapons program in Dimona.

Peres was elected to the Knesset on the Mapai list from 1959 to 1965, but joined Ben-Gurion's Rafi party in 1965. In the 1970s Peres served as defense minister in Labor party governments, which merged Mapai and Rafi. He became acting prime minister in April 1977 when his longtime rival Yitzhak Rabin resigned because of a financial scandal. The Peres-led Labor party suffered defeat in elections in 1977 and 1981, but Peres returned to power as prime minister for two years in a coalition government with Likud (1984–1986). During that time, he brought triple-digit inflation under control, reached an amicable agreement with Egypt on a disputed piece of land in Sinai, withdrew most of the Israeli troops from Lebanon, and proposed a peace accord with Jordan. Those policies remained in abeyance while he subsequently served as foreign minister (1986–1988) and finance minister (1988–1989), because the hard-line Likud party was the dominant partner in the coalition government.

When Labor returned to power in July 1992 under Rabin, Peres became foreign minister. Rabin and Peres overcame their rivalry sufficiently to craft peace accords with the PLO and Jordan, undertake several rounds of diplomacy with Syria, and establish trade relations with Arab countries in the Gulf and North Africa. Peres shared the Nobel Peace Prize with Rabin and Arafat in 1994. Peres suddenly became prime minister after Rabin's assassination in November 1995, but he lost the election in May 1996 in the context of escalating violence by Islamist groups inside Israel and continued tension on the Lebanese border.

In the 1950s, Peres was perceived as a hawk who based Israel's strength on military might. In the 1990s, he was viewed as a visionary who sought comprehensive regional peace that would lead to economic renewal throughout the Middle East.

Rabin, Yitzhak (1922–1995)

The Israeli military leader and prime minister who signed peace accords with the PLO and Jordan, Yitzhak Rabin was born in Jerusalem on March 1, 1922, to parents who were born in East Europe and had also lived in the United States. A graduate of the Kadoury Agricultural School, Rabin became active in Histadrut and the Mapai party. During World War II, he was a leader in the Palmach (the commando units of the Haganah), which assisted the British army in fighting Vichy French forces in Lebanon and Syria. Rabin became deputy commander of the Palmach in 1948, playing a key role in the effort to capture all of Jerusalem and combating Egyptian forces in the Negev and Sinai. He participated in the armistice negotiations on Rhodes in 1949.

Rabin later commanded the northern front (1956–1959) and, as chief of staff starting in January 1964, led the army during the June war of 1967. He then gained diplomatic experience by serving as Israel's ambassador to the United States. He returned to Israel to run for election in December 1973 and joined the government as minister of labor.

Rabin suddenly became prime minister when Golda Meir resigned in April 1974 in the wake of the October war. As the architect of the victory of 1967, he was not tarred with the failures in planning that were evident in the fighting in 1973. Rabin, the first Israeli-born prime minister, projected the image of the no-nonsense soldier. Nonetheless, Rabin was forced to resign in April 1977, after it was revealed that his wife had bank accounts in the United States that she had kept illegally after he completed his term as ambassador and returned to Israel. His resignation came just a month before the election, which the rival Likud party won.

Rabin became defense minister in the coalition government formed with Likud in 1984. He adopted tough policies toward the Palestinians in the Occupied Territories, including deporting dissidents and demolishing houses of suspects. When the Palestinian *intifada* (uprising) broke out in December 1987, he cracked down hard on the demonstrators. Nonetheless, when he returned to power in July 1992 as prime minister, he engaged in negotiations that led to peace accords with the PLO and Jordan and that came close to reaching an agreement on the Golan Heights with Syria. He shared the Nobel Peace Prize in 1994 with Peres and Arafat.

Rabin's tough image held him in good stead when he made diplomatic concessions: He could not be accused of being soft on the Palestinians. And yet polarization inside Israel was so severe that some Israelis viewed him as a traitor for reaching an accord with Arafat and conceding the principle of land-for-peace. At the end of a peace rally in Tel Aviv on November 4, 1995, Rabin was assassinated by a militant religious law student.

Sadat, Anwar (1918–1981)

The Egyptian president who signed the peace treaty with Israel, Anwar Sadat was born in 1918 in the Nile Delta village of Mit Abul-Kum. Gamal Abdel Nasser and Sadat were colleagues at the Military Academy in Cairo in the late 1930s. Sadat shared in the Free Officers' conspiracy to overthrow the monarchy, but almost missed participating in the takeover because he went to see a double-feature movie that crucial night. Sadat subsequently served as speaker of the National Assembly and then vice president, playing a minor role under the charismatic Nasser.

When Nasser died of a heart attack in September 1970, Sadat automatically became president. He consolidated his power within a few months by jailing or co-opting his rivals. He began to alter basic policies, particularly once he gained prestige from Egypt's diplomatic successes in the wake of the October war. The two disengagement agreements with Israel enabled him to reopen the Suez Canal and regain control over the oil fields in Sinai. Sadat moved from dependence on the Soviet Union to trade and diplomatic ties with the United States. He also began to allow foreign investment and privatization through his *infitah* (opening) policies and permitted a small amount of criticism inside the parliament and in the press.

His dramatic trip to Jerusalem in November 1977 won him international stature as a peacemaker but led to his isolation in the Arab world. Most Arab governments broke diplomatic relations with Egypt, and the Arab League pulled its headquarters out of Cairo. The peace treaty with Israel, signed in March 1979, did not achieve the economic transformation of Egypt for which he had hoped. Moreover, Israel's policies in the Occupied Territories and Lebanon severely embarrassed Sadat. In the summer of 1981 he cracked down on his increasingly vocal critics inside Egypt, which triggered a violent reaction. Members of the Islamist-oriented Jihad group assassinated Sadat on October 6, 1981, while he viewed the annual parade that celebrated the October war.

Sadat never achieved the stature and respect inside Egypt that he gained internationally. Egyptians remain ambiguous about his diplomatic legacy and dubious of the depth of his commitment to political change.

Weizmann, Chaim (1874–1952)

The initiator of the Balfour Declaration and first president of Israel, Chaim Weizmann was born in Motol village near Pinsk (Russia) in 1874 and educated in Germany and Switzerland, where he received his doctorate in chemistry. He started teaching chemistry at the University of Manchester (England) in 1904. Weizmann was an early activist in the Zionist movement. He attended the second Zionist congress (1898) and headed the Zionist Federation in England during World War I. He was commended for his research as head of the British Admiralty Laboratories, which created synthetic acetone for explosives.

Weizmann was instrumental in persuading the British government to issue the Balfour Declaration in November 1917 in support of the establishment of a Jewish national home in Palestine. When the British army occupied Palestine the next year, Weizmann led efforts by the World Zionist Organization (WZO) to turn that dream into a reality. Weizmann served as president of WZO from 1920 to 1931. From his base in London he could ensure that the British government did not temporize on its commitments, despite strong opposition by the Arab residents of Palestine. When, for example, government officials suggested in 1930 that British obligations to the Arabs were equal to London's obligations to the Jewish residents, Weizmann persuaded the prime minister to disown that suggestion and reassert that Jewish needs took priority over those of the Arabs.

Weizmann moved to Palestine in 1937, where his influence within the Jewish community waned because he was perceived as not sufficiently militant, as cool to Labor Zionism, and as too supportive of the British. Nonetheless, his diplomatic skills remained vital to the Zionist movement. In 1947, while he headed the Jewish Agency delegation to the United Nations, he helped to persuade U.S. President Harry Truman to endorse the partition of Palestine and the establishment of a Jewish state. He served as the first president of Israel from 1948 until he died in 1952.

Primary Documents of the Arab-Israeli Conflict

Document 1
THE BASEL DECLARATION, AUGUST 1897

The 197 participants in the First Zionist Congress, convened in Basel (Switzerland) in August 1897, articulated the political aims of Jewish nationalism, which they insisted must focus on Palestine, the site of the ancient Jewish kingdom. They spelled out practical means by which the new World Zionist Organization intended to achieve statehood, including forming a political structure, colonization, and gaining the approval of the Ottoman rulers for their program.

The aim of Zionism is to create for the Jewish people a home in Palestine secured by public law. The Congress contemplates the following means to the attainment of this end:

1. The promotion, on suitable lines, of the colonization of Palestine by Jewish agricultural and industrial workers.

2. The organization and binding together of the whole of Jewry by means of appropriate institutions, local and international, in accordance with the laws of each country.

3. The strengthening and fostering of Jewish national sentiment and consciousness.

4. Preparatory steps towards obtaining government consent, where necessary, to the attainment of the aim of Zionism.

Source: Bernard Reich, ed., *Arab-Israeli Conflict and Conciliation* (Westport, CT: Praeger, 1995), 19.

Document 2
HUSSEIN-MCMAHON CORRESPONDENCE, 1915–1916

The British High Commissioner in Egypt exchanged letters with Sharif Hussein of Mecca between July 14, 1915, and March 10, 1916. Those letters specified the conditions under which the Arabs would revolt against Ottoman rule. The British government thereby promised the Arabs independence in all their territories, except those that were specifically excluded in the correspondence. Such territories were not solely Arab in population, were claimed by France, or were sought for strategic and economic reasons by Great Britain. The Sharif joined the revolt before he gained iron-clad guarantees as to the territorial boundaries of the Arab state, because he expected that, at the end of the war, British officials would not only honor their explicit pledges but would grant him some of the additional lands that he considered part of the Arab nation.

A. SIR HENRY MCMAHON'S SECOND NOTE TO THE SHARIF HUSSEIN; CAIRO, OCTOBER 24, 1915

The two districts of Mersin and Alexandretta, and portions of Syria lying to the west of the districts of Damascus, Homs, Hama, and Aleppo, cannot be said to be purely Arab, and should be excluded from the limits demanded. . . .

As for those regions . . . wherein Great Britain is free to act without detriment to the interests of her ally France, I am empowered . . . to give the following assurances . . . :

(1) Subject to the above modifications, Great Britain is prepared to recognise and support the independence of the Arabs in all the regions within the limits demanded by the Sharif of Mecca. . . .

(3) When the situation admits, Great Britain will . . . assist [the Arabs] to establish . . . the most suitable forms of governments in those various territories. . . .

(5) With regard to the *vilayets* [districts] of Baghdad and Basra [in Iraq], the Arabs will recognise that [the] established position and interests of Great Britain necessitate special administrative arrangements. . . .

I am confident that this declaration will convince you, beyond all doubt, of Great Britain's sympathy with the aspirations of her friends the Arabs; and that it will result in a lasting and solid alliance with them, of which one of the immediate consequences will be the expulsion of the Turks from the Arab countries and the liberation of the Arab peoples from the Turkish yoke which has weighed on them all these long years.

B. THE SHARIF HUSSEIN'S THIRD NOTE TO SIR HENRY MCMAHON; MECCA, NOVEMBER 5, 1915

(1) . . . [W]e renounce our insistence on the inclusion of the *vilayets* of Mersin and Adana in the Arab Kingdom. But the two *vilayets* of Aleppo and Beirut and their seacoasts are purely Arab *vilayets*, and there is no difference between a Muslim and a Christian Arab: they are both descendants of one forefather.

(2) As the Iraqi *vilayets* [Baghdad and Basra] are parts of the pure Arab Kingdom . . . and as in them began the civilisation of the Arabs . . . they are greatly valued by all Arabs. . . . But . . . taking into consideration the assurances . . . [in] your letter . . . we might agree to leave under the British administration for a short time those districts . . . against a suitable sum paid as compensation to the Arab Kingdom for the period of occupation.

C. SIR HENRY MCMAHON'S THIRD NOTE TO THE SHARIF HUSSEIN; CAIRO, DECEMBER 14, 1915

I am gratified to observe that you agree to the exclusion of the districts of Mersin and Adana from [the] boundaries of the Arab territories. . . .

With regard to the *vilayets* of Aleppo and Beirut, the Government of Great Britain have fully understood . . . your observations, but, as the interests of our ally France are involved in them both, the question will require careful consideration and a further communication on the subject will be addressed to you in due course. . . .

[Y]ou may rest assured that Great Britain has no intention of concluding any peace in terms of which the freedom of the Arab peoples from German and Turkish domination does not form an essential condition.

D. THE SHARIF HUSSEIN'S FOURTH NOTE TO SIR HENRY MCMAHON; MECCA, JANUARY 1, 1916

[A]t the first opportunity after this war is finished, we shall ask you . . . for what we now leave to France in Beirut and its coasts. . . . [It] is impossible to allow any derogation that gives France, or any other Power, a span of land in those regions.

Source: Excerpted and adapted by the authors from George Antonius, *The Arab Awakening* (New York: Capricorn Books, 1965), 419–24, and Bernard Reich, ed., *Arab-Israeli Conflict and Conciliation* (Westport, CT: Praeger, 1995), 21–25.

Document 3
THE BALFOUR DECLARATION, 1917

The British Foreign Minister Arthur James Balfour sent the following statement by the Cabinet to Lord Rothschild, a private British citizen, on November 2, 1917. Balfour asked him to convey the statement to the Zionist Federation. The letter was drafted by the Cabinet in close consultation with Chaim Weizmann, head of the London office of the World Zionist Organization. The carefully worded letter was deliberately ambiguous in its use of the term "a national home" and in its statement of the "civil and religious rights" (but not political rights) of the "non-Jewish" majority. It also included a strong statement that the creation of a Jewish national home must not undermine the newly acquired political rights of Jews in Western Europe and elsewhere.

Foreign Office
November 2nd, 1917

Dear Lord Rothschild,

I have much pleasure in conveying to you, on behalf of His Majesty's Government, the following declaration of sympathy with Jewish Zionist aspirations which has been submitted to, and approved by, the Cabinet:

"His Majesty's Government view with favour the establishment in Palestine of a national home for the Jewish people, and will use their best endeavours to facilitate the achievement of this object, it being clearly understood that nothing shall be done which may prejudice the civil and religious rights of existing non-Jewish communities in Palestine, or the rights and political status enjoyed by Jews in any other country."

I should be grateful if you would bring this declaration to the knowledge of the Zionist Federation.

Yours sincerely,

Arthur James Balfour

Source: Bernard Reich, ed., *Arab-Israeli Conflict and Conciliation* (Westport, CT: Praeger, 1995), 29.

Document 4
ROYAL COMMISSION (PEEL) WHITE PAPER, 1937

The Royal Commission represented the highest level of investigation mounted by the British government. Its report, issued on June 22, 1937, recommended the territorial partition of Palestine, with Britain retaining control over Jerusalem. The White Paper provides a succinct statement of why the Mandate was doomed from the start, why Jewish and Palestinian nationalism were by then irreconcilable, and why, in the Commission's view, partition was the only feasible solution.

The Jewish Agency accepted partition in principle, but rejected the proposed boundaries on the grounds that they created too small a Jewish state and excluded Jerusalem. The Arab Higher Committee rejected partition in principle, maintaining its insistence that the Arab majority had the right to a unitary state. One Palestinian political party, aligned with Emir Abdullah, accepted the principle of partition and agreed to unite the Palestinian portion with Transjordan but rejected the exclusion of the Galilee from the Arab state. Palestinians universally opposed the provision in article 36 that the quarter-million Arabs living in the territory of the future Jewish state be compelled to leave and to resettle in the Arab world.

THE FORCE OF CIRCUMSTANCES. . .

2. Under the stress of the World War the British Government made promises to Arabs and Jews in order to obtain their support. . . .

3. The application to Palestine of the Mandate System . . . implied the belief that the obligations thus undertaken towards the Arabs and Jews respectively would prove in course of time to be mutually compatible owing to the conciliatory effect on the Palestinian Arabs of the material prosperity which Jewish immigration would bring to Palestine as a whole. That belief has not been justified. . . .

5. . . . irrepressible conflict has arisen between two national communities within the narrow bounds of one small country. About 1,000,000 Arabs are in strife . . . with some 400,000 Jews. . . . They differ in religion and in language. Their cultural and social life, their ways of thought and conduct, are as incompatible as their national aspirations. . . . The War and its sequel have inspired all Arabs with the hope of reviving in a free and united Arab world the traditions of the Arab golden age. The Jews similarly are inspired by their historic past. They mean to show what the Jewish nation can achieve when restored to the land of its birth. . . .

6. This conflict was inherent in the situation from the outset. . . .

10. . . . Saudi Arabia, the Yemen, Iraq and Egypt are already recognized as sovereign states, and Trans-Jordan as an "independent government." In less than three years' time Syria and the Lebanon will attain their national sovereignty. The claim of the Palestinian Arabs to share in the freedom of the Asiatic Arabia will thus be reinforced. . . .

11. . . . [T]he hardships and anxieties of the Jews in Europe are not likely to grow less in the near future. . . .

17. . . . . [W]e cannot . . . both concede the Arab claim to self-government and secure the establishment of the Jewish National Home.

A PLAN OF PARTITION

1. . . . Partition [is] the only method we are able to propose for dealing with the root of the trouble. . . .

6. . . . [T]wo sovereign independent States would be established—the one an Arab State, consisting of Trans-Jordan united with that part of Palestine which lies to the east and south of a frontier such as we suggest . . . ; the other a Jewish State consisting of that part of Palestine which lies to the north and west of that frontier. . . .

36. If Partition is to be effective in promoting a final settlement . . . there should be . . . an exchange of population.

CONCLUSION

1. "Half a loaf is better than no bread" is a peculiarly English proverb; and . . . we think it improbable that either party will be satisfied at first sight with the proposals we have submitted for the adjustment of their rival claims. For Partition means that neither will get all it wants. . . .

2. The advantages to the Arabs of Partition . . . :

(i) They obtain their national independence. . . .

(ii) They are finally delivered from the fear of being "swamped" by the Jews and . . . subjection to Jewish rule.

(iii) . . . [T]he final limitation of the Jewish National Home within a fixed frontier and the enactment of a new Mandate for the protection of the Holy Places . . . removes all anxiety lest the Holy Places should ever come under Jewish control. . . .

3. The advantages of Partition to the Jews . . . :

(ii) Partition . . . converts [the National Home] into a Jewish State. Its citizens will be able to admit as many Jews into it as they themselves believe can be absorbed. They will attain the primary objective of Zionism—a Jewish nation, planted in Palestine, giving its nationals the same status in the world as other nations give theirs. They will cease at last to live a "minority life."

Source: Bernard Reich, ed., *Arab-Israeli Conflict and Conciliation* (Westport, CT: Praeger, 1995), 45–52.

Document 5
PALESTINE NATIONAL COVENANT, 1964/1968

The Palestine National Covenant was adopted by the Palestine National Council (PNC) meeting at which the Palestine Liberation Organization (PLO) was created in June 1964 and was revised in July 1968 to reflect the enhanced role of the guerrilla organizations. These excerpts come form the amended Covenant (1968).

In its meeting in Gaza on April 22–24, 1996, the PNC revoked the articles that called for the destruction of Israel and that thereby violated the 1993–1995 accords with Israel. On January 19, 1997, the PNC authorized the PLO legal committee to begin drafting a new PLO charter.

Article 1: Palestine is the homeland of the Arab Palestinian people. . . .

Article 3: The Palestinian people possess the legal right to their homeland and have the right to determine their destiny after achieving the liberation of their country. . . .

Article 4: . . . The Zionist occupation and the dispersal of the Palestinian Arab people . . . do not make them lose their Palestinian identity. . . .

Article 6: The Jews who had normally resided in Palestine until the beginning of the Zionist invasion will be considered Palestinians. . . .

Article 9: Armed struggle is the only way to liberate Palestine. . . .

Article 13: Arab unity and the liberation of Palestine are two complementary objectives. . . . Arab unity leads to the liberation of Palestine; the liberation of Palestine leads to Arab unity. . . .

Article 19: The partition of Palestine in 1947 and the establishment of the State of Israel are entirely illegal . . . because they were contrary to the will of the Palestinian people and to their natural right in their homeland, and inconsistent with the principles embodied in the Charter of the United Nations, particularly the right to self-determination.

Article 20: The Balfour Declaration, the Mandate for Palestine and everything that has been based upon them, are deemed null and void. . . . Judaism, being a religion, is not an independent nationality.

Source: Bernard Reich, ed., *Arab-Israeli Conflict and Conciliation* (Westport, CT: Praeger, 1995), 93–96.

Document 6
UN SECURITY COUNCIL RESOLUTION 242, 1967

This resolution, passed after lengthy debate on November 22, 1967, served as the framework for all subsequent negotiations and peace agreements between Israel and the Arab states. Its principles were accepted by Egypt and Jordan in 1967, by Israel in 1970, by Syria in 1973, and by the PLO in 1988. The wording was deliberately ambiguous concerning the amount of territory from which Israel should withdraw and the meaning of a "just" peace. Moreover, Palestinians were only referred to indirectly, as individual refugees, not as a nation. The regional governments continue to debate the meaning of the resolution and differ as to whether it is merely a declaration of principles or a blueprint for a peace settlement.

The Security Council,

Expressing its continued concern with the grave situation in the Middle East,

Emphasizing the inadmissibility of the acquisition of territory by war and the need to work for a just and lasting peace in which every State in the area can live in security,

Emphasizing further that all member States in their acceptance of the Charter of the United Nations have undertaken a commitment to act in accordance with Article 2 of the Charter,

1. Affirms that the fulfillment of Charter principles requires the establishment of a just and lasting peace in the Middle East which should include the application of both the following principles:

(i) Withdrawal of Israeli armed forces from territories occupied in the recent conflict;

(ii) Termination of all claims or states of belligerency and respect for the acknowledgement of the sovereignty, territorial integrity and political independence of every State in the area and their right to live in peace within secure and recognized boundaries free from threats or acts of force.

2. Affirms further the necessity

(a) For guaranteeing freedom of navigation through international waterways in the area;

(b) For achieving a just settlement of the refugee problem;

(c) For guaranteeing the territorial inviolability and political independence of every state in the area, through measures including the establishment of demilitarized zones:

3. Requests the Secretary-General to designate a Special Representative to proceed to the Middle East to establish and maintain contacts with the States concerned in order to promote agreement and assist efforts to achieve a peaceful and accepted settlement in accordance with the provisions and principles in this resolution;

4. Requests the Secretary-General to report to the Security Council on the progress of the efforts of the Special Representative as soon as possible.

Source: Bernard Reich, ed., *Arab-Israeli Conflict and Conciliation* (Westport, CT: Praeger, 1995), 101–2.

Document 7
A FRAMEWORK FOR PEACE IN THE MIDDLE EAST, 1978

President Anwar Sadat of Egypt, Prime Minister Menachem Begin of Israel, and U.S. President Jimmy Carter signed the Camp David accord on September 17, 1978, following twelve days of arduous negotiations. The Framework represented the first time that an Arab government committed itself to a full peace accord with Israel. Its terms included provisions for Israeli negotiations with Jordan and Palestinians living on the West Bank and Gaza Strip, even though they were not party to the talks. Because the Framework excluded the PLO and was not based even on consultations with Jordan and Palestinians, they rejected its terms. Nonetheless, by stressing that negotiations were based on UNSC Resolution 242 and by referring to Palestinian "legitimate rights," the Framework provided the first official indication that Israel might consider limiting its presence in and control over the Palestinian-populated Occupied Territories.

The agreed basis for a peaceful settlement of the conflict between Israel and its neighbors is United Nations Security Council Resolution 242, in all its parts. . . .

The historic initiative of President Sadat in visiting Jerusalem and the reception accorded to him by the Parliament, government and people of Israel, and the reciprocal visit of Prime Minister Begin to Ismailia . . . have created an unprecedented opportunity for peace which must not be lost if this generation and future generations are to be spared the tragedies of war. . . .

Peace requires respect for the sovereignty, territorial integrity and political independence of every state in the area and their right to live in peace within secure and recognized boundaries free from threats or acts of force. . . .

. . . . [T]his framework . . . is intended by them to constitute a basis for peace not only between Egypt and Israel, but also between Israel and each of its other neighbors.

A. WEST BANK AND GAZA

1. Egypt, Israel, Jordan and the representatives of the Palestinian people should participate in negotiations on the resolution of the Palestinian problem in all its aspects. . . .

(a) . . . [T]here should be transitional arrangements for the West Bank and Gaza for a period not exceeding five years. In order to provide full autonomy to the inhabitants, . . . the Israeli military government and its civilian administration will be withdrawn as soon as a self-governing authority has been freely elected by the inhabitants of these areas. . . .

(b) Egypt, Israel, and Jordan will agree on the modalities for establishing the elected self-governing authority in the West Bank and Gaza. The delegations of Egypt and Jordan may include Palestinians from the West Bank and

Gaza or other Palestinians as mutually agreed. . . . A withdrawal of Israeli armed forces will take place and there will be a redeployment of the remaining Israeli forces into specified security locations. . . . A strong local police force will be established, which may include Jordanian citizens. . . .

   (c) . . . [N]ot later than the third year after the beginning of the transitional period, negotiations will take place to determine the final status of the West Bank and Gaza and its relationship with its neighbors, and to conclude a peace treaty between Israel and Jordan by the end of the transitional period. These negotiations will be conducted among Egypt, Israel, Jordan, and the elected representatives of the inhabitants of the West Bank and Gaza. . . . The negotiations shall be based on all the provisions and principles of UN Security Council Resolution 242. . . . The solution . . . [must] recognize the legitimate rights of the Palestinian people and their just requirements. . . .

   3. . . . [R]epresentatives of Egypt, Israel, Jordan, and the self-governing authority will constitute a continuing committee to decide by agreement on the modalities of admission of persons displaced from the West Bank and Gaza in 1967. . . .

   4. Egypt and Israel will work with each other and with other interested parties to establish agreed procedures for a prompt, just and permanent implementation of the resolution of the refugee problem.

B. EGYPT-ISRAEL

   1. Egypt and Israel undertake not to resort to the threat or the use of force to settle disputes. . . .

   2. In order to achieve peace between them, the parties agree to negotiate in good faith with a goal of concluding within three months . . . a peace treaty between them, while inviting the other parties to the conflict to proceed simultaneously to negotiate and conclude similar peace treaties. . . .

C. ASSOCIATED PRINCIPLES

   1. Egypt and Israel state that the principles and provisions described below should apply to peace treaties between Israel and each of its neighbors—Egypt, Jordan, Syria and Lebanon.

   2. . . . [Those principles] include:

   (a) full recognition;

   (b) abolishing economic boycotts . . .

Source: Bernard Reich, ed., *Arab-Israeli Conflict and Conciliation* (Westport, CT: Praeger, 1995), 147–50.

Document 8
EGYPTIAN-ISRAELI TREATY OF PEACE, 1979

President Anwar Sadat of Egypt and Prime Minister Menachem Begin of Israel signed this peace treaty in Washington, D.C., on March 26, 1979. It was witnessed by President Jimmy Carter of the United States. The two governments quickly exchanged ambassadors; signed bilateral economic, touristic, and cultural accords; and opened land and air communication routes. Criticism within Egypt because the treaty did not include the Palestinians, Jordan, and Syria led to bureaucratic resistance against implementing trade agreements and the boycott of visiting Israelis by most academics and journalists. Egypt withdrew its ambassador from Tel Aviv between September 1982 and September 1986 in protest against Israeli policies in Lebanon and its continued control over Taba, a small strip of land on the Gulf of Aqaba, just south of Eilat. Relations improved when Israel accepted the authority of a panel of arbiters established by the International Court of Justice, which ruled that Taba was part of Egypt.

The provision to place United Nations peacekeeping forces in Sinai was not implemented, because the Soviet Union threatened to veto that provision. Instead, the United States assembled a multinational force (MNF) under its own leadership, outside the UN framework. That MNF continues to monitor the on-the-ground situation in Egypt's Sinai peninsula.

Convinced of the urgent necessity of the establishment of a just, comprehensive and lasting peace in the Middle East in accordance with Security Council Resolutions 242 and 338;

Reaffirming their adherence to the "Framework for Peace in the Middle East Agreed at Camp David," dated September 17, 1978; . . .

[The governments of Egypt and Israel] agree to . . . :

Article I:

1. The state of war between the Parties will be terminated and peace will be established between them upon the exchange of instruments of ratification of this Treaty.

2. Israel will withdraw all its armed forces and civilians from the Sinai behind the international boundary between Egypt and mandated Palestine . . . and Egypt will resume the exercise of its full sovereignty over the Sinai.

3. Upon completion of the interim withdrawal . . . the Parties will establish normal and friendly relations. . . .

Article III:

1. The Parties will apply . . . the provisions of the Charter of the United Nations. . . . In particular:

   a. They recognize and will respect each other's sovereignty, territorial integrity and political independence;

   b. They recognize and will respect each other's right to live in peace within their secure and recognized boundaries;

   c. They will refrain from the threat or use of force, directly or indirectly, against each other and will settle all disputes between them by peaceful means; . . .

3. The Parties agree that the normal relationship . . . will include full recognition, diplomatic, economic and cultural relations, termination of economic boycotts and discriminatory barriers to the free movement of people and goods. . . .

Article IV:

1. In order to provide maximum security for both Parties on the basis of reciprocity, agreed security arrangements will be established including limited force zones in Egyptian and Israeli territory, and United Nations forces and observers. . . .

Article V:

1. Ships of Israel, and cargoes destined for or coming from Israel, shall enjoy the right of free passage through the Suez Canal and its approaches through the Gulf of Suez and the Mediterranean Sea on the basis of the Constantinople Convention of 1888. . . .

2. The Parties consider the Strait of Tiran and the Gulf of Aqaba to be international waterways open to all nations for unimpeded and non-suspendable freedom of navigation.

Source: Bernard Reich, ed., *Arab-Israeli Conflict and Conciliation* (Westport, CT: Praeger, 1995), 155–57.

Document 9
FEZ SUMMIT PEACE PROPOSAL, 1982

A summit conference of the Arab League convened in Fez (Morocco) in September 1982 following the Israeli invasion of Lebanon, the expulsion of the PLO from Beirut, and U.S. President Ronald Reagan's articulation of a peace plan on September 1. The Fez Proposal (September 9) implicitly linked endorsement of UN Security Council Resolution 242 with support for a Palestinian state on the West Bank and the Gaza Strip, with its capital in East Jerusalem. It also implied that refugees would return only to the territory governed by the proposed Palestinian state. The Proposal provided the first clear articulation of the Arab states' consensus following the divisive Egypt-Israel treaty and became the basis for diplomatic efforts during the 1980s.

[T]he conference has decided to adopt the following principles:

1. The withdrawal of Israel from all Arab territories occupied in 1967 including Arab Al-Quds [East Jerusalem].

2. The dismantling of settlements established by Israel on the Arab territories after 1967.

3. The guarantee of freedom of worship and practice of religious rites for all religions in the holy shrines.

4. The reaffirmation of the Palestinian people's right to self-determination and the exercise of its imprescriptible and inalienable national rights under the leadership of the Palestine Liberation Organization (PLO), its sole and legitimate representative, and the indemnification of all those who do not desire to return.

5. Placing the West Bank and Gaza Strip under the control of the United Nations for a transitional period not exceeding a few months.

6. The establishment of an independent Palestinian state with Al-Quds [Jerusalem] as its capital.

7. The Security Council guarantees peace among all states of the region including the independent Palestinian state.

8. The Security Council guarantees the respect of these principles.

Source: Bernard Reich, ed., *Arab-Israeli Conflict and Conciliation* (Westport, CT: Praeger, 1995), 180.

Document 10
DECLARATION OF THE PALESTINIAN STATE, 1988

This declaration was issued by the Palestine National Council at its meeting in Algiers on November 15, 1988. Its recognition of the validity of the UN resolution that partitioned Palestine superseded the statements in the PLO covenant that rejected partition. The declaration also explicitly rejected terrorism and implicitly recognized UN Security Council Resolution 242. Because it did not explicitly mention that resolution, however, U.S. officials refused to open a dialogue with the PLO following its proclamation.

Despite the historical injustice inflicted on the Palestinian Arab people resulting in their dispersion and depriving them of their right to self-determination, following upon U.N. General Assembly Resolution 181 (1947), which partitioned Palestine into two states, one Arab, one Jewish, yet it is this Resolution that still provides those conditions of international legitimacy that ensure the right of the Palestinian Arab people to sovereignty. . . .

The massive national uprising, the *intifada* . . . has elevated awareness of the Palestinian truth and right. . . . The *intifada* has set siege to the mind of official Israel, which has for too long . . . den[ied] Palestinian existence altogether. . . .

In pursuance of Resolutions adopted by Arab Summit Conferences and relying on the authority . . . [of] the Resolutions of the United Nations Organizations since 1947 . . .

The Palestine National Council . . . hereby proclaims the establishment of the State of Palestine on our Palestinian territory with its capital Jerusalem (Al-Quds Al-Sharif).

The State of Palestine is the state of Palestinians wherever they may be. . . . In it will be safeguarded their political and religious convictions and their human dignity by means of a parliamentary democratic system of governance. . . .

The state of Palestine herewith declares that it believes in the settlement of regional and international disputes by peaceful means, in accordance with the U.N. Charter and resolutions. Without prejudice to its natural right to defend its territorial integrity and independence, it therefore rejects the threat or use of force, violence and terrorism against its territorial integrity or political independence, as it also rejects their use against the territorial integrity of other states.

Source: Bernard Reich, ed., *Arab-Israeli Conflict and Conciliation* (Westport, CT: Praeger, 1995), 213–17.

Document 11
ARAFAT'S PRESS CONFERENCE, 1988

In response to U.S. dissatisfaction with the wording of the PNC's declaration on November 14, 1988 (Document 10), Yasir Arafat recognized Israel's right to exist, renounced terrorism, and explicitly accepted UN Security Council Resolutions 242 and 338 at his press conference in Geneva on December 14, 1988. That statement opened the door to a direct dialogue between the PLO and the U.S. government, conducted by the U.S. ambassador in Tunis, where the PLO had its headquarters.

Our desire for peace is a strategy and not an interim tactic. . . . Our statehood provides salvation to the Palestinians and peace to both Palestinians and Israelis. . . .

Yesterday in my speech I made reference to United Nations Resolution 181 as the basis for Palestinian independence. I also made reference to our acceptance of Resolutions 242 and 338 as the basis for negotiations with Israel within the framework of the international conference. These three resolutions were endorsed by our Palestine National Council session in Algiers.

. . . [W]e mean our people's rights to freedom and national independence, according to Resolution 181, and the right of all parties concerned in the Middle East conflict to exist in peace and security . . . including the state of Palestine, Israel and other neighbors, according to Resolutions 242 and 338.

. . . I repeat for the record that we totally and absolutely renounce all forms of terrorism, including individual, group and state terrorism.

Source: Bernard Reich, ed., *Arab-Israeli Conflict and Conciliation* (Westport, CT: Praeger, 1995), 218–19.

Document 12
ISRAEL-PLO DECLARATION OF PRINCIPLES, 1993

The Declaration of Principles (DOP) resulted from secret negotiations by the Israeli government and the PLO in Oslo (Norway) during the spring and summer of 1993. The parties signed the DOP in Washington, D.C., on September 13, 1993. For the first time, the two parties recognized their peoples' mutual rights and issued a joint call for peace. The DOP was followed by intense and complex negotiations on its implementation, which led to bilateral accords in May 1994, September 1995, and January 1997. The implementation of those accords remains incomplete and final-status negotiations, which were supposed to begin by May 1997, have not begun as of this writing.

The Government of the State of Israel and the P.L.O. team . . . agree that it is time to put an end to decades of confrontation and conflict, recognize their mutual legitimate and political rights, and strive to live in peaceful coexistence and mutual dignity and security and achieve a just, lasting and comprehensive peace settlement and historic reconciliation through the agreed political process. Accordingly, the two sides agree to the following principles:

Article I . . . The aim of the Israeli-Palestinian negotiations . . . is . . . to establish a Palestinian Interim Self-Government Authority, the elected Council, for the Palestinian people in the West Bank and the Gaza Strip, for a transitional period not exceeding five years, leading to a permanent settlement based on Security Council Resolutions 242 and 338. . . .

Article IV . . . Jurisdiction of the Council will cover West Bank and Gaza Strip territory, except for issues that will be negotiated in the permanent status negotiations. The two sides view the West Bank and the Gaza Strip as a single territorial unit, whose integrity will be preserved during the interim period.

Article V . . .

1. The five-year transitional period will begin upon the withdrawal from the Gaza Strip and Jericho area.

2. Permanent status negotiations will commence as soon as possible, but not later than the beginning of the third year of the interim period, between the Government of Israel and the Palestinian people['s] representatives.

3. It is understood that these negotiations shall cover [the] remaining issues, including: Jerusalem, refugees, settlements, security arrangements, borders. . . .

4. The two parties agree that the outcome of the permanent status negotiations should not be prejudiced or preempted by agreements reached for the interim period.

Source: Bernard Reich, ed., *Arab-Israeli Conflict and Conciliation* (Westport, CT: Praeger, 1995), 230–32.

Document 13
TREATY OF PEACE: ISRAEL AND THE HASHEMITE KINGDOM OF JORDAN, 1994

Prime Minister Yitzhak Rabin (Israel) and Prime Minister Abdul Salam Majali (Jordan) signed this treaty on October 26, 1994, at the Eilat/Aqaba crossing. It was witnessed by U.S. President William J. Clinton. The treaty called for the exchange of ambassadors within one month; the signing of tourism accords in three months; the conclusion of a civil aviation agreement and the establishment of economic and environmental cooperation within six months, including arrangements for trade, border-crossings, and connecting the electric grids in Eilat-Aqaba; and the demarcation of boundaries, conclusion of cultural and scientific agreements, opening of direct telephone and fax lines, and arranging joint development in Aqaba-Eilat within nine months. Most of the practical agreements were implemented on schedule.

Preamble . . . Aiming at the achievement of a just, lasting and comprehensive peace in the Middle East based on Security Council resolutions 242 and 338 in all their aspects; Bearing in mind the importance of maintaining and strengthening peace based on freedom, equality, justice and respect for fundamental human rights, thereby overcoming psychological barriers and promoting human dignity; . . . Desiring to develop friendly relations and co-operation between them in accordance with the principles of international law governing international relations in time of peace; Desiring as well to ensure lasting security for both their States and in particular to avoid threats and the use of force between them; . . . Have agreed as follows:

Article 1. Establishment of Peace . . .

Article 2 . . .

1. They recognise and will respect each other's sovereignty, territorial integrity and political independence;

2. They recognise and will respect each other's right to live in peace within secure and recognised boundaries;

3. They will develop good neighbourly relations of co-operation between them to ensure lasting security, will refrain from the threat or use of force against each other and will settle all disputes between them by peaceful means; . . .

Article 3 . . .

1. The international boundary between Israel and Jordan is delimited with reference to the boundary definition under the Mandate . . .

2. The boundary, as set out in Annex I (a), is the permanent, secure and recognised international boundary between Israel and Jordan, without prejudice to the status of any territories that came under Israeli military government control in 1967.

Article 4. Security . . .

4. Consistent with the era of peace . . . the Parties further agree to refrain from the following: a. joining or in any way assisting, promoting or co-operating with any coalition, organisation or alliance with a military or security character with a third party, the objectives or activities of which include launching aggression or other acts of military hostility against the other Party, in contravention of the provisions of the present Treaty. b. allowing the entry, stationing and operating on their territory, or through it, of military forces, personnel or materiel of a third party, in circumstances which may adversely prejudice the security of the other Party.

5. Both Parties will take necessary and effective measures, and will co-operate in combating terrorism of all kinds. . . .

Article 6. Water . . .

1. The Parties agree mutually to recognise the rightful allocations of both of them in Jordan River and Yarmouk River waters and Araba/Arava ground water in accordance with the agreed acceptable principles, quantities and quality as set out in Annex II . . .

Article 7. Economic Relations . . .

2. [T]he Parties agree . . . a. to remove all discriminatory barriers to normal economic relations, to terminate economic boycotts directed at each other, and to co-operate in terminating boycotts against either Party by third parties. . . .

Article 9. Places of Historical and Religious Significance

1. Each party will provide freedom of access to places of religious and historical significance.

2. In this regard . . . Israel respects the present special role of the Hashemite Kingdom of Jordan in Muslim Holy shrines in Jerusalem. When negotiations on the permanent status will take place, Israel will give high priority to the Jordanian historic role in these shrines. . . .

Article 14. Freedom of Navigation . . .

3. The Parties consider the Strait of Tiran and the Gulf of Aqaba to be international waterways open to all nations for unimpeded and non-suspendable freedom of navigation and overflight. . . .

Article 20. Rift Valley Development

The Parties attach great importance to the integrated development of the Jordan Rift Valley area, including joint projects in the economic, environmental, energy-related and tourism fields.

Source: Bernard Reich, ed., *Arab-Israeli Conflict and Conciliation* (Westport, CT: Praeger, 1995), 263–71.

Document 14
GUIDELINES OF THE GOVERNMENT OF ISRAEL, 1996

These policy guidelines were approved by all the political parties that joined the Cabinet formed by Israeli Prime Minister Benjamin Netanyahu in June 1996. They provided an indication of the preferred outcome of negotiations, including retention of the Golan Heights and East Jerusalem, prevention of the establishment of a Palestinian state on the West Bank and the Gaza Strip, and expansion of Israeli settlements throughout the Occupied Territories. In this sense, they partially contradicted the assumptions behind the Israeli-Palestinian accords of 1993–1995 and articulated a strategy toward Syria that differed substantially from the previous Labor government.

The Government presented to the Knesset will act on the premise that the right of the Jewish people to the Land of Israel is eternal and indisputable, that the State of Israel is the State of the Jewish people. . . .

The government will work to achieve the following goals:

1. Achieving peace with all our neighbors, while safeguarding national and personal security.

2. Reinforcing the status of Jerusalem as the eternal capital of the Jewish people.

3. Increasing immigration to Israel, and integrating new immigrants in all walks of life.

4. Creating conditions for a free, thriving economy and social welfare.

5. Strengthening, broadening and developing settlement in Israel.

1. PEACE, SECURITY AND FOREIGN RELATIONS . . .

2. The Government of Israel will propose to the Palestinians an arrangement whereby they will be able to conduct their lives freely within the framework of self-government. The Government will oppose the establishment of a Palestinian state or any foreign sovereignty west of the Jordan River, and will oppose "the right of return" of Arab populations to any part of the Land of Israel west of the Jordan River. . . .

8. In any political arrangement, Israel shall insist on ensuring the existence and security of Jewish settlements and their affinity with the State of Israel. . . .

9. The Government views the Golan Heights as essential to the security of the state and its water resources. Retaining Israeli sovereignty over the Golan will be the basis for an arrangement with Syria.

2. JERUSALEM

1. Jerusalem, the capital of Israel, is one city, whole and undivided, and will remain forever under Israel's sovereignty.

2. Freedom of worship and access to the holy places will be guaranteed to members of all faiths.

3. The Government . . . will prevent any action which is counter to Israel's exclusive sovereignty over the city. . . .

6. SETTLEMENT

1. Settlement in the Negev, the Galilee, the Golan Heights, the Jordan Valley, and in Judea, Samaria and Gaza is of national importance to Israel's defense and an expression of Zionist fulfillment. The Government will . . . develop the settlement enterprise in these areas, and allocate the resources necessary for this.

2. The government of Israel will safeguard its vital water supplies, from water sources on the Golan Heights and in Judea and Samaria.

Source: Report on Israeli Settlement in the Occupied Territories (Washington, DC: Foundation for Middle East Peace), volume 6 (July 1996), 6.

Glossary of Selected Terms

Alawi or **Alawite:** Member of the Alawi sect, a tenth-century offshoot of Shia Islam; also known as the Nusairi sect. Alawis today form approximately 10 percent of Syria's population and are particularly influential under the regime of Hafiz al-Asad, himself an Alawi.

Alignment: See *Labor Alignment*.

Altalena **Affair:** The attack by the Israeli Defense Forces in June 1948 on the *Altalena* transport ship that had docked near Tel Aviv, carrying arms and reinforcements to the Irgun. Prime Minister David Ben-Gurion ordered the ship's destruction, partly because it publicly violated the terms of the truce that was then in force but primarily because he feared that the Irgun would use the arms to seize power from the new Israeli government.

Anglo-American Committee of Inquiry: Joint investigative committee formed in 1946 by the United States and Great Britain, charged with recommending policy toward Palestine. The committee reached a compromise by recommending the eventual admission of one hundred thousand Jews from displaced persons camps in Europe and the creation of a single state to include both Jews and Arabs.

Arab League: A regional organization of Arab states founded in 1945 by Egypt, Lebanon, Transjordan, Saudi Arabia, Syria, and Yemen. Palestine had observer status. As additional Arab countries became independent, they also joined the League, which served as an important forum for meetings of Arab leaders.

Arab trade boycott: The ban on trade with Israel instituted by the Arab League after the 1948–1949 war with Israel.

Armistice agreements: The truce accords signed by Israel in 1949 with Egypt, Jordan, Lebanon, and Syria, which ended the fighting without resolving the underlying political issues or establishing final borders between Israel and its neighbors.

Ashkenazim: Jews of European origin, in contrast to Mizrahi Jews who came from the Middle East or North Africa.

Aswan High Dam: A dam constructed on the Nile River in upper Egypt in the late 1950s and early 1960s that regulates the flow of the river and provides vital hydroelectric power for industries and for residents of cities. The denial in June 1956 of American, British, and World Bank funding to build the dam triggered the decision by Egyptian President Gamal Abdul Nasser to nationalize the Suez Canal Company.

Avodat Ivrit: See *Histadrut.*

Baath Party: Pan-Arab socialist party that has ruled Syria and Iraq since the 1960s.

Baghdad Pact: An anti-Soviet alliance that linked Turkey, Iran, Pakistan, Britain, and Iraq. Iraq left the Pact in 1959, which was then renamed the Central Treaty Organization (CENTO).

Balfour Declaration: Statement by the British Foreign Minister Arthur James Balfour to Lord Rothschild on November 2, 1917, which declared the British government's sympathy for establishing a Jewish national home in Palestine.

Constantinople Convention: An 1888 international convention that established the rights of maritime traffic through international waterways, notably the Dardanelles and the Suez Canal.

Demilitarized zones (DMZs): Areas whose control was contested at the time of the armistice agreements between Israel and the Arab states and which were therefore placed off-limits to both sides' military forces and outside the sovereign authority of Israel or the Arab states. The Syrian-Israeli DMZs became particular points of friction during the 1950s and early 1960s.

Dimona: Israel's nuclear complex in the northern Negev desert, which was initiated with French assistance in 1959.

Displaced persons: Individuals who could neither return to nor remain in their countries of origin in the wake of World War II.

Dreyfus trial: The trial in Paris in 1894 of the Jewish Captain Alfred Dreyfus, who was falsely accused of treason for passing French military secrets to the Germans. Dreyfus was found guilty by a military court and sent to Devil's Island in French Guiana. After evidence accumulated that Dreyfus was framed by brother officers, he was pardoned by the French president in 1899. His trial, however, had triggered anti-Semitic outbursts in France and led Theodor Herzl to conclude that anti-Semitism was endemic in Europe.

Druze: A religious sect that traces its origins to the eleventh century as an offshoot of Islam. Its adherents are primarily found in Lebanon, Syria, and Israel.

Entebbe Raid: The rescue in July 1976 by Israeli airborne commandos of 103 hostages held by German and Palestinian terrorists who had hijacked an Air France jetliner to Entebbe, Uganda. Yonatan Netanyahu, who led the Israeli operation, was the only Israeli to die in the raid.

Fatah: Palestinian group founded by Yasir Arafat and his colleagues in Kuwait in 1959, which became the dominant body in the Palestinian national movement by the late 1960s.

Fidayiin: Arabic term used for Palestinian guerrillas, which means "self-sacrificers."

Gaza Strip: The portion of Palestine that was controlled by the Egyptian army at the time of the Egypt-Israel armistice in 1949. Egypt established a military government and partial self-rule in Gaza, which was seized by Israel in 1967. Two-thirds of Gaza is now part of the area controlled by the Palestinian Authority.

Golan Heights: Syrian territory overlooking the Jordan River and the Sea of Galilee that was captured by Israel in June 1967 and remains subject to negotiations.

Gulf of Aqaba/Eilat: An international waterway bordered by Egypt, Israel, Jordan, and Saudi Arabia. Threats to close Israeli access to the Gulf helped trigger Israeli attacks on Egypt in 1956 and 1967.

Gush Emunim: The Hebrew term for the Bloc of the Faithful, an Israeli religious nationalist movement formed after the 1967 war that views the West Bank as land holy to the Jewish people. Gush Emunim actively colonizes that land in order to ensure its permanent incorporation into Israel.

Haganah: The Jewish defense force (1920–1948) that initially guarded Jewish residential areas and kibbutzim in Palestine and later became the nucleus for the Israeli Defense Forces.

Hamas: The armed wing of the Palestinian branch of the Muslim Brotherhood, formed in 1988 during the intifada. Hamas calls for an Islamic state in all of Palestine and claims responsibility for numerous terrorist attacks and suicide bombings in Israel.

Histadrut: The General Federation of Jewish Labor, which organized Jewish rural and urban workers in Palestine under the leadership of David Ben-Gurion and the Labor Zionists. Histadrut pressured Jewish farmers and businesses to fire their Arab workers and employ only Jews, following the concept of *Avodat Ivrit* (Jewish labor). After independence, Histadrut diversified to form economic enterprises and became a key base of power for the Labor party.

Hizballah: A Lebanese political movement that was formed after Israel's invasion in 1982 in order to fight against the U.S. and Israeli presence in Lebanon and to create an Islamic state inside Lebanon. Hizballah receives funding from Iran for its military and charitable activities, participates in the elected

Lebanese parliament, and works closely with Syria to challenge the presence of Israeli forces in south Lebanon.

Holocaust: The genocide of the Jewish people, undertaken systematically by Germany's Nazi government during World War II. The Holocaust virtually wiped out the Jewish communities throughout western and central Europe.

Intifada: Arabic term for the Palestinian uprising that began on the West Bank and the Gaza Strip in late 1987. The word literally means "shaking off," a reference to its aim of ending Israeli's military occupation.

Irgun: Militant Jewish underground organization that attacked British soldiers and Palestinian civilians during the 1940s in an effort to establish an exclusively Jewish state in all of Palestine and Transjordan. *See* Altalena *Affair.*

Jewish Agency: The international Jewish organization that was authorized by the League of Nations and the British Mandate to represent world Jewry in dealing with the British administration in Palestine. The Jewish Agency continued to raise funds and facilitate immigration after Israel became independent.

Jewish National Fund (JNF): An organization established by the World Zionist Organization in 1901 to pay for land purchases in Palestine. Land was purchased in the name of the JNF and became inalienable Jewish property.

Kibbutz: Term for collective farming settlements that the Labor Zionists founded in Palestine as both economic and military outposts. Members shared the income from their agricultural labor and lived communally, rather than in family units, with children living by age group in special houses and members eating in the collective dining room. Since independence, kibbutz members have played key roles in elite units of the armed forces, although they constitute only 3 percent of the population. Collective living has mostly given way to family living units and meals eaten at home. Moreover, kibbutzim now rely on manufacturing and services more than agriculture for their survival, and they hire Mizrahim and Palestinians to work in all aspects of their operations.

Knesset: Hebrew term for the Israeli parliament, located in West Jerusalem. The Knesset has 120 members, elected according to party affiliation.

Kurds: A twenty-five-million strong people, who are Muslim and have distinct languages and cultures. They are divided among Turkey, Iran, Iraq, and Syria.

Labor Alignment: A bloc of left-wing and moderate political parties formed under the leadership of the Mapai party in 1968.

Lavon Affair: A covert attempt by Israel in 1954 to prevent Egypt and Britain from signing a treaty that would complete the British military evacuation from Egypt.

League of Arab States: See *Arab League.*

League of Nations: The international organization formed after World War I that sponsored the mandates system, through which Britain and France legitimized their control over Arab provinces of the Ottoman Empire.

Likud: The bloc of right-wing political parties that has ruled Israel almost continuously since May 1977. Likud generally advocates Israel's retaining control over the West Bank, East Jerusalem, and the Golan Heights, but did negotiate withdrawal from the Sinai peninsula in return for peace with Egypt.

Mapai: See *Labor Alignment.*

Maronite: Christian denomination centered in Lebanon, founded by St. Maron in the fifth century. The Maronites, who constitute at most 20 percent of the population, control the presidency and have disproportionate representation in the Lebanese parliament.

Mecca and **Medina:** Muslim holy cities in the Hejaz, a province of Saudi Arabia that was an autonomous entity until 1924–1925.

Mizrahim: Jews of Asian, Middle Eastern, or African origin.

Muslim Brotherhood: A sociopolitical movement founded in Egypt in 1929 that seeks to establish Islamic-oriented regimes in Muslim countries. The branches formed in other Arab countries are now mostly autonomous. The Palestinian branch was largely oriented toward charitable and religious activities until 1988, when it formed an armed wing called Hamas.

National Water Carrier: Israeli system of canals and pipes that conducts water from the Sea of Galilee to the Negev. Construction of the carrier in the early 1960s angered the Arab states. Syria tried to divert part of the headwaters of the Jordan River in order to deny Israel that vital water.

Occupied Territories: The land captured by Israel in the June 1967 war, namely the Sinai peninsula, Golan Heights, West Bank, Gaza Strip, and East Jerusalem. According to international law, their legal status can not be altered until negotiations determine whether the territories return to the Arab states or fall under Israeli sovereignty.

Organization of Petroleum Exporting Countries (OPEC): International coordinating body for most of the governments that produce and export oil. Its Arab members have attempted to coordinate diplomatic as well as economic policies.

Ottoman Empire: A Turkish-origin empire that spread from Anatolia through the Middle East, North Africa, and east/central Europe. The Ottomans captured Constantinople in 1453, which they renamed Istanbul. As a result of its alignment with Germany and the Austro-Hungarian Empire in World War I, the Empire was dismembered by the end of 1918.

Palestine Liberation Organization (PLO): The umbrella organization for Palestinian guerrilla and civilian groups, formed by the Arab League in 1964. The PLO was recognized in 1974 by the Arab League as the sole representative of the Palestinian people and gained observer status at the United Nations the same year.

Palestine National Council (PNC): The parliament of the PLO, which first met in May 1964. The PNC elects the PLO's executive committee and serves as the forum for major changes in policy.

Pogrom: Term given to violent and massive assaults on Jews, with the tacit approval—if not active participation—of the government. The pogroms in czarist Russia in the late nineteenth and early twentieth centuries led to a massive exodus of Jews to the United States, with smaller migratory flows to Palestine and western Europe.

Popular Front for the Liberation of Palestine (PFLP): Radical Palestinian guerrilla group that hijacked planes and killed Israeli civilians. The PFLP sought to overthrow conservative Arab regimes in order to create a united Arab state that could be strong enough to defeat Israel. The PFLP continues to criticize the PLO's agreements with Israel. It refused to participate in elections for the Palestinian legislative council in 1996.

Rogers Plan and Peace Initiative: The Plan by U.S. Secretary of State William Rogers in December 1969 called for indirect negotiations leading to Israeli withdrawal from nearly all occupied territories in exchange for Arab recognition of Israel's right to exist in peace. The less-ambitious Peace Initiative in June 1970 called for a cease-fire as a prelude to indirect negotiations aimed at exchanging an unspecified amount of territory in return for peace.

Sabra and Shatila: Palestinian refugee camps in Beirut whose civilian population was decimated by Maronite Lebanese Forces in September 1982—with the tacit approval of the commanders of the Israeli Defense Forces who controlled Beirut.

Settlements: Jewish civilian or semimilitary residential communities established in the territories occupied by Israel in 1967 in order to stake political claims to that land.

Shatt al-Arab: The estuary leading to the Persian (Arab) Gulf that is formed by the confluence of the Tigris and Euphrates Rivers. The Shatt al-Arab separates Iraq and Iran.

United Arab Republic (UAR): The union between Egypt and Syria that lasted from February 1958 to September 1961.

United Nations Emergency Force (UNEF): The international force sent by the UN to Egypt in 1957 to monitor the border with Israel.

Village Leagues: Israeli-sponsored local groups on the West Bank that the Israeli military government hoped would gain credibility among Palestinian villagers.

West Bank: The part of Palestine controlled by Transjordan's Arab Legion at the time of the Israel-Jordan armistice agreement, which was incorporated into the renamed Jordan in 1950. Israel captured the West Bank in 1967. Parts of the territory are now ruled by the Palestinian Authority, but more than half remains under total Israeli military and political control.

Western (Wailing) Wall: Remnant of Herod's wall adjacent to the site of the ancient temple in Jerusalem, the holiest site in Judaism. Before 1967 it was legally the property of the Muslim community. Because Jewish Israelis did not have access to this important holy place from 1948 to 1967, when Jordan controlled East Jerusalem, regaining control of the Wall became a central goal of religious Israelis. The Israeli government seized control over the Wall in June 1967 and demolished Arab houses adjacent to it in order to create a large plaza for Jewish worshipers.

World Zionist Organization (WZO): Jewish national body founded in 1897 in order to create the conditions conducive to forming a Jewish state.

Yishuv: The organized Jewish community in mandated Palestine.

Zionism: The ideology that expresses Jews' longing to return to their historical homeland (Zion). In the late nineteenth century this concept was embodied in a political movement to create a Jewish state on the site of the ancient Jewish kingdom.

Annotated Bibliography

ARAB-ISRAELI CONFLICT

Bickerton, Ian J., and Carla L. Klausner. *A Concise History of the Arab-Israeli Conflict*, 2nd ed. Englewood Cliffs, NJ: Prentice-Hall, 1995. A thorough textbook on the Arab-Israeli conflict, including the civil war in Lebanon, with useful documents and maps.

Carter, Jimmy. *The Blood of Abraham*. Boston: Houghton Mifflin Company, 1985. Ex-president Carter's reflections on the Arab-Israeli conflict, which led him to call for increased efforts to bring peace to the Middle East.

Elon, Amos, and Sana Hassan. *Between Enemies: An Arab-Israeli Dialogue*. London: Andre Deutsch, 1974. A candid debate between an Israeli and an Egyptian after the October war, which examines the meaning of the Holocaust for Israelis, the prospects for negotiations, and the hopes and fears of both peoples.

Fernea, Elizabeth Warnock, and Mary Evelyn Hocking, eds. *The Struggle for Peace: Israelis and Palestinians*. Austin: University of Texas Press, 1992. Profiles of Israeli and Palestinian peace activists are combined with topical essays on peacemaking. This serves as a study guide for the video on peace activism. Produced by Fernea and Hocking.

Gerner, Deborah J. *One Land, Two Peoples: The Conflict over Palestine*. Boulder: Westview Press, 1994. A clearly written textbook on the Israeli-Palestinian conflict, completed just as the Oslo accords were being negotiated.

Gilbert, Martin. *Atlas of the Arab-Israeli Conflict*, 6th ed. New York: Oxford University Press, 1993. A useful compendium of the battles and border changes.

Halabi, Rafik. *The West Bank Story*. New York: Harcourt, Brace, Jovanovich Publishers, 1985. An Israeli Druze journalist describes the first decade of occupation of the West Bank and Gaza. Written from the perspective of a loyal non-Jewish Israeli who is troubled by Israeli policies.

Heikal, Mohamed. *Cutting the Lion's Tail: Suez through Egyptian Eyes*. New York: William Morrow, 1987. An Egyptian perspective on the Suez crisis of 1956 by a confidante to Nasser.

————. *The Road to Ramadan*. New York: Quadrangle, 1975. A frank commentary on the background to the October war.

Heller, Mark A. *A Palestinian State: The Implications for Israel*. Cambridge: Harvard University Press, 1983. A pioneering Israeli proposal, which argues that ending the occupation and establishing a Palestinian state on the West Bank and Gaza will enhance Israel's security.

Heller, Mark A., and Sari Nusseibeh, *No Trumpets, No Drums: A Two-State Settlement of the Israeli-Palestinian Conflict*. New York: Hill and Wang, 1991. A wide-ranging dialogue between an Israeli and a Palestinian scholar on key issues, including refugees, settlements, Jerusalem, water, and security.

Hurewitz, J. C. *The Struggle for Palestine*. New York: Schocken Books, 1976 (reprint of 1950 original). The classic chronicle of the clash of British, Zionist, and Arab political goals under the mandate.

Lesch, Ann, and Mark Tessler. *Israel, Egypt and the Palestinians: From Camp David to Intifada*. Bloomington: Indiana University Press, 1989. A collection of essays on Egyptian-Israeli relations and Israeli policies toward the Palestinians.

Quandt, William. *Camp David: Peacemaking and Politics*. Washington, DC: Brookings Institution, 1986. An authoritative account of the Camp David talks by an American participant.

Reich, Bernard, ed. *Arab-Israeli Conflict and Conciliation: A Documentary History*. Westport, CT: Praeger, 1995. A valuable compilation covering the period from 1896 to 1995.

Shipler, David K. *Arab and Jew: Wounded Spirits in the Promised Land*. New York: Times Books, 1986. A compassionate portrait of the peoples in Israel and the Occupied Territories by a former correspondent for the *New York Times*.

Tessler, Mark. *A History of the Israeli-Palestinian Conflict*. Bloomington: Indiana University Press, 1994. A lengthy and balanced survey that envisions a political solution to end Palestinian statelessness and ensure Israeli security.

PALESTINIANS

Abu-Amr, Ziad. *Islamic Fundamentalism in the West Bank and Gaza: Muslim Brotherhood and Islamic Jihad*. Bloomington: Indiana University Press,

1994. An analysis of the political programs of Palestinian Islamist movements, which emphasizes the impact of the intifada on their ideologies and actions.

Abu Iyad with Eric Rouleau. *My Home, My Land.* New York: Times Books, 1981. An impassioned account of the Palestinian national movement by Salah Khalaf (Abu Iyad), a founder of Fatah.

Aruri, Naseer H., ed. *Occupation*, 2nd ed. Belmont, MA: AAUG Press, 1989. Detailed essays on legal, socioeconomic, and political conditions on the West Bank and Gaza Strip.

Brand, Laurie A. *Palestinians in the Arab World: Institution Building and the Search for State.* New York: Columbia University Press, 1988. A careful examination of the circumstances facing Palestinians in Egypt, Kuwait, and Jordan.

Cobban, Helena. *The Palestinian Liberation Organization.* New York: Cambridge University Press, 1984. A detailed overview of the pivotal role of Fatah within the PLO.

Cossali, Paul, and Clive Robson. *Stateless in Gaza.* London: Zed Books, 1986. British observers re-create through the words of Palestinians their experiences in 1948, the conditions in Gaza under Israeli rule, and the social and political changes with which they are struggling.

Ghabra, Shafeeq. *Palestinians in Kuwait: The Family and Politics of Survival.* Boulder: Westview Press, 1987. An examination of the migration of Palestinians to Kuwait and their complex roles in Kuwaiti social and economic life, prior to the disruption caused by the Gulf crisis in 1990–1991.

Gharaibeh, Fawzi A. *The Economics of the West Bank and Gaza Strip.* Boulder: Westview, 1985. A Jordanian economist's assessment of the major economic transformations under Israeli rule.

Gresh, Alain. *The PLO: The Struggle Within.* London: Zed Books, 1985. A French journalist's analysis of the ideological positions and debates among Palestinian groups and of the evolving official positions of the PLO through the early 1980s.

Hiltermann, Joost. *Behind the Intifada.* Princeton: Princeton University Press, 1991. A detailed examination of the grass-roots mobilization of women and workers that presaged the intifada.

Institute for Palestine Studies. *The Palestinian-Israeli Peace Agreement: A Documentary Record.* Washington, DC: Institute for Palestine Studies, 1994. U.S., Israeli, and Palestinian documents from the Madrid Conference and Oslo accords, along with the texts of prior agreements and declarations.

Khalidi, Rashid. *Under Siege: PLO Decisionmaking during the 1982 War.* New York: Columbia University Press, 1986. An insider's account of the negotiations that led to the PLO's withdrawal from Beirut.

Khalidi, Walid, ed. *All That Remains: The Palestinian Villages Occupied and Depopulated by Israel in 1948*. Washington, DC: Institute for Palestine Studies, 1992. Detailed information on more than four hundred villages destroyed during and after the war in 1948–1949.

————. *Before Their Diaspora: A Photographic History of the Palestinians, 1876–1948*. Washington, DC: Institute for Palestine Studies, 1984. Striking visual evidence of family life, culture, and customs among Palestinian Arabs prior to 1948.

Lesch, Ann M. *Arab Politics in Palestine, 1917–1939: The Frustration of a Nationalist Movement*. Ithaca: Cornell University Press, 1979. A concise overview of the radicalization of Palestinian politics during the British mandate.

————. *Transition to Palestinian Self-Government*. Bloomington and Cambridge, MA: Indiana University Press and American Academy of Arts and Sciences, 1992. An outline of the political, economic, and security systems on the West Bank and of measures that might ensure stable self-rule; written just before the Oslo accords.

Mattar, Philip. *The Mufti of Jerusalem: Al-Hajj Amin al-Husayni and the Palestinian National Movement*. New York: Columbia University Press, 1988. A careful account of Husayni's life, with emphasis on the shift in his role after 1936, when accommodation with the British proved impossible.

Morris, Benny. *The Birth of the Palestinian Refugee Problem 1947–1949*. New York: Cambridge University Press, 1987. A detailed account of the flight of Palestinians by an Israeli scholar, based on Israeli archives.

Muslih, Muhammad Y. *The Origins of Palestinian Nationalism*. New York: Columbia University Press, 1988. A thoughtful analysis of changing Palestinian political attitudes at the end of the Ottoman period and the advent of British rule.

————. *Toward Coexistence: An Analysis of the Resolutions of the Palestine National Council*. Washington, DC: Institute for Palestine Studies, 1990. A useful outline of the changes in PLO positions from 1964 to 1988.

Najjar, Orayb Aref, with Kitty Warnock. *Portraits of Palestinian Women*. Salt Lake City: University of Utah Press, 1992. Vivid images of women's lives through interviews with twenty-one women on the West Bank.

Peretz, Don. *Intifada*. Boulder: Westview, 1990. A succinct overview of the causes of the intifada and its impact on Palestinians and Israelis.

Peteet, Julie. *Gender in Crisis: Women and the Palestinian Resistance Movement*. New York: Columbia University Press, 1991. A portrait of politically active Palestinian women in Lebanon from 1968 to 1982.

Quandt, William B., Fuad Jabber, and Ann M. Lesch. *The Politics of Palestinian Nationalism*. Berkeley: University of California Press, 1973. A basic text on the early years of the PLO and its confrontation with Jordan in 1970.

Said, Edward. *The Question of Palestine.* New York: Random House, 1992. A leading Palestinian intellectual's reflections on the evolution of the concept of Palestinian nationalism.

Sayegh, Rosemary. *Palestinians: From Peasants to Revolutionaries.* London: Zed Books, 1979. A pioneering analyis of the political awakening of Palestinian refugees in Lebanon.

Warnock, Kitty. *Land before Honour: Palestinian Women in the Occupied Territories.* New York: Monthly Review Press, 1990. A study of women's lives on the West Bank, covering family roles, education, work in agriculture and industry, women's organizations, and political life.

ISRAEL AND ZIONISM

Allon, Yigal. *The Making of Israel's Army.* New York: Bantam Books, 1971. An analysis of the formation of the Haganah and the battles of 1948–1949 by a senior commander.

Arian, Asher. *Politics in Israel: The Second Generation*, Rev. ed. Chatham, NJ: Chatham House Publishers, 1989. A clear outline of the peoples, economy, and politics of Israel, which stresses the importance of political parties and elections.

Avineri, Shlomo. *The Making of Modern Zionism: The Intellectual Origins of the Jewish State.* New York: Basic Books, 1981. An overview of the principal Zionist thinkers and politicians from Herzl and Rabbi Kook through Ben-Gurion.

Avishai, Bernard. *The Tragedy of Zionism.* New York: Farrar, Straus, Giroux, 1985. A lively analysis of political and cultural Zionism and the painful contradictions created by the occupation of the West Bank.

Ben-Zadok, Efraim. *Local Communities and the Israeli Polity.* Albany: State University of New York, 1993. A scholarly look at major social divisions within Israel and their impact on political mobilization at the local level.

Caplan, Neil. *Palestine Jewry and the Arab Question, 1917–1925.* London: Frank Cass, 1978. An analysis of the encounter between Jewish immigrants and indigenous Arabs during the period following the Balfour Declaration of November 1917. The immigrants' expectation of rapidly attaining Jewish statehood clashed with the reality of an Arab majority that feared that the Zionist movement would block their own aspiration to independence.

Flapan, Simha. *The Birth of Israel: Myths and Realities.* New York: Pantheon Books, 1987. A passionate dissection of Israel's founding myths concerning the war of independence and the flight of Palestinian refugees, by a prominent Israeli dove.

————. *Zionism and the Palestinians.* New York: Barnes and Noble, 1979. A critical look at the views of Chaim Weizmann, David Ben-Gurion, the Revisionist movement, and Jewish binationalists toward the Palestinians, Jewish labor, and partition.

Garfinkle, Adam. *Politics and Society in Modern Israel: Myths and Realities.* Armonk, NY: M. E. Sharpe, 1997. A comprehensive analysis of Israeli politics and foreign policy that also conveys a sense of everyday life and the nuances of Israeli society.

Hattis, Susan Lee. *The Bi-National Idea in Palestine during Mandatory Times.* Haifa: Shikmona Publishing Company, 1970. A carefully balanced analysis of groups and individuals who sought to promote binationalism under the mandate and of official Arab, British, and Jewish attitudes toward binationalist programs for Palestine.

Hertzberg, Arthur, ed. *The Zionist Idea.* New York: Doubleday and Company, 1959 (Greenwood Press reprint 1970). The classic compilation of writings by Zionists from the mid-nineteenth century to the 1940s.

Krausz, Ernest, ed. *Politics and Society in Israel: Studies of Israeli Society.* Vol III. New Brunswick and Oxford: Transaction Books, 1985. A broad and valuable collection of studies of Israel's historical development, political culture and ideology, political institutions, and politics.

Laqueur, Walter. *A History of Zionism.* New York: Weidenfeld and Nicholson, 1974. A classic history of the Zionist movement and the establishment of Israel.

Lustick, Ian. *Arabs in the Jewish State: Israel's Control of a National Minority.* Austin: University of Texas Press, 1980. A systematic inquiry into the political status of Arabs in Israel and the means by which the Israeli government regulates their lives.

————. *For the Land and the Lord: Jewish Fundamentalism in Israel.* New York: Council on Foreign Relations, 1988. Analysis of the writings and practices of the Jewish settlement movement on the West Bank.

Newman, David, ed. *The Impact of Gush Emunim: Politics and Settlement in the West Bank.* New York: St. Martin's Press, 1985. A collection of essays examining the ideology and practice of settlement activity under the banner of religious nationalism.

Oz, Amos. *In the Land of Israel.* New York: Harcourt, Brace, Jovanovich, 1983. An Israeli writer encounters Israelis of various political views and social backgrounds in West Bank settlements and Israeli cities, and discusses the Israeli occupation with Palestinian journalists.

Safran, Nadav. *Israel: The Embattled Ally.* Cambridge, MA: Belknap Press, 1978. Lengthy analysis of Israeli foreign policy and relations with the United States.

Schiff, Ze'ev, and Ehud Ya'ari. *Israel's Lebanon War.* New York: Simon and Schuster, 1984. A revealing account of Israel's policies in Lebanon by two senior Israeli military correspondents.

Segev, Tom. *1949: The First Israelis.* New York: Free Press, 1993. Insights into Israel's first year as a sovereign state.

Shafir, Gerson. *Land, Labour and the Origins of the Israeli-Palestinian Conflict 1882–1914*. New York: Cambridge University Press, 1989. A historical study stressing the centrality of control over land to Jewish settlement.

Shindler, Colin. *Israel, Likud and the Zionist Dream: Power, Politics and Ideology from Begin to Netanyahu*. New York: I. B. Tauris, 1995. A comprehensive analysis of Likud ideology and practices.

Smooha, Sammy. *Arabs and Jews in Israel*. 2 vols. Boulder: Westview, 1989, 1992. Analysis of the relations between Jews and Arabs in Israel, based on extensive survey research.

Sprinzak, Ehud. *The Ascendance of Israel's Radical Right*. New York: Oxford University Press, 1991. Powerful critique of the rightist political forces that control the settlement movement in the West Bank.

ARAB STATES

Antonius, George. *The Arab Awakening*. New York: Capricorn Books, 1965. The seminal account of the rise of Arab nationalism in the nineteenth century, the clash between Arab and Turkish aspirations, and the Arab revolt during World War I. Antonius details the promises made by the British government to Sharif Hussein and the failure of the postwar settlement to fulfill those promises.

Brand, Laurie. *Jordan's Inter-Arab Relations: The Political Economy of Alliance Making*. New York: Columbia University Press, 1994. An analysis of Jordanian foreign policy from the 1970s until 1991 that emphasizes the extent to which internal economic problems determine the government's foreign policy orientation. She applies her argument to Jordan's relations with Egypt, Iraq, Kuwait, Saudi Arabia, and Syria.

Drysdale, Alasdair, and Raymond A. Hinnebusch. *Syria and the Middle East Peace Process*. New York: Council on Foreign Relations Press, 1991. A clear-headed commentary on the problems and prospects for Syrian-Israeli negotiations.

Mishal, Shaul. *West Bank/East Bank: The Palestinians in Jordan, 1949–1957* New Haven: Yale University Press, 1978. Assessment of the complex relations between Palestinians and the Jordanian regime.

Randal, Jonathan A. *Going All the Way: Christian Warlords, Israeli Adventurers and the War in Lebanon*. New York: The Viking Press, 1983. A vivid picture of Gemayel's rise to power and his sudden demise after the Israeli invasion of 1982.

Salibi, Kamal. *The Modern History of Jordan*. New York: I. B. Tauris, 1993. An up-to-date account of Jordan's historical development by a leading Lebanese scholar.

Shlaim, Avi. *Collusion across the Jordan: King Abdullah, the Zionist Movement, and the Partition of Palestine*. New York: Columbia University Press,

1988. A detailed account of King Abdullah's negotiations with Zionist leaders in the 1940s.

Smith, Charles D. *Palestine and the Arab-Israeli Conflict*, 2nd ed. New York: St. Martin's Press, 1992. A balanced study of historical trends and diplomatic issues.

Tschirgi, Dan, ed. *The Arab World Today*. Boulder: Lynne Rienner Publishers, 1994. A collection of essays by experienced students of the Middle East, assessing the implications of major political, social, and economic currents in the post-Gulf war Arab world.

THE UNITED STATES AND THE ARAB-ISRAELI CONFLICT

Ball, George. *Error and Betrayal in Lebanon*. Washington, DC: Foundation for Middle East Peace, 1984. A strong critique of U.S. involvement in Lebanon under the Reagan administration by a former government official, who charges that Washington was unduly influenced and manipulated by Israel.

Findley, Paul. *They Dare to Speak Out: People and Institutions Confront Israel's Lobby*. Westport, CT: Lawrence Hill and Company, 1985. A veteran congressman details what he views as excessive political influence by the pro-Israel lobby in Washington.

Finer, Herman. *Dulles over Suez*. Chicago: Quadrangle, 1964. An assessment of U.S. policy toward the Suez crisis of 1956.

Neff, Donald. *Fallen Pillars: U.S. Policy towards Palestine and Israel since 1945*. Washington, DC: The Institute for Palestine Studies, 1995. A critical appraisal of the U.S. approach to the Palestine problem from Truman to Clinton.

Quandt, William B. *Decade of Decisions: American Policy toward the Arab-Israeli Conflict, 1967–1976*. Berkeley: University of California Press, 1977. An examination of U.S. policy toward the Arab-Israeli conflict that emphasizes the role of presidential involvement in policymaking. The author served on the staff of the National Security Council under Nixon and Carter.

Reich, Bernard. *The United States and Israel: Influence in the Special Relationship*. New York: Praeger Publishers, 1984. A study that concludes that U.S.-Israeli relations are marked by a community of interests and by mutual influence.

Sayed-Ahmed, Muhammed Abd el-Wahab. *Nasser and American Foreign Policy: 1952–1956*. London: LAAM, 1989. An analysis based on archival research, which sheds light on pre-Suez relations between Washington and Nasser's regime.

Suleiman, Michael W., ed. *U.S. Policy on Palestine from Wilson to Clinton*. Normal, IL: AAUG Press, 1994. Chapters by eleven authors depicting each president's policies toward the clash between Israel and the Palestinians.

Tschirgi, Dan. *The American Search for Mideast Peace*. New York: Praeger, 1989. An analysis of the dynamics and consequences of the U.S. pursuit of Arab-Israeli peace between 1967 and the PLO's acceptance of Israel's legitimacy in 1988.

————. *The Politics of Indecision: Origins and Implications of American Involvement with the Palestine Problem*. New York: Praeger, 1983. A heavily documented look at U.S. policy-making and its consequences in Palestine during the years 1939–1948, with particular attention to assessing Washington's responsibility for the anarchy attending the end of the British mandate.

MEMOIRS AND PERSONAL ACCOUNTS

Abdullah, King. *My Memoirs Completed*. London: Longman, 1978. Reflections by the Jordanian monarch on his rule and on Jordan's status in the Middle East.

Ashrawi, Hanan. *This Side of Peace: A Personal Account*. New York: Simon and Schuster, 1995. An account of the author's role in Israeli-Palestinian negotiations.

El-Asmar, Fouzi. *To Be an Arab in Israel*. London: Frances Pinter, 1975. A Palestinian poet, who was a child when Lydda fell to Israel in 1948, describes his family's experiences within Israel, his relations with Jewish Israelis, his growing politicization, and his imprisonment in 1968–1970.

Begin, Menachem. *The Revolt*. New York: Nash, 1981. Autobiography of the leader of the Irgun, which employed terror against the British and Palestinians under the mandate. Begin subsequently became prime minister of Israel.

Ben-Gurion, David. *Israel: Years of Challenge*. New York: Holt, Rinehart and Winston, 1963. Autobiography that depicts the former Israeli prime minister's role in the struggle for independence in 1948–1949 and the Suez crisis of 1956.

Binur, Yoram. *My Enemy, My Self*. New York: Penguin Books, 1989. An Israeli Jewish journalist pretends to be Palestinian so that he can experience the living conditions of Palestinians in Tel Aviv and in the Occupied Territories as well as the attitudes of Israelis toward Palestinians.

Chacour, Elias. *Blood Brothers*. Old Tappan, NJ: Chosen Books, 1984. A Christian Palestinian priest, who is a citizen of Israel, describes the destruction of his village in northern Galilee by the Israeli army after the 1948 war and his lifelong search for brotherly relations between Arabs and Jews inside Israel.

Dayan, Moshe. *Breakthrough: A Personal Account of the Egypt-Israel Peace Negotiations.* New York: Alfred A. Knopf, 1981. An analysis of the Camp David talks by a leading Israeli participant.

————. *Diary of the Sinai Campaign.* London:.Weidenfeld and Nicolson, 1966. A dramatic account of the Suez war as seen through the eyes of a daring military commander.

Doughty, Dick, and Mohammed El Aydi. *Gaza: Legacy of Occupation, A Photographer's Journey.* West Hartford, CT: Kumarian Press, 1995. A deeply human account of the lives of Palestinian refugees in Gaza by a young American photojournalist and a Palestinian living in Gaza.

Elon, Amos. *Flight into Egypt.* New York: Pinnacle Books, 1981. An Israeli writer visits Egypt in 1979, just after the peace accord, and meets a wide range of Egyptians. He stresses the psychological impact of the October war on Egyptians and the continuing skepticism of Israelis toward the possibility of peace.

Friedlander, Saul. *When Memory Comes.* New York: Farrar, Straus and Giroux, 1979. A Prague-born Israeli historian traces his family's flight to France in 1938, their suffering during World War II, his rediscovery of his Jewish identity, and the attraction of Zionism. Writing in 1977, he intersperses comments on Israeli reactions to Sadat's visit.

Gorkin, Michael. *Days of Honey, Days of Onion: The Story of a Palestinian Family in Israel.* Berkeley: University of California Press, 1991. A Jewish psychologist gains insight into the dilemmas facing Arab citizens of Israel through his friendship with a family in Kufr Qara village.

Grossman, David. *The Yellow Wind.* New York: Farrar, Straus and Giroux, 1988. An Israeli writer talks to Palestinians in refugee camps, villages, and universities and meets Israeli settlers and security officers. He reflects on the price paid by both Palestinians and Israelis as a result of twenty years of occupation.

Meir, Golda. *My Life.* New York: Putnam, 1975. Autobiography by Israel's leading female politician.

Netanyahu, Benjamin. *A Place among the Nations: Israel and the World.* New York: Bantam Books, 1993. The views of the leader of Israel's Likud party toward the peace process and Israeli identity.

Peres, Shimon. *Battling for Peace: A Memoir.* New York: Random House, 1995. An inside view of the complexities of peacemaking by the Israeli politician who orchestrated the Oslo accords.

Rabin, Leah. *Rabin: Our Life, His Legacy.* New York: G. P. Putnam's Sons, 1997. This moving account by the widow of Israel's assassinated prime minister provides interesting information on Yitzhak Rabin as well as on key events and personalities that have shaped the Arab-Israeli conflict.

Sadat, Anwar. *In Search of Identity*. New York: Fontana, 1978. The Egyptian president depicts himself as a courageous but pragmatic leader searching for a fruitful peace.

Shehadeh, Raja. *The Third Way: A Journal of Life in the West Bank*. New York: Quartet Books, 1982. Rejecting both hatred and submission, a Palestinian lawyer seeks a "third way" by which he can live on the West Bank under Israeli rule. He reflects on his encounters with Palestinians and Israelis as well as his frustrated efforts to uphold basic standards of law.

Tawil, Raymonda Hawa. *My Home, My Prison*. New York: Holt, Rinehart and Winston, 1980. A Palestinian woman describes her childhood in Israel, her marriage and restricted life on the West Bank, and her political and feminist awakening during the Israeli occupation. She fosters dialogue between Israelis and Palestinians but is placed under house arrest by the military government.

Turki, Fawaz. *The Disinherited: Journal of a Palestinian Exile*. New York: Monthly Review Press, 1972. A Palestinian intellectual angrily describes his life as a refugee in Lebanon and his profound sense of political alienation.

Weizmann, Chaim. *Trial and Error*. Westport, CT: Greenwood Press, 1971. Reflections by a leading Zionist on the founding of Israel.

Winternitz, Helen. *A Season of Stones: Living in a Palestinian Village*. New York: Atlantic Monthly Press, 1991. A personal account by an American journalist of a West Bank village that was radically affected by the intifada and by the expansion of Israeli settlements.

Yermiya, Dov. *My War Diary: Lebanon, June 5 - July 1, 1982*. Boston: South End Press, 1984. A Jewish Israeli reserve officer describes his painful experiences with the Israeli forces in Lebanon, where he was in charge of civilian relief in Sidon. He critiques the army's treatment of Lebanese and Palestinian civilians.

BIOGRAPHIES

Golan, Matti. *Shimon Peres: A Biography*. New York: St. Martin's Press, 1982. An account of the role played by this leading Israeli politician in his country's fortunes.

Hart, Alan. *Arafat: A Political Biography*. Bloomington, IN: Indiana University Press, 1989. A laudatory portrait of Arafat, based on wide-ranging interviews.

Horovitz, David, ed. *Shalom, Friend: The Life and Legacy of Yitzhak Rabin*. New York: Newmarket, 1996. Eulogies of Rabin written by the staff of *Jerusalem Report*, a liberal Israeli English-language newspaper.

Perlmutter, Amos. *The Life and Times of Menachem Begin*. Garden City, NY: Doubleday, 1987. A sympathetic portrait of the former Israeli prime minister.

Seale, Patrick. *Asad: The Struggle for the Middle East.* Berkeley, CA: University of California Press, 1988. The principal biography of the Syrian president.

FICTION

Adnan, Etel. *Sitt Marie Rose.* Sausalito, CA: Post-Apollo Press, 1982. A heart-wrenching novel about the abduction by Maronite militiamen of the Lebanese headmistress of a school for deaf children, on the grounds that she had become a traitor to her Maronite community by assisting Palestinian refugees.

Awwad, Tawfiq Yusuf. *Death in Beirut.* London: Heinemann, 1976. A Lebanese diplomat's analysis of the social upheavals that confronted Lebanon just before the civil war, through the life of a young Shia village woman from south Lebanon who moves to Beirut.

Azrak, Michel, trans. *Modern Syrian Short Stories.* Washington, DC: Three Continents Press, 1988. Eighteen stories by Syrian writers that depict social issues in the countryside and cities, and comment elliptically on Syria's authoritarian rule.

Barakat, Halim. *Days of Dust.* Washington, DC: Three Continents Press, 1974. A Lebanese sociologist evokes the trauma of the June 1967 war through the eyes of Lebanese and Palestinian narrators living in Beirut, Amman, and the West Bank.

Grossman, David. *The Smile of the Lamb.* New York: Washington Square Press, Simon and Schuster, 1990. A disturbing novel about a troubled Israeli soldier serving in the occupation forces on the West Bank.

Gur, Batya. *Murder on a Kibbutz: A Communal Case.* New York: HarperCollins Publishers, 1994. A lively murder mystery that unravels the complex layers of Israel's insular kibbutz society.

Habiby, Emile. *The Secret Life of Saeed, The Ill-Fated Pessoptimist.* New York: Vantage Press, 1985. The contradictions facing Arab citizens of Israel are reflected in the adventures of the novel's non-hero Saeed, who remains both optimistic and pessimistic.

Herzl, Theodor. *Old New Land.* New York: Marcus Wiener Publishing and the Herzl Press, 1987. A utopian novel written in 1900, in which the founder of the World Zionist Organization imagines a cosmopolitan and secular Jewish entity in Palestine that is at the forefront of industrialization and free of conflict with its Arab neighbors.

Jabra, Jabra Ibrahim. *Hunters in a Narrow Street.* Washington, DC: Three Continents Press, 1990. A Palestinian novel about a young man who flees Jerusalem in 1948 and becomes a professor in Baghdad, Iraq, where he is caught up in the social and political tensions of a tradition-bound society.

Jayyusi, Salma Khadra, ed. *Anthology of Modern Palestinian Literature.* New York: Columbia University Press, 1992. A unique compilation of Palestinian poetry and prose, providing literary expression to life before 1948, during the wars of 1948 and 1967, in exile, and under Israeli occupation. Biographical sketches place the authors in their historical contexts.

Kanafani, Ghassan. *Men in the Sun*. Washington, DC: Three Continents Press, 1983. Short stories by a Palestinian political activist, which include the difficulties facing men who travel to Kuwait for work, the flight from Galilee in 1948, and one person's decision to remain in Gaza rather than live in exile.

Khalifa, Sahar. *Wild Thorns*. London: Al Saqi Books, 1985. Palestinians struggle with the meaning of nationalism, resistance, and steadfastness as they cope with daily life under Israeli military rule on the West Bank.

Oz, Amos. *Where the Jackals Howl*. London: Harcourt, Brace, and Jovanovich, 1981. In eight haunting stories about life on a kibbutz in the 1960s, this leading Israeli novelist intertwines the personal and the political.

Al-Qa'id, Yusuf. *War in the Land of Egypt*. London: Al Saqi Books, 1986. An Egyptian novel that portrays the tensions between rich landlords and poor peasants at the time of the October war of 1973.

Shalev, Meir. *The Blue Mountain*. New York: HarperCollins Publishers, 1991. A passionate novel about the loves, hates, feuds, and ventures in a rural community in Israel over the span of three decades.

Al-Shaykh, Hanan. *The Story of Zahra*. London: Quartet Books, 1986. This Lebanese novel depicts vividly the terror and fear during the civil war, from the perspective of a young Lebanese woman.

Tamer, Zakaria. *Tigers on the Tenth Day and Other Stories*. London: Quartet, 1985. Stories by a Syrian novelist that range across personal, social, and political issues, including a daring allegory on how those in power can break and tame even the strongest person.

Yehoshua, A. B. *The Lover*. London: Heinemann Press, 1979. This novel depicts the disorientation and sense of loss in Israel during and after the October war (1973), focusing on the doomed love between a Jewish and Palestinian couple, who are both Israeli citizens and live in the port city of Haifa.

VIDEOS AND FILMS

Arab-Israeli Struggle for Peace. Landmark Media, 1993, fifty-five-minute video. Analysis using historic footage of the Arab-Israeli wars and highlighting the careers of Nasser, Begin, and Shamir.

The Arabs and Israel since 1947. BBC Films, 1989, sixty-minute video. A critical look at the evolution of relations between Israel and the Arabs.

Ben-Gurion: One Place, One People. Learning Corporation of America, 1986, twenty-four-minute video. The role of Ben-Gurion as Zionist leader and prime minister.

Children of Fire. BBC, 1991, fifty-minute video. Personal perspective on the uprising on the West Bank, seen through the eyes of Palestinian children.

Holy Land: Judaism, Christianity, and Islam in the Middle East. Encyclopedia Britannica, 1984, twenty-five-minute 16mm film. The conflictive relations among the three religions in Jerusalem.

Inside God's Bunker. London, 1995, forty-minute video. Interviews with Israeli settlers in Hebron by an Israeli journalist. Available from WLIW, 1790 Broadway, New York, NY 10019.

Journey to the Occupied Lands. PBS Video, 1992, eighty-six-minute video. *Frontline* commentary on the West Bank, including interviews with Israelis and Palestinians.

Middle East. Landmark Films, 1991, two-part video, sixty minutes each. The history of the region from 1915 to 1991.

The Mountain. Hanna Elias, 1992, twenty-four-minute video. Elegantly photographed drama about a Palestinian girl in Galilee whose parents oppose her marriage to a vegetable vendor from Gaza.

Nasser: People's Pharaoh. Learning Corporation of America, 1986, twenty-four-minute video. Emphasizes the difficulty Nasser had fulfilling popular expectations within Egypt and in the Arab world.

Oasis of Peace. Landmark Media, 1995, twenty-eight-minute video. The story of a unique village in Israel, whose Jewish and Palestinian residents seek to be a model for a wider peace.

The Shadow of the West. Landmark Films, 1985, fifty-minute video. Analysis of the Palestinian refugee situation as the result of the modern encounter between the Arabs and the colonizing West.

Women of South Lebanon. 1991, seventy-minute video. Docudrama about Lebanese villagers' complex reactions to the Israeli occupation in 1982.

Women under Siege. Icarus Films, 1982, twenty-six-minute 16mm film. Documentary on a Palestinian refugee camp in Lebanon, filmed in 1981.

USS "Liberty" Survivors: Our Story. Sligo Productions, 1991, seventy-minute video. Eyewitness accounts by survivors of the Israeli attack on a U.S. reconnaissance ship in June 1967.

Index

About the Authors

ANN M. LESCH is Professor of Political Science at Villanova University. She has published seminal analyses of the Arab-Israeli conflict, including *Arab Politics in Palestine, 1917–1939* (1979), *Political Perceptions of the Palestinians on the West Bank and Gaza Strip* (1980), and *Transition to Palestinian Self-Government* (1992), and is co-author (with Mark Tessler) of *Israel, Egypt, and the Palestinians* (1989). She has served as president of the Middle East Studies Association and is a member of the advisory committee for Human Rights Watch/Middle East.

DAN TSCHIRGI is Professor of Political Science at the American University in Cairo. He is the author of *The Politics of Indecision: Origins and Implications of American Involvement with the Palestine Problem and the American Search for Mideast Peace* (Praeger, 1983), *The American Search for Mideast Peace* (Praeger, 1989), and is editor of *The Arab World Today* (1994). He has been a visiting scholar at the Harry S. Truman Institute for the Advancement of Peace at the Hebrew University of Jerusalem and at the Institute of Oriental Studies in Moscow.